"The Gospel is firmly rooted in a story of that which once happened. The story is familiar. But we should observe that the situation into which Jesus Christ came was genuinely typical (the outcome of much previous history) and too long to tell here. The forces with which he came into contact were such as are permanent factors in history: — government, institutional religion, nationalism, social unrest. . . ."

C. H. Dodd, "The Kingdom of God and the Present Situation," *Christian News-Letter,* May 29, 1940, supplement no. 31

The Politics of Jesus

Vicit Agnus Noster

• •

SECOND EDITION

JOHN HOWARD YODER

WILLIAM B. EERDMANS PUBLISHING COMPANY
GRAND RAPIDS, MICHIGAN / CAMBRIDGE, U.K.

First edition 1972
Second edition 1994

Wm. B. Eerdmans Publishing Co.
2140 Oak Industrial Drive N.E., Grand Rapids, Michigan 49505 /
P.O. Box 163, Cambridge CB3 9PU U.K.

Printed in the United States of America

12 11 10 09 08 18 17 16 15

Library of Congress Cataloging-in-Publication Data
Yoder, John Howard.
The politics of Jesus: vicit Agnus noster / John H. Yoder. — Rev. ed.
p. cm.
Includes bibliographical references (p. xxx-xxx) and index.
ISBN 978-0-8028-0734-2 (pbk.)
1. Jesus Christ — Political and social views. 2. Jesus Christ — Example. 3. Social ethics.
4. Pacifism — Religious aspects — Christianity. 5. Bible. N.T. Luke — Criticism,
interpretation, etc. I. Title.
BT202.Y63 1993
232 — dc20 93-39532
CIP

www.eerdmans.com

Contents

Preface to the Second Edition

Each of the chapters of the 1972 book was *then* a summary of the widely known scholarship of the time. *As New Testament scholarship* it was popularization, not fresh research. Its preparation back then had required a few years' attention to the then current scholarly publications, but I never pretended to be a professional New Testament scholar.

Obviously I am farther from being a specialized scholar in that field today than I was a quarter-century ago. Meanwhile, each of the major subfields represented in the book has seen considerable new scholarly work since I wrote. These themes have continued to receive attention during the past twenty years, not because of what I wrote in 1972, but because what I wrote then was representative of the lively research agenda in the field.

It would therefore have been quite inappropriate, in the frame of reference of such a brief text as this, that I should have attempted to rewrite the text proper to catch up with a quarter-century of frontier scholarship on all its topics. After all, the original purpose of the book had not been to offer a compendium of New Testament scholarship for its own sake, but only to select a few representative specimens pertinent to the general thesis of the book.

That "general thesis" belongs in the field not of exegesis but of ethical methodology. It has to do not with the substance of the moral testimony of the New Testament texts for its own sake, but with whether their total witness is "political."

Nevertheless the reader will be right to wonder whether the kinds of insights summarized in the synthesis of 1972 have been supported or left behind by ongoing research. By and large, the answer is "supported," but of course only study in detail could validate that summary. What that state of affairs means for this present revision of *The Politics of Jesus* is that while leaving the text proper with only minimal changes, most chapters will be followed by a brief epilogue, by way of update, in which I seek to identify the lines that further research has taken. In the preparation of these epilogues and in other updating details I have been aided by Kim Paffenroth.

Two things that I generally cannot and should not do in an update like this are: (a) to give an overall accounting for "how my mind has changed in a quarter-century," or (b) to respond in detail to criticisms of particular passages. There are of course numerous points where my original statement in the 1972 text would need to be corrected or retracted. There are others where it would be fitting to defend it against misinterpretations or to argue it further against interlocutors who understand it correctly but disagree. That kind of argument would, however, usually call for much more text, and a more fine-grained kind of argument, than the original passage. To do that generally would unduly burden the revision.

A separate matter is the style changes needing to be introduced within the original text for reasons of tone, and to take account of today's sensitivities as to gender-related overtones. In this editing the most important contributions have been made by the Reverends Augustus and Laurel Jordan.

My first preface referred to "biblical realism" as characterizing my mode of reading Scripture. That phrase was current among specialists in the 1960s. It was, like the substance of the survey, no idea of my own. Yet it never became widely known, nor did the scholars whom it then described try in any concerted way to work together as a team or a "school." It named an approach which sought to take full account of all of the tools of literary and historical criticism, without any traditional scholasticism, yet without letting the Scriptures be taken away from the church. In a way foreign to my intentions, this book has been taken by some as representing an original way to relate the Bible to the church or to ethics.[1] Others have called it "fundamentalist"; also a misreading.

1. This was done, e.g., by Bruce Birch and Larry Rasmussen, whose two editions of *Bible and Ethics in the Christian Life* (Minneapolis: Augsburg, 1976 and 1989) used me

If I had known the book would be put on review as a prototype of something methodologically ambitious or profound, I might have gone further into the discussion of theoretical prolegomena — or I might have refused to do so, since one can very soon come to a point, in the abstract discussions of method, where that very discussion gets in the way of letting the text play its role as the documentary spine of the church's identity.

in different ways, citing different texts; similarly Charles F. Curran and Richard A. McCormick (eds.), *The Use of Scripture in Moral Theology,* Readings in Moral Theology No. 4 (New York: Paulist, 1981).

Preface to the First Edition

The meaning of this book is not immediately or easily classified. On the least sophisticated, most argumentative level, it is the simple rebound of a Christian pacifist commitment as it responds to the ways in which mainstream Christian theology has set aside the pacifist implications of the New Testament message.

On the deepest level, it represents an exercise in fundamental philosophical hermeneutics, trying to apply in the area of the life of the Christian community the insights with regard to the distinct biblical worldview which have previously been promoted under the name of "biblical realism." Since the pioneer statements of Hendrik Kraemer, Otto Piper, Paul Minear, Markus Barth, and Claude Tresmontant, it has become thinkable that there might be about the biblical vision of reality certain dimensions which refuse to be pushed into the mold of any one contemporary worldview, but which stand in creative tension with the cultural functions of our age or perhaps of any age. The main thrust of the "biblical realist" movement a generation ago was in the areas of metaphysics and the personality of God. It led to a renewal of concern for ecclesiology and for eschatology without which neither ecumenical developments since then nor Christian thinking about hope since then would have been understandable. What the present volume offers is a late ripening, in the field of ethics, of the same biblical realist revolution, in which precisely ecclesiology and eschatology come to have a new import for the substance of ethics.

Between the argumentative and the philosophical levels, this work testifies to the conviction that, well beyond the questions of formal orientation, there is a bulk of specific and concrete content in Jesus' vision of the divine order which can speak to our age as it seldom has been free to do before, if it can be unleashed from the bonds of inappropriate a prioris.

The preparation of this text has been facilitated by the support, here gratefully acknowledged, of the Institute of Mennonite Studies and the Schowalter Foundation, and by the counsel and critique of many friends and colleagues.

Abbreviations

ASTI	*Annual of the Swedish Theological Institute in Jerusalem* (Leiden)
BJRL	*Bulletin of the John Rylands Library* (Manchester)
BR	*Biblical Research* (Amsterdam; Chicago)
CBQ	*Catholic Biblical Quarterly* (Washington)
CC	*Christian Century* (Chicago)
CR	*Cahiers de la reconciliation* (Paris)
EvT	*Evangelische Theologie* (Munich)
HTR	*Harvard Theological Review* (Cambridge, Mass.)
HzNT	Handbuch zum Neuen Testament (Tübingen)
JBL	*Journal of Biblical Literature*
JES	*Journal of Ecumenical Studies* (Philadelphia)
JJS	*Journal of Jewish Studies* (London)
MQR	*Mennonite Quarterly Review* (Goshen, Ind.)
NovT	*Novum Testamentum* (Leiden)
NTS	*New Testament Studies* (Cambridge)
RHPR	*Revue d'histoire et de philosophie religieuses* (Strasbourg; Paris)
SBT	Studies in Biblical Theology (London: SCM; Naperville: Allenson)
SJT	*Scottish Journal of Theology* (Edinburgh)
ST	*Studia theologica* (Lund)
ThEx	*Theologische Existenz heute* (Munich)
ThSt	Theologische Studien, ed. K. Barth (Zurich)

TQ	*Theologische Quartalschrift* (Tübingen; Ravensburg; Stuttgart)
TT	*Theology Today* (Princeton)
TZ	*Theologische Zeitschrift* (Basel)
USQR	*Union Seminary Quarterly Review* (New York)
ZNW	*Zeitschrift für die neutestamentliche Wissenschaft* (Berlin)
ZTK	*Zeitschrift für Theologie und Kirche* (Tübingen)

CHAPTER 1

The Possibility of a Messianic Ethic

The Problem

The peculiar place of Jesus in the mood and mind of many young "rebels" is a sore spot in the recent intergenerational tension of Western post-Christendom, and one of the inner contradictions of our age's claim to have left Christendom behind. It may be a meaningless coincidence that some young men wear their hair and their feet like the Good Shepherd of the Standard Press Sunday school posters; but there is certainly no randomness to their claim that Jesus was, like themselves, a social critic and an agitator,[1] a drop-out from the social climb, and the spokesman of a counterculture.

1. The bellwether of this trend is probably Stephen Rose's article "Agitating Jesus," in *Renewal* (Oct. 1967), reprinted in his booklet *Alarms and Visions* (New York: Association, 1967), p. 125. Somewhat similar are Jean-Marie Paupert, *The Politics of the Gospel* (New York: Holt, 1969), and John Pairman Brown, *The Liberated Zone* (Richmond: John Knox, 1969). Paupert and Brown are more serious than Rose, but their style is still sufficiently impressionistic that the theological reader is not sure how much of what they say about "Mahatma Jesus" should really be taken seriously as exegesis, and how much is simply the new symbolic dress for something they could say without it.

Still closer to the concerns of this study, but focusing only on Jesus' death, and with detailed textual analysis, is William Stringfellow's "Jesus the Criminal," in *Christianity and Crisis,* 30/8 (June 8, 1970), 119ff.

The most parallel stance of all is that of my Brethren brethren Dale Brown (*The Christian Revolutionary* [Grand Rapids: Eerdmans, 1971]) and Art Gish (*The New Left and Christian Radicalism* [Eerdmans, 1970]); they presuppose a view like that of this book, but without arguing it at length on New Testament grounds.

The equation is so glib, and so surrounded by the not-sure-I-really-mean-it indirection of the age of McLuhan, that the Christian ethicist can just as glibly pass it off as not only irreverent but also irrelevant to the real business of ethics. But is it that simple? Or might it be that in this half-spoofing exaggeration there is breaking into common awareness a dimension of biblical truth that we — precisely the reverent and relevant ethicists — had been hiding from ourselves?

This study makes that claim. It claims not only that Jesus is, according to the biblical witness, a model of radical political action, but that this issue is now generally visible throughout New Testament studies, even though the biblical scholars have not stated it in such a way that the ethicists across the way have had to notice it.[2]

This "stating it" is all the present study tries to do; to let the Jesus story so speak that the person concerned with social ethics, as accustomed as such a person is to a set of standard ways to assume Jesus not to be relevant to social issues, or at least not relevant *immediately*, can hear.

Such an effort at interdisciplinary "translation" has its own set of serious perils. To both the parties whom it attempts to bring into hailing range of one another it must seem to be oversimplifying, since it begins by disrespecting the boundaries, and the axioms, of each discipline, and since the "translator" or bridge-builder is always somehow partly an alien, partly a layperson blundering beyond his or her depth. We may plead only that if the experts had built the bridge we need, the layperson would not have needed to.

Our study, then, seeks to describe the connection which might relate New Testament studies[3] with contemporary social ethics, espe-

2. "Despite a greater readiness now frankly to face the problems that inevitably result regarding a historical person as the incarnation of God, there is still a curious reluctance to consider the possibility that Jesus might have had political views." S. G. F. Brandon, *Jesus and the Zealots* (Manchester University Press, 1967), p. 24. Brandon is an outsider in the New Testament guild. It would probably be a more correct description of contemporary New Testament scholarship if he had said that in particular texts scholars are quite ready to recognize the political dimension of the ministry of Jesus but that there is a reluctance to synthesize these observations. Cf. below, p. 50n.52, the comment of Etienne Trocmé.

3. The kernel of this material was presented to the second "Puidoux" Conference on Church and Peace at Iserlohn (Germany) in July 1957, and expanded in *Nachfolge Christi als Gestalt politischer Verantwortung* (Basel: Agape Verlag, 1964), pp. 37ff. Its present

cially since this latter discipline is currently preoccupied with the problems of power and revolution.[4] Theologians have long been asking how Jerusalem can relate to Athens; here the claim is that Bethlehem has something to say about Rome — or Masada.

By what right dare one seek to throw a cable across the chasm which usually separates the disciplines of New Testament exegesis and contemporary social ethics? Normally any link between these realms of discourse would have to be extremely long and indirect. First there is an enormous distance between past and present to be covered by way of hermeneutics from exegesis to contemporary theology; then still another long leg must be covered from theology to ethics via secular sociology and Ernst Troeltsch. From the perspective of the historical theologian, normally perched on an island between these two spans and thus an amateur on both banks, I can justify leaping into the problem in such an amateur way on only two grounds. For one thing, it seems that the experts who set out to go the long way around never get there. The Scripture scholars in their hermeneutic meditations develop vast systems of crypto-systematics, and the field of ethics remains as it was; or, if anything new happens there, it is usually fed from some other sources.[5]

---

outline (up to p. 114) reflects a paper prepared for presentation April 27, 1968, to the Chicago Society for Biblical Research, as a strictly New Testament study. It has been released for publication in this expanded form by the editors of *Biblical Research.* Its preparation has benefited from numerous suggestions of William Klassen and John E. Toews.

4. The wide visibility of the question dealt with in this book goes back at least to the writings of the brothers Niebuhr in the 1930s; yet it reaches a new height of intensity in the current of ecumenical thought on political ethics, especially strong in Latin America, which found strong expression in the Geneva Conference on Church and Society in July 1966. Here "revolution" becomes the key term (e.g., Richard Shaul, *Containment and Change* [New York: Macmillan, 1967], pp. 215ff.). In this context there is often an appeal to Jesus as a revolutionary and political figure; yet this appeal is a slogan-like formal one. It is not linked to a substantial concern for the *kind* of politics Jesus incarnated. It sometimes even pointedly rejects the relevance of the concrete guidance of Jesus while still claiming his mandate. It is thus marked by the absence of precisely the concerns to which the present book is devoted. I referred in n. 1 above to other attempts in recent religious journalism to deal with "Jesus as an Agitator" but without posing seriously the questions, either of biblical hermeneutics or of contemporary systematic social ethics, that would enable such a parallelism to stand serious criticism.

5. In 1993 I stand by the accuracy of this description of the lay of the academic

The other reason for my boldness, which would be in its own right also a subject for debate in the exegetical guild, is the radical Protestant axiom, which more recently has been revitalized and characterized as "biblical realism," according to which it is safer for the life of the church to have the whole people of God reading the whole body of canonical Scripture than to trust for enlightenment only to certain of the filtering processes through which the learned folk of a given age would insist all the truth must pass.[6]

It is thus not unawares, nor irresponsibly, that in the present book I take the risk of synthesis in proposing to bring the Jesus of the canonical Gospels into juxtaposition with the present. This hazardous venture involves no disrespect for the many kinds of historical questions which might be appropriately asked about the link between Jesus of the canonical Gospels and the other Jesuses whom scholarship can project.

Mainstream Ethics: Jesus Is Not the Norm

The classically naive approach once could assume an immediate connection between the work or the words of Jesus and what it would mean today to be faithful "In His Steps."[7] To this there is an equally

---

land in the 1960s. The respective epilogues to the several following chapters will demonstrate that there has been some improvement.

6. The case for the continued legitimacy of theological recourse to the wholeness of the Gospel texts in their received form has been persuasively restated by Floyd Filson in the article, "Thinking with the Biblical Writer," *BR* 11 (1966); and similarly by Theodore Wedel, *The Gospel in a Strange, New World* (Philadelphia: Westminster, 1963), pp. 17ff. Hans Conzelmann, in his *Theology of St. Luke* (London: Faber & Faber, 1960), pp. 9ff., likewise argues that although it is part of the scholar's task to seek to evaluate his documents and reconstruct the events behind them, the *first* interest of the student of any text must be what the author of that text means to say. In saying this of Luke, Conzelmann cites a similar argument of M. Dibelius concerning Acts. Yet our concentration for present purposes on the text as we have it by no means concedes that further research into events behind the text would weaken what it says to our point; cf. pp. 12, 41n.35, 101. Concerning the label "biblical realism," I have added a few clarifying comments in the Preface to the 1993 Edition, p. viii above.

7. The classic of turn-of-the-century popular Protestantism which Charles Sheldon published under this title is not a serious sample of the vision of discipleship which I am here describing. The values to which the devoted disciple Henry Maxwell is committed

classic nonnaive answer, which can be played back from every age in the history of Christian thought about society. Thus if we can restate this mainstream answer we will have set the stage for our argument. The first and most substantial affirmation of this classic defense against an ethic of imitation is the observation that Jesus is simply not relevant in any immediate sense to the questions of social ethics. The great variety of ways of grounding this negative statement can perhaps not unfairly be summarized in three theses, the first being the sixfold claim of Jesus' irrelevance.[8]

1. The ethic of Jesus is an ethic for an "Interim" which Jesus thought would be very brief. It is possible for the apocalyptic Sermonizer on the Mount to be unconcerned for the survival of the structures of a solid society because he thinks the world is passing away soon. His ethical teachings therefore appropriately pay no attention to society's need for survival and for the patient construction of permanent institutions. The rejection of violence, of self-defense, and of accumulating wealth for the sake of security, and the footlooseness of the prophet of the kingdom are not permanent and generalizable attitudes toward social values. They make sense only if it be assumed that those values are coming to an imminent end. Thus at any point where social ethics must deal with problems of duration, Jesus quite clearly can be of no help. If the impermanence of the social order is an axiom underlying the ethic of Jesus, then obviously the survival of this order for centuries has already invalidated the axiom. Thereby the survival of society, as a value in itself, takes on a weight which Jesus did not give it.[9]

---

are not *materially* related to Jesus. "Do what Jesus would do" means for Sheldon simply, "do the right at all costs"; but *what* is the right thing to do is knowable for Sheldon apart from Jesus. Sheldon is rather an advocate of the mainstream view being characterized here, which finds the substantial norms of ethics elsewhere than in the Gospels. For a serious advocacy of Jesus' exemplarity in social ethics one would need to go back to Franciscan, Czech Brethren, or Anabaptist models. The beginnings of a modern restatement of the claim can be found in G. H. C. MacGregor, *The New Testament Basis of Pacifism* (New York: Fellowship of Reconciliation, 1936). Cf. also C. H. Dodd, below, p. 94n.3 and above, p. i.

8. In the epilogue a few more dimensions of this claim have been added.

9. The classic American statement of the dependence of Jesus' ethic upon his expectation of an early end to history was Reinhold Niebuhr's *Interpretation of Christian Ethics* (New York: Harper, 1935); it is followed by Paul Ramsey and many others.

2. Jesus was, as his Franciscan and Tolstoyan imitators have said, a simple rural figure. He talked about the sparrows and the lilies to fishermen and peasants, lepers and outcasts. His radical personalization of all ethical problems is only possible in a village sociology where knowing everyone and having time to treat everyone as a person is culturally an available possibility. The rustic "face-to-face model of social relations" is the only one he cared about. There is thus in the ethic of Jesus no intention to speak substantially to the problems of complex organization, of institutions and offices, cliques and power and crowds.

3. Jesus and his early followers lived in a world over which they had no control. It was therefore quite fitting that they could not conceive of the exercise of social responsibility in any form other than that of simply *being* a faithful witnessing minority. Now, however, that Christianity has made great progress in history, represented symbolically by the conversion of Constantine and practically by the "Judeo-Christian" assumptions underlying our entire Western culture, the Christian is obligated to answer questions which Jesus did not face. The individual Christian, or all Christians together, must accept responsibilities that were inconceivable in Jesus' situation.[10]

4. The nature of Jesus' message was ahistorical by definition. He dealt with spiritual and not social matters, with the existential and not the concrete. What he proclaimed was not a social change but a new self-understanding, not obedience but atonement. Whatever he said and did of a social and ethical character must be understood not for its own sake but as the symbolic or mythical clothing of his spiritual

10. "Jesus deals only with the simplest moral situation . . . the case of one person in relation to but one other. He does not undertake to say how men, who themselves ought not to resist at all . . . when they themselves alone receive the blows, ought to act in more complex cases. . . ." Paul Ramsey, *Basic Christian Ethics* (New York: Scribner, 1950), pp. 167ff. A representative of the tendency to dehistoricize Jesus' teaching even when intending to take it seriously is Ernest C. Colwell, *Jesus and the Gospel* (New York: Oxford, 1963). Although the thrust of Colwell's book is a reaffirmation of the basic historical reliability of the Gospel reports, he says this must not be so read as to include social concreteness. The temptation legend (p. 47) is a dramatic parable of humility, not a temptation. The frequency of economic topics in parables and ethical teaching should not be taken to indicate an attitude to wealth or labor (p. 60). What is wrong with greed is not that it takes bread from someone else but that it is spiritually seductive.

message.[11] If the Gospel texts were not sufficiently clear on this point, at least we are brought to a definitive clarity by the later apostolic writings. Especially Paul moves us away from the last trace of the danger of a social misunderstanding of Jesus and toward the inwardness of faith.

5. Or to say it just a little differently, Jesus was a radical monotheist. He pointed people away from the local and finite values to which they had been giving their attention and proclaimed the sovereignty of the only One worthy of being worshiped. The impact of this radical discontinuity between God and humanity, between the world of God and human values, is to relativize all human values. The will of God cannot be identified with any one ethical answer, or any given human value, since these are all finite. But the practical import of that relativizing, for the substance of ethics, is that these values have become autonomous. All that now stands above them is the infinite.[12]

6. Or the reason may be more "dogmatic" in tone. Jesus came, after all, to give his life for the sins of humankind. The work of atonement or the gift of justification, whereby God enables sinners to be restored to his fellowship, is a forensic act, a gracious gift. For Roman Catholics this act of justification may be found to be in correlation with the sacraments, and for Protestants with one's self-understanding,

11. A standard statement of this stance is that of Roger Mehl, "The Basis of Christian Social Ethics," in John C. Bennett (ed.), *Christian Social Ethics in a Changing World* (New York: Association, 1966), pp. 44ff. According to Mehl, Jesus' concern was centered exclusively on the individual. He was indifferent to social and political issues, and far from the Zealots' preoccupations. It is thus an innovation (according to Mehl a salutary one) when Christian ethics, only in modern times and in response to socialism's challenge, comes to deal with matters of social structure.

It could be shown at greater length how this pattern of thought may often persist even under the cover of language that would seem to mean quite the opposite. When, e.g., Jesus is spoken of as "unveiling true humanity," or when incarnation is spoken of as revelation, this could well mean that we could or should go to the man Jesus in all his contingent humanity to see what kind of person God wants. Yet in the actual practice of contemporary "incarnational theology" this language generally serves as the preamble to or as validation for a definition of essential or common humanity derived from quite other sources, which incarnation is held to have ratified.

12. This is the central thrust of H. Richard Niebuhr already in his *Christ and Culture* (New York: Harper, 1951), esp. pp. 234ff., and further in his *Radical Monotheism and Western Culture* (Harper, 1960) and *The Responsible Self* (Harper, 1963).

in response to the proclaimed Word; but never should it be correlated with ethics. Just as guilt is not a matter of having committed particular sinful acts, so justification is not a matter of proper behavior. How the death of Jesus works our justification is a divine miracle and mystery; how he died, or the kind of life which led to the kind of death he died, is therefore ethically immaterial.

It results from this consideration of the type of thinking and teaching Jesus was doing, that it cannot have been his intention — or at least we cannot take it to have been his achievement — to provide any precise guidance in the field of ethics. His apocalypticism and his radical monotheism may teach us to be modest; his personalism may teach us to cherish the values of face-to-face relationships, but as to the stuff of our decision-making, we shall have to have other sources of help.

What Other Norm Is There?

The second substantial affirmation of the mainstream ethical consensus follows from the first. Since, as we have seen, Jesus himself (either his teachings or his behavior) is not finally normative for ethics, there must be some kind of bridge or transition into another realm or into another mode of thought when we begin to think about ethics. This is not simply a bridge from the first century to the present, but from theology to ethics or from the existential to the institutional. A certain very moderate amount of freight can be carried across this bridge: perhaps a concept of absolute love or humility or faith or freedom. But the substance of ethics must be reconstructed on our side of the bridge.

Third, therefore, the reconstruction of a social ethic on this side of the transition will derive its guidance from common sense and the nature of things. We will measure what is "fitting" and what is "adequate"; what is "relevant" and what is "effective." We shall be "realistic" and "responsible." All these slogans point to an epistemology for which the classic label is the *theology of the natural:* the nature of things is held to be adequately perceived in their bare givenness; the right is that which respects or tends toward the realization of the essentially given. Whether this ethic of natural law be encountered in the reformation form, where it is called an ethic of "vocation" or of the "station," or in the currently popular form of the "ethic of the situation," or in the older catholic forms where "nature" is known in other ways, the structure of the argument is the same: it is by studying the realities around us, not by hearing a proclamation from God, that we discern the right.[13]

Once these assumptions about the sources of a relevant social ethic and about the spirituality of Jesus' own message have been made, we may then observe a kind of negative feedback into the interpretation of the New Testament itself. We now know, the argument runs, that Jesus could not have been practicing or teaching a relevant social ethic. Then the Jewish and Roman authorities, who thought he was doing just that and condemned him for it, must have misunderstood very seriously what he was about. This is an evidence of the hardness of their hearts. Matthew as well, who organized and interpreted the teachings of Jesus so as to make of them a simple kind of ethical catechism, misunderstood Jesus: from his misunderstanding arises that regrettable phenomenon which Protestant historians call "Early Catholicism."[14]

Fortunately before long, the explanation continues, things were put into place by the apostle Paul. He corrected the tendency to neo-Judaism or to early catholicism by an emphasis upon the priority of grace and the secondary significance of works, so that ethical matters could never be taken too seriously.

> Let those who have wives live as though they had none,
> And those who mourn as though they were not mourning,
> Those who rejoice as though they were not rejoicing,
> And those who buy as though they had no goods,
> And those who deal with the world as though they had no dealings with it. (1 Cor. 7:29ff.)

13. That this source of ethical substance is "other than Jesus" of course need not signify that it is unrelated to revelation. It may well be spoken of in terms of the order created by God the Father, or as an imperative discerned in the situation by the work of the Holy Spirit, or as the "Cosmic Christ" or "God at work in history." All such popular phrasings, as they currently function in ethical thought, point away from the concreteness of Jesus to some other source of norms. More examples of the stand that relativizes Jesus in the name of "revelation" are noted below, pp. 99ff.

14. Ecumenical manners have somewhat improved in recent decades. "Early catholic" is no longer a pejorative epithet. Yet the idea that developing a moral catechism was a step away from the original radicality of Jesus still prevails.

The second Pauline correction was that the apparent social radicality of Jesus himself (not only the Judaizing misinterpretation of Jesus) was clarified and put in its place.[15] Positive respect for the institutions of society, even the subordination of woman and slavery, acceptance of the divinely sanctioned legitimacy of the Roman government, and the borrowing of Stoic conceptions of ethics conformed to nature were some of the elements of Paul's adjustment, so that the church was ready to construct an ethic to which the person and character — and especially the career — of Jesus made no unique or determining contribution.

Looking back over this hastily sketched pattern of prevalent structures of ethical thought, systematic and historical theology will need to ask some careful questions. There is the question of the authority of these hermeneutic assumptions.[16] If the meaning of Jesus is this different from what he was understood by his Palestinian disciples and adversaries to mean, and if those ordinary meanings need to be filtered through a hermeneutic transposition and replaced by an ethic of social survival and responsibility, what then has come of the concept of revelation? Is there such a thing as a *Christian* ethic at all? If there be no specifically Christian ethic but only natural human ethics as held to by Christians among others, does this thoroughgoing abandon of particular substance apply to ethical truth only? Why not to all other truth as well?

A second kind of question we will need to ask is: What becomes of the meaning of incarnation if Jesus is not normatively human? If he is human but not normative, is this not the ancient ebionitic heresy? If he be somehow authoritative but not in his humanness, is this not a new gnosticism?

There could be problems of inner consistency as well. Why should it be important for Christians to exercise social responsibility within the power structures, if what they do there is to be guided by the same standards which non-Christians apply?

But this would not be biblical study if we were to pursue those

15. Cf. our fuller description of this view below, pp. 162ff.

16. Graydon F. Snyder, *The Continuity of Early Christianity* (Unpub. Ph.D. diss., Princeton Theological Seminary, 1961), pp. 18ff., makes clear that much of this analysis was dictated by the prior philosophical commitment (to Hegel) of the scholars of the Tübingen school.

questions now from the systematic and historical end. What I propose here is rather that, once we are sensitized by those questions, we might begin at the front again by seeking to read one portion of the New Testament without making the usual prior negative assumptions about its relevance. Or let me say it more sharply: I propose to read the Gospel narrative with the constantly present question, "Is there here a social ethic?" I shall, in other words, be testing the hypothesis that runs counter to the prevalent assumptions: the hypothesis that the ministry and the claims of Jesus are best understood as presenting to hearers and readers not the avoidance of political options, but one particular social-political-ethical option.

This study is then addressed to two quite discrete tasks. In substance and procedure the two will be distinct, calling for different kinds of methods and demonstration.

1. I will attempt to sketch an understanding of Jesus and his ministry of which it might be said that such a Jesus would be of direct significance for social ethics. This is a task of New Testament research immediately within the concerns of biblical scholarship.

2. I will secondly state the case for considering Jesus, when thus understood, to be not only relevant but also normative for a contemporary Christian social ethic.

Let us be fully aware that the endeavor will have any meaning at all only if both of the answers turn out to be affirmative. If for general reasons of systematic and philosophical theology such as have been widely dominant in theological ethics for a long time, Jesus, whoever he was, is no model for ethics, it then becomes immaterial just who he was and what he did.

If, on the other hand, Jesus was not like everyone else a political being, or if he demonstrated no originality or no interest in responding to the questions which his sociopolitical environment put to him, it would be pointless to ask about the meaning of his stance for today.

To simplify the question and bring it within workable dimensions, I propose to concentrate largely on one document, on the canonical text of the Gospel according to Luke. Luke's story line provides us with a simple outline, and his editorial stance is often taken to have been a concern to deny that the Christian movement was any threat to Mediterranean society or Roman rule. This centering upon Luke for our scattered soundings is not meant to slant the reading; any other Gospel text could equally well have been used, and we shall occasionally observe the parallels and contrasts in the other Gospels.

Nor is our simply beginning with the canonical text meant to convey any lack of respect for the significance of the critical and historical problems which lie behind the canonical text. But the distance between the canonical text and the "historical Jesus" as he "actually was" is not the subject of my present study. The bridge from the canon to the present is already long enough.[17]

The case I am seeking to make has to do not narrowly with the New Testament text but with the modern ethicists who have assumed

17. This simplification of the present task by setting aside the critical questions is not done with the intent of avoiding contrary evidence. Critical studies tend to confirm this study's thesis; cf. below, p. 41n.35.

It should not be thought that by failing to deal at length with such historical-critical problems the present book makes any neo-fundamentalist assumptions about the composition of the Gospel text, or about diversities within the development of the early churches and during the formation of the canonical texts. Neither are any particular "old quest" or "new quest" assumptions being made about how to reach behind the Gospel texts in their received form to an understanding of the "historical Jesus." Further debate on the construction of hypotheses about these matters is here set aside not because it is felt unimportant, and not because I have settled in my own mind just what they would have to produce, but only because a careful reading of the canonical text suffices to make the present point. It would, of course, be a count against my reading of the Jesus story if the historical questers were to come up with solid demonstrations that the "real Jesus" they find is quite incompatible with what we find in the canonical account. We shall need to meet that challenge if and when it arises, but thus far neither the old questers nor the new questers nor the nonquesters have done so. Thus far, the more skeptically the critics root around behind the documents for what they can recognize as "hard fact," under the assumption that the Gospel writers were less concerned for such data, and the more confidently the critics project their new vision of how it must really have been instead, the less likely it will become that interpretations can result that will support the traditional dogmatic picture of the apolitical Jesus, and the more likely will be the confirmation of the believability of those elements of the picture with which we are here dealing.

The traditional dogmatic rejection of the relevance of Jesus' social example for ethics was not based upon an alternative critical reconstruction of "what really happened," and therefore a challenge to that tradition need not await new agreed critical results.

Yet after having stated my serious openness to the critical task, it may be in order to testify to some skepticism about the degree of clarity that can be promised by the techniques currently used in that field of research. Anyone comparing the present effort to be honest with the canonical text with the highly confident and creative reconstructions of Carmichael or Schonfield, Brandon or Hamilton, would hardly conclude that the latter are self-critically hesitant to risk questionable hypotheses.

that the only way to get from the gospel story to ethics, from Bethlehem to Rome or to Washington or Saigon, was to leave the story behind. I shall be looking more at the events than at the teachings, more at the outlines than at the substance. The next pages present soundings rather than a thorough survey.

Nor is it the intention of this book to be exegetically original. At no point do I mean to be hazarding unheard-of textual explanations. All that I add is the focusing effect of a consistent, persistent question. It is because I claim no originality at this point that I may dispense with some of the pedantic paraphernalia which would be helpful or needful if I were making claims never heard before.

EPILOGUE

The Basic Thesis

In taking stock of the responses which *The Politics of Jesus* called forth, my first step must be to review the state of the debate in New Testament studies, with regard to whether Jesus was in principle a political person. There continues to be deep diversity among the scholars as to detail, but less than ever does any of them make Jesus apolitical. Two of the profession's senior authorities, Ernst Bammel and C. F. D. Moule, for instance, recently edited a massive symposium, *Jesus and the Politics of His Day.*[18] Their intention was to counteract especially the extreme thesis of Brandon; yet in so doing they could not avoid meeting him partway.

This massive flow of scholarship in the field,[19] representative of

18. Cambridge University Press, 1984.

19. N. Thomas Wright and Marcus Borg speak of a "third quest of the historical Jesus." Cf. Borg, "Portraits of Jesus in Contemporary American Scholarship," *Harvard Theological Review,* 84/1 (1991), 1-22. Of the five major interpreters whom Borg reviews, he says that three accentuate Jesus' sociopolitical impact in a way that is "fresh in Jesus scholarship."

a much broader body of writing, did not come about in response to *The Politics of Jesus.* Some of it was responding directly, as already indicated, to the farther-out thesis of Brandon,[20] according to which Jesus was very political, but in a very traditional way, that is, in a violent, state-oriented, military way.

Some scholars review the theme "was Jesus political?" by means of innovative modes of reading ("postmodern," "poststructuralist," or "sociological") which were not present in the same way in the 1960s. What it means that every reader of a text has and owns a specific perspective, as over against seeking or claiming some kind of quasi-neutral "objectivity," is itself part of a continuing debate among scholars about proper method. This debate has proliferated enormously since 1970. I have no intention of claiming the capacity to evaluate what can come through these new grids, but in no case can it be the previous precritical, apolitical Jesus.[21]

Some of the ongoing retrieval of awareness of the political dimension in the work of Jesus has been fostered by the perspectives of specific interpretative constituencies, notably in the broad spectrum of "theologies of liberation." As a somewhat informed amateur I have opinions on these matters,[22] but the thesis of *The Politics of Jesus* is not dependent on my claiming expertise of my own in the new subfield of "liberation." The prerequisite for appropriate reading of *any* text is the reader's empathy or congeniality with the intention and genre of the text. We do not ask someone hostile to the discipline of

20. Brandon's text has been referred to several times in my study (see the Index); other more popular uses of the same theme have been numerous: Schonfeld, Joel Carmichael, James Pike, etc.

21. E.g., John Dominic Crossan, *The Historical Jesus: The Life of a Mediterranean Jewish Peasant* (San Francisco: Harper/Collins, 1991). Crossan exemplifies the renewed acceptability of the term "historical Jesus" as more than a theme for skepticism (cf. n. 19 above). Likewise John P. Meier, *A Marginal Jew: Rethinking the Historical Jesus,* I (Garden City, N.Y.: Doubleday, 1992). Borg (n. 19) says of two "portraits" that they describe Jesus apolitically, but this is only the case if the term "political" is defined more narrowly than in this study.

22. My interpretative writing on the theme was last summarized in my "The Wider Setting of 'Liberation Theology,'" *The Review of Politics,* 52 (Spring 1990), 285-96. Cf. also my symposium summary in Daniel S. Schipani (ed.), *Freedom and Discipleship: Liberation Theology in an Anabaptist Perspective* (Maryknoll, N.Y.: Orbis, 1989), pp. 159-68.

mathematics to read a mathematics text expertly. To read a text of the genre *gospel* under the a priori assumption that there could be no such thing as "good news" (whether as a true message or as a genre) would be no more fitting.

I do not mean with this comment to brush off the numerous criticisms properly addressed to some of the oversimplifications and short-circuits that have surfaced in theologies under the heading of "liberation";[23] but for such critique to be valid it must be text- and context-based. It cannot be held to be wrong for the New Testament text to be read as the testimony of a liberation movement *sui generis.*

Why Not Jesus?

A second component of my continuing conversation with comments since 1972 must engage the reasons (pp. 16ff. in the 1972 version, pp. 5ff. above) that various schools of ethics give for not taking Jesus straightforwardly as moral model. There I identified six reasons; there are more:

There is historical-critical skepticism about whether the text says anything clear enough to guide us in the moral life, assuming that we would want to follow Jesus. This kind of expert attention to the canyon within the canon, between "whatever really happened" and "what the text actually says," has continued to develop in complexity during the last generation. There continue to be scholars who are very skeptical about the historical accuracy of details in the ancient accounts, and others who affirm a greater level of trust that there is within the texts a reliable historical core.[24] In either case, scholarly developments have not had the effect of discovering an apolitical Jesus, nor has any of the most astute scholars given up making appeals to the authority of the figure behind the text.[25]

23. Some reviewers in the 1970s, notably James McCord, saw in this book an especially valid expression of "liberation theology"; others read it as a critique of that movement. Both were correct, since "liberation" is a field or a theme, not a single position.

24. Cf. the survey of Borg (n. 19, above) and the "proverbs" school represented by Crossan (n. 21, above).

25. My previous reference was to scholars who believe that reliable testimony to

There is another historical-critical debate going on, not about whether there is something clear to be found in the old texts but about whether what is there is internally consistent. Every New Testament author had his own sources and his own readership. Even the same author could address different guidance to different readers in different settings. Any redactor could pass on differing traditions from more than one source. This observation would be damaging against the claims of fundamentalism, or of high Protestant scholasticism, in which the content of belief to which people seek to be faithful is not really the Bible but the seamlessly consistent system of propositions in which one believes all its revelatory "teachings" cohere. This same awareness of diversity, however, does nothing to undercut a postcritical or narrative understanding, for which the witness of a text consists in the direction in which it pointed, along the trajectory from earlier tradition to present challenge, within the actual life of the community for and to which it spoke. From this perspective, unity within diversity is more credible, and more helpful, than simple uniformity would have been.

There is the general theological bias of more recent scholars against the historical/particular quality of the narrative and prophetic strands of Scripture which proclaim a "God Who Acts"[26] and in favor of "Wisdom,"[27] that is, in favor of moral insights less tied to time and place. No one will deny that numerous genres of witness are present in Old Testament and New.[28] It does not follow, however, either a priori or

---

Jesus can be found in the sources; now I am saying that there are those who ascribe to him, if found, some authority.

26. Protestant academic understanding of the Bible beginning in the 1950s was strongly influenced by *God Who Acts* by G. Ernest Wright. Any theme which becomes a dominant mode for a while will be respected less by the next generation.

27. These words characterize a sea change in theology at large, not specific to interpreting Jesus, or to one date. An early specimen was Walter Brueggemann's *In Man We Trust* (Richmond: John Knox, 1973), a treatment of the prophetic message, which the author introduced in a very time-conscious way as a corrective for the "neo-orthodox" and "pietist" thought of his own past. Reading Jesus can also be a corrective for neo-orthodox and pietist prior bias.

28. Some will argue that the pendulum swing in Scripture studies, away from "history" and toward "wisdom," is overdone; that is not my present concern. Republishing a book after over twenty years frees one from concern for where the pendulum is.

empirically, that Jesus seen as sage,[29] as rabbi,[30] or as incarnate Wisdom,[31] would be any less politically relevant than Jesus the nonviolent Zealot.

There is the effort which some systematic theologians make to filter the Gospel witness through some much later epistemological grid. One very popular such grid is the "distributive" epistemological understanding of the Trinity promoted by H. Richard Niebuhr.[32] One should not make Jesus too important for ethics, Niebuhr argued, since God the Father would call for a different (perhaps more institutionally conservative) social ethic, based on an understanding of creation or providence whose content is derived otherwise than from Jesus. God the Spirit might guide us toward another, also different ethic, based on the further revelations received since Pentecost, during the history of the church.[33] This widely

29. That the genre of parable intends to startle its hearer/reader into a new vision of things is widely agreed by the most creative interpreters; cf. John Dominic Crossan, *In Parables: The Challenge of the Historical Jesus* (New York: Harper, 1973), and *In Fragments: The Aphorisms of Jesus* (San Francisco: Harper, 1983). Parables are like Wisdom literature in that they are not anchored to particular stories, yet at the same time they burst out of the traditional Wisdom categories of proverb and cosmology. It is an error common to "mainstream" moral thought to assume that the *literary* genre of "wisdom" must correlate with a conservative or mediating bias in the *substance* of moral thought. As A. E. Harvey, *Strenuous Commands: The Ethic of Jesus* (London/Philadelphia: SCM/Trinity, 1990), 62ff. makes clear, this is not true either of pagan or hebraic models. Harvey describes the cynic's intention to "change the currency."

30. The entire Sermon on the Mount, most pointedly Matthew 5, illustrates the rabbi's concentration on the outer and inner meaning of the *halakah* (although most of what we know about rabbis is from sources later than the Gospels). This book underemphasizes the Sermon on the Mount, because of its overemphasis in previous debates.

31. *Logos,* the name used by the Fourth Gospel for the divine Wisdom that came into our life in Jesus, is formally parallel to what is said about *Hokma* (Wisdom) in Proverbs 8. Yet when that Word enters human experience it is countercultural; it is rejected by its own. Cf. my "Glory in a Tent," in *He Came Preaching Peace* (Scottdale, Pa.: Herald, 69ff.).

32. Helmut Richard Niebuhr, "The Doctrine of the Trinity and the Unity of the Church," *TT* (Oct. 1946), pp. 371ff.; reprinted in the same journal, vol. 40/2 (July 1983), 150-57. Further conversation with Niebuhr's argument is projected in a possible publication with Diane Yeager and Glen Stassen.

33. Some of our contemporaries would take these phrases about the Spirit in a "charismatic" way; i.e., to mean that contemporary words of wisdom might give believers fresh contextual moral guidance. H. R. Niebuhr, however, did not mean that as much as he meant the "lessons of history," the adjustments made by the churches over the centuries to the intractable constancies of the fallen world, i.e., structures like ethnicity, the state, or the economy, which one can appeal to the guidance of the Holy Spirit to validate.

influential scheme is worthy of careful criticism,[34] but since it is derived from a modern epistemology alien to the New Testament, that argument does not belong here. Niebuhr's analysis does not make one person of the Trinity more or less political than the others. If such a distinction were to make any substantive difference at all,[35] it would be to come out in favor of a different political ethic, not of apoliticism. It would presuppose that Jesus is political.[36]

Jesus did not come to teach a way of life; most of his guidance is not original. His role is that of Savior, and for us to need a Savior presupposes that we do not live according to his stated ideals.[37] The classical Lutheran tradition designates as *usus elenchticus* the claim that the function of the law is less to tell us what we can do than to bring us to our knees because we cannot do it.

A. E. Harvey[38] provides a very illuminating discussion of ways in which various intellectual forces, driving toward a generalizable ethic, set aside the most characteristic teachings of Jesus. The considerations he cites overlap more or less with those listed above, although with different language. Harvey's project differs from that of the present book: (a) He centers on a handful of "strenuous" and "distinctive" texts, mostly on the Sermon on the Mount, whereas I protest against those few chapters' being singled out. (b) He trusts more than I do the scholar'scapacity to reconstruct, behind the texts, varieties of strands and strata of tradition corresponding to various styles and shadings of belief and carried by various first-century subcommunities. (c) He

34. Cf. n. 32 above.

35. Whether Niebuhr's intention was at all to deal differently with the *substance* of ethics as related differentially to Father, Son, and Spirit, as he seems *prima facie* to do, is part of the discussion cited above in n. 15.

36. Borg ("Portraits of Jesus," p. 21) notes that previous interpreters' discussions of whether Jesus was "political" or not presupposed that there are only two options: Zealot revolution or apolitical nonviolence. This disjunction sets aside the simple Gospel data on a priori grounds, not on the basis of the text. In general, the fivefold variety of images of Jesus which Borg surveys is a difference based more on people's a priori hermeneutical commitments than on the text.

37. "The Good News of the Gospel is not the law that we ought to love one another. The good news . . . is that there is a resource of divine mercy. . . ." Reinhold Niebuhr, "Why the Christian Church is not Pacifist," in *Christianity and Power Politics* (New York: Scribner, 1940), p. 2. This view is a refinement of negation 6 in the original list.

38. *Strenuous Commands,* pp. 7ff.

posits a clear disjunction between "aphorisms" and what was "meant to be" rules for community life. (d) He omits, during most of the exposition, the possibility that the reason for Jesus' radicality in "taking a maxim to its logical conclusion" might be the Kingdom's coming.[39]

If Not Jesus, Then What?

If our concern here were to spell out the substance of social ethics, it would be appropriate to widen the theme "what other norm is there?" (pp. 8ff. above).[40] The classical theological appeals for this purpose are to "nature," "reason," "creation," and "reality." What these four terms have in common is:

(a) that one claims that their meaning is self-evident,
(b) that said meaning is very hard to define with the concreteness that would provide strong moral guidance, especially with a view to guiding and motivating dissent,
(c) that these guides differ in their moral substance (i.e., in what we should actually do) from the teachings and example of Jesus; and
(d) that those guides are ascribed a priori a higher or deeper authority than the "particular" Jewish or Christian sources of moral vision, whether these be the Bible in general, or Jesus in particular.[41]

The connection of this discussion to the theme of the present book is of course that the impact of these several arguments, each in

39. This dimension is largely missing in the earlier chapters; it is present on pp. 192ff.

40. See also my discussion of "the other lights" in my *The Original Revolution* (Scottdale, Pa.: Herald Press, 1982), pp. 127ff., soon to be reissued in Michael Cartwright (ed.), *The Royal Priesthood* (Grand Rapids: Eerdmans, pp. 182ff.).

41. Cf. my "Does Natural Law Provide a Basis for a Christian Witness to the State?" in *Brethren Life and Thought,* 7 (Spring 1962), 18-22. This exchange with Donald Miller was the result of his critique of the argument on pp. 33ff. in my *Christian Witness to the State* (Newton, Kans.: Faith and Life Press, 1964). Similar arguments about the appeal to "nature" are made by Jacques Ellul, *The Theological Foundation of Law* (Garden City, N.Y.: Doubleday, 1960), and by Stanley Hauerwas in *The Peaceable Kingdom* (Notre Dame, Ind., 1983), pp. 51-60, 99-101.

its own way, is to set the authority of Jesus aside, not by avowing that one chooses not to follow him, nor by reading the story and finding in it a different message, but by claiming that in one way or another Jesus' claims on the disciple's life are set aside a priori, on systematic logical grounds. The inquiry to which this volume is dedicated aims to test whether being thus set aside is fair to the intent or the substance of the New Testament texts.

CHAPTER 2

The Kingdom Coming

The Annunciation: Luke 1:46ff., 68ff.; cf. 3:7ff.

We are not used to thinking of the maiden Myriam as a Maccabean. Yet if it were not for the history of repetition in the liturgical use of the *Magnificat,* we should all have been impressed that that is precisely what she sounds like:

> "He has shown strength with his arm,
> He has scattered the proud in the imagination of their hearts,
> He has put down the mighty from their thrones,
> And exalted those of low degree;
> He has filled the hungry with good things,
> And the rich he has sent away empty."

It is not important for our present purposes what kind of literary source Luke is drawing upon, nor what kind of liturgical source Mary might have been drawing upon.[1] In the present testimony of the gospel

1. Nor does it make a deep difference if, as some radical critics suggest, the earlier sources of this narrative may have had these words in the mouth of Elizabeth; cf. Paul Winter, "Magnificat and Benedictus — Maccabean Psalms?" *BJRL,* 37 (1954-55), 328ff.

The Jewish contemporary would likely have heard in this song the echoes of the song of Hannah (1 Sam. 2), whose imagery is not only revolutionary ("Those who were full have hired themselves out for bread, but those who were hungry have ceased to hunger") but also military: "the bows of the mighty are broken . . . the adversaries of the LORD shall be broken to pieces. . . ." Winter holds that this was a Maccabean battle song, embedded in an earlier document circulating among the disciples of John the Baptist,

we are being told that the one whose birth is now being announced is to be an agent of radical social change. The preoccupations of those who await the "consolation of Israel," with which he comes to deal, are not cultic nor doctrinal, and thus in the narrow sense they are not "religious" preoccupations; he comes to break the bondage of his people.

A few verses later Zechariah, as soon as his lips are loosened, proclaims as the meaning of the birth of John,

> "That we should be saved from our enemies,
> And from the hand of all who hate us;
> . . . to grant us that we,
> Being delivered from the hand of our enemies,
> Might serve him without fear."

This expectation is all the more clear when John himself spells it out:

> "Even now the ax is laid to the root of the trees;
> Every tree that does not bear good fruit is cut down and thrown into the fire. . . .
> His winnowing fork is in his hand,
> To clear his threshing floor,
> To gather the wheat into his granary,
> But the chaff he will burn with unquenchable fire."

This is the language with which John "preached good news to the people." Too hastily we have passed all of this language of annunciation through the filter of the assumption that, of course, it is all to be taken "spiritually."[2] Of course, John was wrong in what he was expecting, was he not?

---

which Luke took over. To posit such a borrowing would make Luke's assumption of political meaning in the text all the more conscious.

2. The current epithet, especially in the writings of those who interpret the social teachings of the councils of churches, for this kind of dehistoricizing interpretation is "pietistic." I reject the use of this simpler label because of the injustice it does to the historical movement known by that name, which was creative and critical in social ethics. Cf. my paragraph on "The Bogey of Pietism," in *Christian Witness to the State* (Newton, Kans.: Faith and Life, 1964), p. 84; and Dale Brown's article by the same title in the *Covenant Quarterly*, 25 (Feb. 1967), 12ff.

We shall see later in what sense the fulfillment which Jesus brought differed from the expectations of John; but certainly the difference was not that John's hopes were socio-political and the fulfillment Jesus brought was "spiritual." If the difference had been of that character, Luke would have had to begin his story differently. There would have had to be some hint in these first three chapters to warn us of the impropriety of the hopes of Mary and Zechariah as well as of John. Failing such a warning flag, we can only conclude that even at that late date when Luke compiled his story for Theophilus, presumably with some apologetic concern to avoid giving the impression that Christians were insurrectionists, he still had no choice but to report that the pious hopes which awaited Jesus were those in which the suffering of Israel was discerned in all its social and political reality, and the work of the Awaited One was to be of the same stuff.

For the sake of brevity we shall skip over the birth narrative, with the prominence there given to Caesar's census, with all its meaning for a subject people: registration, taxation, policing identities. We need not dwell on the evident political significance of Bethlehem's being identified by Luke as the city of David; on the angels' proclamation of "peace on earth," or the expectations of Simeon and Anna, or Matthew's reporting Herod's fear and the massacre of the infants; it will have to suffice to pick up the threads again where the account becomes public.

We could also have followed further than we do the theme of Jesus' relation to John the Baptist, as being of evident political import. John's ministry had a pronounced political character, and to some extent Jesus took up his succession (note the time linkage in Matt. 3:12). The instruction John gave his hearers called for an immediate community of consumption (Luke 3:11); the only categories of listeners indicated by Luke in addition to the "multitudes" (Matthew names Pharisees and Sadducees) are the socio-politically slanted publicans (3:12) and soldiers (3:14). According to Josephus, John's imprisonment was connected with Herod Antipas's fear that he might foment an insurrection.[3] Luke's account of John's offense speaks not only of "Herodias his brother's wife," but also of "all the evil things Herod had done," which might

3. *Antiquities* 18.5.2. Cf. Carl H. Kraeling, *John the Baptist* (New York: Scribner, 1951), pp. 85ff.

well involve some substantial political critique. Herod's putting away his first wife and taking in her place Herodias was itself a public political issue, as it brought on a war with the first wife's father, Aretas IV of Nabatea. Even if John's judgment upon the remarriage was motivated first by his rejection of divorce and adultery, his imprisonment had a political symbolic meaning, as did perhaps the choice of Machaerus, the fortress on the Nabatean border, as the place of John's imprisonment and execution. Jesus' answer to the emissaries of John (7:22) is directly reminiscent of his first Nazareth sermon (4:18). The report of his ministry leads Herod to see him as a possible successor to John (9:7ff.). He sets in juxtaposition his fate and that of John (16:16 and par.).

This scanty summary must suffice to show that in whichever direction we might have turned, fuller study of the tributaries would constitute further reinforcement of what we find in the mainstream of the story.

The Commissioning and Testing: Luke 3:21–4:14

"Thou art my beloved Son;
With Thee I am well pleased."

We need not speculate about how explicitly in the mind of Jesus — or of John, or of Luke — these words from heaven were understood as an allusion to Psalm 2:7 or to Isaiah 42:1b. If the double allusion is clearly intended, this is then an explicit merging of the themes of enthronement (Ps. 2) and suffering servanthood (Isa. 42). Be that as it may, with or without *explicit* messianic cross-reference, we certainly have to do here with the conferring of a mission in history. "Thou art my Son" is not the definition or accreditation of a metaphysically defined status of sonship; it is the summons to a task. Jesus is commissioned to be, in history, in Palestine, the messianic son and servant, the bearer of the goodwill and the promise of God. This mission is then further defined by the testing into which Jesus moves immediately.

The tempter's hypothetical syllogism "If you are the Son of God, then . . ." is reasoning not from a concept of metaphysical sonship but from kingship. "Son of God" cannot very well in Aramaic have pointed to the ontological coessentiality of the Son with the Father, so that it would then be appropriate for the tempter, as the first Chalcedonian, to contemplate how, sharing the divine attributes, Jesus is by definition omnipotent and subject to the temptation to put his omnipotence to improper use. The "Son of God" in Psalm 2:7 is the King; all the options laid before Jesus by the tempter are ways of being king.[4]

Luke's report of the testing begins with the economic option. The spiritual filter through which we are now used to reading has dealt with the attraction of this temptation as a purely personal and carnal one. Jesus was hungry: would he by miracle abuse his omnipotence selfishly to feed himself? But one does not break a fast of forty days with crusty bread, certainly not with a whole field of boulder-sized loaves. The option here, suggested or reinforced by Jesus' own renewed sensitivity to the pangs of

4. Rudolf Schnackenburg, "Der Sinn der Versuchung Jesu bei den Synoptikern," *TQ*, 132 (1952), 297ff., agrees that the title is meant messianically and not metaphysically (p. 317, n. 37).

The same is true in other Synoptic usages: e.g., Luke 22:76–23:21 (substantially the same in the parallels) equates "Messiah" and "Son of God" (in a Jewish context) with "King of the Jews" (before Pilate). All three titles referred in standard usage not to incarnate deity but to a divinely mandated royal man; cf. R. H. Strachan, in *The Interpreter's Bible,* VII, 15; and W. J. Foxell, *The Temptation of Jesus* (London: S.P.C.K., 1920), p. 81.

Following suggestions of Dupont and Grant, R. W. Stegner posits both a contemporary cultural rootage of the vision of "testing in the desert" within the Qumran tradition, and a scriptural model for it in the story of Israel's testing in the desert ("Wilderness and Testing in the Scrolls and in Matt. 4:1-11," *BR,* 12 [1967], 18ff.). Neither of these dimensions stands in the way of discerning as well a dimension of political choice, unless it be argued that the temptation narratives were *fabricated* out of the scriptural and cultural models.

Erich Fascher surveyed the opinions of historical-critical scholarship in his *Jesus und der Satan: Eine Studie zur Auslegung der Versuchungsgeschichte* (Halle, 1949). The themes he surveys are numerous: whether the story goes back to Jesus himself or was composed by later preachers; whether it is reported as having been a vision, a poetic meditation, or a more literal (and therefore less believable) physical translation of Jesus by the tempter from desert to temple to mountaintop; where this concept of Satan's authority came from, and so on. Yet it does not occur to Fascher to ask whether the account has real social meaning. The theme of Jesus' clash with diabolical forces (which Fascher then pursues beyond the temptation accounts) is located for Fascher in Jesus' inner spiritual experience.

Birger Gerhardsson, *The Testing of God's Son,* Coniectanea Biblica (Lund, 1966), illuminates the temptation with a wealth of parallels to the testing of Israel in the desert, but avoids any social concreteness in Jesus' own situation.

hunger, was that his messianity would be expressed by his providing a banquet for his followers. That this is no idle imagination, the later story was to demonstrate. Feed the crowds and you shall be king.[5]

The second temptation according to the sequence of Luke is the one most widely recognized as socio-political in character.[6] The voice from heaven (3:22) had quoted Psalm 2:7; now the tempter simply goes on to the promise of 2:8. Here there is no ambiguity about the political nature of the promised reward, "All the kingdoms of the world; . . . all this authority and their glory"; the question is rather what it would have meant to "Bow the knee before me." Are we to imagine some sort of Satan cult? Or does it not yield a much more concrete meaning if we conceive of Jesus as discerning in such terms the idolatrous character of political power hunger and nationalism?

Then Jesus was taken to the "pinnacle of the temple." Niels Hyldahl[7] ingeniously combines the Mishnah's prescriptions for the execution of the death penalty with some ancient accounts of the martyrdom of James, and concludes that being thrown down from a

5. Cf. below the "fulfillment" in Luke 9 (p. 42), ". . . surely it was not his own hunger alone that was in Jesus' thoughts in these desert days. There was the hunger of the great multitudes of the world's poor. . . . It was a question of the regular method to be adopted for his whole public career. . . . First the earthly paradise, then the heavenly paradise — was that not the right order?" James Stuart Stewart, *The Life and Teaching of Jesus Christ* (London: SCM, 1933), pp. 39ff. Schnackenburg, "Der Sinn der Versuchung Jesu," p. 315, is one of the commentators who accentuate the parallel to Deut. 8:3.

6. "Certainly the story means that secular power is not to be acquired at the price of worship of Satan; but do we grasp the import of the story fully if we think the only thing wrong with the offer is that it came from Satan. . . ? The offer is not rejected because Satan is unable to deliver what he promises; it is rejected because secular power is altogether inept for the mission of Jesus, indeed because the use of secular power is hostile to his mission." John L. MacKenzie, S.J., *Authority in the Church* (New York: Sheed and Ward, 1966), pp. 28-29.

Robert Morgenthaler, by a careful analysis of the difference between Matthew and Luke, concludes that the sequence and vocabulary of Luke's account of the temptation are intended especially to point up the political nature of the temptation in its relevance for Luke's contemporaries. "Roma–Sedes Satanae," *TZ*, 12 (May 1956), 289ff. I cannot go into the speculation about the difference between Matthew and Luke as to the sequence of the temptations.

7. *ST*, 15 (1961), 113ff. H. A. Kelly, "The Devil in the Desert," *CBQ*, 26 (1964), 213, suggests an alternative reading of the pinnacle symbolism; it is equally messianic-political in character. Similarly Fitzmyer I, 517.

tower in the temple wall (which might well be called *pterygion,* the term usually translated "pinnacle") into the Kidron valley, followed by stoning, if necessary, to bring death, was the prescribed penalty for blasphemy. The testing would then mean that Jesus was tempted to see himself as taking on himself the penalty for his claims to divine authority, yet being miraculously saved from the consequences.[8] Hyldahl does not decide whether the accent should lie on Jesus' contemplating the punishment and counting on the escape, or on his throwing himself down at his own initiative, as a kind of ordeal. In either case, it is the quasi-blasphemous claim to divine kingship which underlies the testing.

If, instead of following Hyldahl's suggestion of a fall *outside* the temple wall, we stay with the more traditional picture of an apparition suddenly from above *within* the temple court, we must in any case agree with Hyldahl that the concern is not with a mere acrobatic marvel as accreditation for Jesus' status as a worker of wonders. This would have been the kind of "sign" which Jesus consistently refused to give to the curious and the dubious. If we seek at all to reconstruct what might have been conceived of as a concrete human possibility in Jesus' testing of the meaning of his mission, would not an unexpected apparition from above have been the most self-evident way for the messenger of the covenant, in the words of Malachi (3:1-3), to come "suddenly to his temple to purify the sons of Levi"? Then (even more clearly in Matthew's account, where this temptation is not the culminating one, but rather leads to the offer of world supremacy) we see Jesus contemplating the role of religious reformer, heavenly messenger, appearing unheralded from above to set things right.

"Would such a descent from such a symbolic place mark the signal for a religio-political freedom fight, making Jesus ultimately the Triumphator, in the way sought after by those pseudo-messianic pretenders, of whom the New Testament and Josephus report examples enough in this period?"[9]

8. Hyldahl discerns here a recurrent motif: "escape-from-the-consequences-of-your-claims," which he sees as well in the other invitations to Jesus to avoid prospective suffering:

- Peter's plea which Jesus explicitly attributes to Satan (Mark 8:31ff.);
- the possible angelic deliverance in Gethsemane (Matt. 26:53);
- the mocking call to come down from the cross (Luke 23:35 and par.).

9. Schnackenburg, "Der Sinn der Versuchung Jesu."

The Platform: Luke 4:14ff.

Luke does not begin with a capsule statement of what Jesus "began to preach." Matthew and Mark do. They both report that Jesus' initial message was in the same words as were used before by John the Baptist (and were to be used later by the disciples): "The kingdom of God is at hand; repent and believe in the good news." The language "kingdom," "evangel," is chosen from the political realm. This peculiar selectivity of vocabulary would be most out of place if Jesus' whole point had been that over against the expectations of John, he was not interested in this realm. It hardly needs to be argued that "kingdom" is a political term; the common Bible reader is less aware that "gospel" as well means not just any old welcome report but the kind of publicly important proclamation that is worth sending with a runner and holding a celebration for when it is received.

Luke also speaks of proclaiming "the evangel of the kingdom" (4:43), yet he does not use just these phrases at the very beginning of the ministry; for Theophilus they would not have had the same density of technical meaning as for Mark's readers. Luke instead unfolds the same claim in a fuller statement in the synagogue at Nazareth.

Here the passage from Isaiah 61 which Jesus turns upon himself[10]

10. We cannot answer the question whether Jesus chose his own text or followed a set cycle of readings. The presence or absence of a fixed lectionary tradition in Jesus' time has become a subject of intense and complex scholarly debate for reasons quite apart from our concern. One school of Gospel critics, working quite independently from the mainstream of commentary writers, claims that the contents of the Gospel narrative are treated in a sequence dictated by the synagogue lectionaries, in such a correlation that the contemporary reader would gather a wealth of between-the-lines meaning from the connection between the Old Testament readings and a given episode from the life of Jesus (A. Guilding for John, P. P. Levertoff for Matthew, R. G. Finch for most of the New Testament). Suggestive as this hypothesis seems to the inventive scholar, it would be very hard to support with any degree of certainty. Cf. Leon Morris, *The New Testament and the Jewish Lectionaries* (London: Tyndale, 1964). The fruit of this debate for our concern seems to be that it points away from the likelihood that the choice of Isa. 61 was dictated by a lectionary. According to Paul Billerbeck (*ZNW,* 55 [1964], 143ff.) there was at that time no regularly prescribed reading of the prophets. That this passage is not included in the (known, but later) lectionaries would tend to indicate Jesus' choosing the passage for his own purposes, rather than his seizing the occasion of the text's having been chosen for him. This then points to a very self-conscious preparation for the claim with which he caps the reading.

Much of the effort to link Jesus' reading in the synagogue with the existence of a

is not only a most explicitly messianic one: it is one which states the messianic expectation in the most expressly social terms.

> "He has anointed me to preach good news to the poor;
> He has sent me to proclaim release to the captives;
> And recovering of sight to the blind;
> To set at liberty those who are oppressed,
> To proclaim the acceptable year of the LORD."[11]

It may well be that "the acceptable year of the LORD" in the book of the prophet referred to some particular event either at the end of the age or in the immediate future of the Babylonian captives (or both); but for rabbinic Judaism and thus for the listeners of Jesus it most likely meant neither of these but rather the jubilee year, the time when the inequities accumulated through the years are to be crossed off and all God's people will begin again at the same point. The expectation is thus not that Jesus is going to take Palestine off the end of the scale of

---

fixed lectionary tradition has been dominated by the desire of scholars to prove that such a lectionary tradition existed in synagogue Judaism at the time. Others are arguing for the hypothesis that dependence upon the Jewish lectionary determined the form of the Gospel redaction, and therefore constitutes a key to Gospel interpretation. These two theses are dependent upon one another in a petitionary way. Neither has been followed far enough that we could conclude either that the passage was chosen for Jesus by the calendar, or that the choice of the passage permits dating the Nazareth event. To understand the claim Jesus makes, the distinction is immaterial; though, of course, its dramatic effect and the immediate sense of eschatological fulfillment would have been greater if it were the case that the text was chosen for him. Cf. L. Crockett, "Luke iv.16-30 and the Jewish Lectionary Cycle: A Word of Caution," in *JJS*, 17/1-2 (1966), 13ff.

11. As this quotation now stands, it breaks off in mid-verse, omitting 61:2b, "the year of the Lord's vengeance." One might surmise that to listeners familiar with the text this omission would have been striking. J. Jeremias, *Jesus' Promise to the Nations* (Naperville: Allenson, 1958), pp. 44ff., builds upon this surmise the suggestion that the omission, rejecting thereby Jewish concepts of vengeance and opening the covenant to the nations, was the whole point of the narrative. This would then see in the abrupt end of the quotation the same issue as is spoken to later in the same chapter, namely Jesus' open attitude to Gentiles. But the talmudic practice of introducing a citation by the first phrases, leaving the reader to fill in the rest of the chapter, probably forbids reading this much meaning into the absence of a phrase. The openness to Gentiles remains, however, as an offense in its own right, in the next episode. (There may be a new narrative beginning v. 22 or 23, or at least some omission between vv. 21 and 22 or between vv. 22 and 23. The pleased surprise of v. 22 is not quite the same as the disbelief of v. 23.)

temporal sequence but rather that there is to come into Palestine the equalizing impact of the sabbath year.

In a most ingenious booklet,[12] André Trocmé has gathered the evidence that Jesus' concept of the coming kingdom was borrowed extensively from the prophetic understanding of the jubilee year. This hypothesis throws light on many allusions and on some of the difficult parables. In the consistency with which Trocmé uses his hypothesis as a key, he may be found too original and imaginative. But it is not the case, as the silence with which continental New Testament specialists have responded to Trocmé's book might indicate, that it is a brand new or unthinkable idea. Such standard commentaries as LaGrange and Plummer had already given the same interpretation of this particular passage.[13] The difference lies rather in the degree of readiness to take seriously the light this passage might throw on the rest of Jesus' ministry and on his self-understanding.

It is not our purpose here to discuss the origins of the sabbatical year and the jubilee, which apparently arose out of some kind of bankruptcy and mortgage arrangement in ancient Israel.[14] Nor need we discuss whether or to what extent the provisions of Leviticus 25 were ever literally observed,[15] either in the form of a fifty-year term on

12. *Jesus and the Nonviolent Revolution* (Scottdale, Pa.: Herald, 1973; French original 1961). A section of Trocmé's text is included below, ch. 3. An earlier book on a similar theme was E. Stanley Jones, *Christ's Alternative to Communism* (New York: Abingdon, 1953), a sermonic elaboration of themes from Jesus' Nazareth declaration, written after Jones's visit to the Soviet Union.

13. Rabbi Stephen Schwarzschild indicates (in personal correspondence) that according to the (perhaps later) talmudic lectionaries, particular prophetic readings were correlated with Torah texts, and in such a way as to link Isa. 61 indirectly with Lev. 25 (the jubilee provisions). Hugh Anderson in a recent survey of the status of criticism on this passage ("Broadening Horizons: The Rejection at Nazareth Pericope of Luke 4:16-30 in Light of Recent Critical Trends," *Interpretation,* 18 [1964], 259ff.) deals with the tension between acceptance and rejection by the audience, and with underlying questions about the pre-Lucan background of the narrative and about Luke's redactional intention; there is, however, no analysis of whether what Jesus is reported as saying had any social meanings. David Hill, "The Rejection of Jesus at Nazareth," *NovT,* 13 (July 1971), 161ff., pursues Anderson's questions. He holds that the linking of the two segments is a construction dictated by Luke's missionary theology.

14. Robert North, S.J., *Sociology of the Biblical Jubilee* (Rome: Pontifical Biblical Institute, 1954).

15. "There is not a single Hebrew who does not, even now, obey his sabbath year

particular obligations or as a sweeping economic realignment redistributing all property at once. Our interest is in the prophetic use of the jubilee vision. The place of Leviticus 25 in the Bible kept alive the vision of an age when economic life would start over from scratch; and the testimony of Isaiah 61 demonstrates its fruitfulness as a vision of the coming renewal.

At least once in Israel's experience it came to life as a concrete experience of national revival. Jeremiah (ch. 34) carries the report of a covenant of renewal in besieged Jerusalem, where King Zedekiah again put into effect the ancient law, proclaiming liberty to all Hebrew slaves. The slaveowners, however, turned around and took back the male and female slaves they had set free, and brought them again into subjection.[16] In immediate response, the prophetic words proclaimed by Jeremiah in the name of YHWH, God of Israel, were a reminder of the place of manumission in the Sinai covenant and the express statement that it was because of this failure to live up to the renewed covenant that Jerusalem would fall to Nebuchadnezzar. "You have not obeyed me by proclaiming liberty, everyone to his brother and to his neighbor; behold, I proclaim to you liberty [i.e., I deliver you] to the sword, to pestilence, and to famine, says the Lord" (v. 17). That the renewal of God's people, both the concrete renewal which is possible and has happened occasionally in past history, and the renewal after the end of the age, will have the form of the jubilee is thus integral to the prophetical vision. The same vision is evident in Isaiah 58:6-12. Thus Jesus' use of Isaiah is in no way arbitrary.[17]

---

legislation just as if Moses were present to punish him for infractions; and this even in cases where violation would pass unnoticed" (Josephus *Antiquities* 3.15.3). North, who cites this claim from Josephus, is inconclusive as to whether the procedure was ever carried out; in any case it was hardly done regularly. Note, however, the emergency revival of it by Zedekiah.

16. The text does not indicate whether we should consider this return to slavery as having been the result of force or of economic difficulties. If the public proclamation of liberation had been clear, it is hardly thinkable that the former slaveowners would simply have gone out and physically seized their former slaves. The point must rather be that the slaves, having no means to make their own way economically, again rapidly fell into debt. Thus the owners are reprimanded not simply for not releasing the slaves but also for not providing them with the wherewithal to function economically and independently.

17. The continuing fecundity of the image is demonstrated as well in creative

We must conclude that in the ordinary sense of his words Jesus, like Mary and like John, was announcing the imminent implementation of a new regime whose marks would be that the rich would give to the poor, the captives would be freed, and the hearers would have a new mentality *(metanoia),* if they believed this news.

We cannot assume that we know *exactly* what was meant by Jesus' statement that "this word is fulfilled." In what sense was Jesus claiming that something was beginning to happen right then in his person? Did anything really happen at all? Was he announcing an event the realization of which was dependent upon the faith of his listeners, so that it could not come to pass after all because of their unbelief? Or was he announcing what actually then did happen, namely nothing very visible for a while?

This is a serious question. But let us recognize that it is a question of systematic hermeneutics which is read into the Lucan text by readers who were not there. It has to do with the sense in which the fulfillment Jesus promised was an historical reality. It does not, however, have anything to do with the clear affirmation that the subject of the text is a social event. We may have great difficulty in knowing in what sense this event came to pass or could have come to pass; but what the event was supposed to be is clear: it is a visible socio-political, economic restructuring of relations among the people of God, achieved by divine intervention in the person of Jesus as the one Anointed and endued with the Spirit.

The second theme of the encounter in the synagogue provides Jesus' first direct offense to his hearers; appealing to prophetic precedent, he proclaims the opening of the New Age to Gentiles. This second thrust does not seem to be derived from the jubilee proclamation; it grows rather out of Jesus' response to the disbelief bred in his hearers by their familiarity with his family. There is rather a negative correlation between the two themes; the undercutting of racial egoism by the second thrust prevented the former from being taken in a nationalistic sense. The prophet's reference to the captive and

twentieth-century theology: "Jubilee is exodus spelled out in terms of social salvation. . . ." Johannes Hoekendijk, "Mission — A Celebration of Freedom," *USQR,* 21 (Jan. 1966), 141.

oppressed can thus not refer to Israel or Judaism at large as collectively oppressed; the liberation is too wide for that. The New Age is for all, and the hesitance of the Nazarenes to believe will only hasten its wider proclamation.

The Platform Reaffirmed: Luke 6:12ff.

After the move to Capernaum (4:31) Luke reports a rising tide of effectiveness among the multitudes, the sick, and the tax-gatherers. Soon the backlash of the religious establishment begins, with objections to Jesus' authority to forgive (5:21) and his disreputable associates (5:30). Almost immediately the opposition mounts to the point of angry scheming (6:11). Luke emphasizes that it was "in these days" that Jesus, after a night-long vigil, named twelve key messengers, first-fruits of a restored Israel. To organized opposition he responds with the formal founding of a new social reality. New teachings are no threat, as long as the teacher stands alone; a movement, extending his personality in both time and space, presenting an alternative to the structures that were there before, challenges the system as no mere words ever could.[18]

Cognate as the *functioning* of this inner circle may have been to the way any other rabbi would live with his favored disciples, there is more to its *formation* than that. Their number, the night of prayer,[19] and the following ceremonial proclamation of woes and blessings all serve to dramatize a new stage of publicness. The opening beyond Judaism which was predicted in the synagogue at Nazareth is now beginning; the "seacoast of Tyre and Sidon" is represented on this great plain. Despite the extensive parallels with the Sermon on the Mount, the emphasis in Luke's report is different. The blessings are balanced with woes, after the fashion of ancient Israel's covenant ceremonies.

18. In connection with the preaching tour of the seventy Jesus sees "Satan fall like lightning from heaven" (10:18). The mission of the church in the world is the destruction of Satan's dominion, as the acceptance of the tempter's shortcut would have been his triumph.

19. Luke 6:12. Reference to Jesus' prayer is one way Luke indicates major landmarks in his story; cf. 3:21; 5:16; 9:18.

The blessing is for the poor, not only the poor in spirit; for the hungry, not only those who hunger for justice. The examples drawn from the sexual realm (Matt. 5:27-32) are missing; only personal and economic conflict are chosen as specimens of the New Way, in which seized property is not reclaimed and the delinquent loan is forgiven. As in the jubilee, and as in the Lord's Prayer, *debt* is seen as the paradigmatic social evil. In short, the announcement of the synagogue is being repeated and spelled out in detail, this time with a structured social base (both the believing multitude and the defined nucleus)[20] and in plain view of the crowds ("in the hearing of all the people," 7:1). An ethic which is to be guided by the twin loci of imitating the boundless love of God for his rebellious children (6:35-36) and being strikingly different from the ordinary "natural law" behavior of others ("what credit is that to you? Even sinners . . ." [6:32-34]) is conceivable only if a new age has begun, and if that age's novelty is at the point of economic realism.

The Bread in the Desert: Luke 9:1-22

The link that binds together the sending of the twelve (9:1-10), the feeding of the multitude (9:11-17), and the first confession of Peter (9:18-22) is worked out much more fully in the account of John 6, which Maurice Goguel has justifiably taken to have serious historical value. This crowd of thousands was not the hard core of tested disciples but the first wave of inquirers coming to see if this kingdom which the twelve had been announcing was for real. As the devil had said it would, the distribution of bread moved the crowd to acclaim Jesus as the New

20. "The physical movement — of the preacher towards the people, of the disciple following the teacher — involves a social and professional uprooting. . . . Thus the decision for the Gospel claimed by preaching is expressed concretely, first of all, in an immediate decision to depart and to follow the teaching." Michel Philibert, *Christ's Preaching — and Ours* (Richmond: John Knox, 1963-64), theses 3 and 7. The realism of Jesus' proclamation included its power to create its own sociological base; without this he would have been no threat.

This awareness is the valid kernel of insight in the otherwise exaggerated article "The Power Tactics of Jesus Christ," in the book of the same name by Jay Haley (New York: Grossman, 1969), pp. 17ff.

Moses, the provider, the Welfare King whom they had been waiting for. His withdrawal from their acclamation is (in all the Gospels) the occasion for his first statement that his ministry was to be one of suffering and that his disciples would need to be ready to bear with him that cross. This is the moment when he elicits and then silences Peter's confession, followed immediately by Peter's first sign of unwillingness to conceive of the Christ as suffering. This is the moment when other disciples draw away from his "hard saying" (John 6:60, 66). This is the moment when he "sets his face to go to Jerusalem." However meager may be the possibility of constructing a continuous narrative biography out of the Gospel records, this episode of the bread in the desert is certainly one of the hinges of whatever did happen.[21] It marks the culmination of the popular Galilean ministry and the transition both to a ministry centered more on the disciples and to the approach to Jerusalem. "Going to Jerusalem" (9:51) is the superscription of the second third of Luke's book.

This first reference to the cross is already most clearly in its context behind the reference to the crown. Not only when Jesus says so, as an element of moral instruction to the disciples (cf. below, p. 37), but also in his own vision of his ministry and in his response to the beckoning acclamation, the cross and the crown are alternatives. He begins to be estranged not only from the Jewish leaders but also from the crowds,

21. Goguel was hardly the type of scholar to be overoptimistic about the chances for writing a biography of Jesus. Nevertheless, he deals with what he calls the "Galilean crisis" as the crucial turning in Jesus' ministry outside of Jerusalem.

In a slightly different way William Manson also makes the wilderness meal the hinge between the Galilean ministry and the later less public ministry. He further suggests that the gathering in the wilderness was precipitated by the public impact of the first sending of the twelve, and by Herod's growing concern about Jesus (with a conjectural dating of Luke 13:31-33 to the time of ch. 9 to coincide with the Tell Galilee movement). Manson takes as historically reliable Mark's report (8:29ff.) that it is from now on that Jesus discourages the use of messianic vocabulary and begins to teach explicitly about the sufferings of the Son of Man and the disciples' cross. W. Manson, *The Way of the Cross* (Richmond: John Knox, 1958), 54ff.

More recently Ernst Bammel has again described this event as the hinge where Jesus marked a turn in his attitude to the messianic vocation. Cf. "The Feeding of the Multitude," in E. Bammel and C. F. D. Moule (eds.), *Jesus and the Politics of His Day* (Cambridge, 1984), pp. 211-40. Bammel reinforces this reading by comparing the different versions of the account and by reconstructing likely connections to the death of John.

because the messianity he proposes to them is not to their tastes; yet what he proposes is not withdrawal into the desert or into mysticism; it is a renewed messianic claim, a mountaintop consultation with Moses and Elijah, and a march to Jerusalem. The cross is beginning to loom not as a ritually prescribed instrument of propitiation but as the political alternative to both insurrection and quietism.

The Cost of Discipleship: Luke 12:49–13:9; 14:25-36

The shadow never lifts from the band on the road to Jerusalem. The fire Jesus is impatient to kindle (12:49-50) already is flaming up; his message has begun to sow division even within the family (vv. 51-53). An atrocity, the massacre of a crowd of Galileans by Pilate, is the kind of provocation one would report to a political figure on the brink of a holy revolution.[22] The falling masonry at the tower of Siloam[23] may well have been relevant because the aqueduct there had been financed by funds Pilate had seized from the temple treasury.[24] Jerusalem's destruction is prefigured in the parable of the fig tree (13:6-9)[25] and

22. "Pilate mingled the Galileans' blood with that of their sacrifices" gives the superficial impression of a massacre in the temple; but Oscar Cullmann argues that the meaning may well rather be "with that of their victims" and may describe a Zealot uprising. *The State in the New Testament* (E.T. New York: Scribner, 1956), p. 14. A. T. Olmstead, *Jesus in the Light of History* (New York: Scribner, 1942), p. 148, identifies this massacre with one reported by Josephus (see below, p. 91).

Josef Blinzler, "Die Niedermetzelung von Galiläern durch Pilatus," *NovT,* 2 (1958), 24ff., rejects on linguistic grounds Cullmann's interpretation of "their sacrifices" as the Zealots' (human) *victims,* but he agrees, filling out with still greater detail, that the massacred Galileans were political enthusiasts in whom Pilate saw the menace of rebellion. Ethelbert Stauffer, *Jesus and His Story* (New York: Knopf, 1959), p. 84, agrees. Blinzler further believes that this slaughter must have taken place at the Passover, just one year before Jesus' passion.

23. This conjecture by Ewald has been widely echoed in the commentaries, but remains pure conjecture. Nonetheless, it looks for meaning in the right direction; the question put to Jesus in this context ("at that very time," 13:1) was not about the mysteries of Providence, which lets some innocent people be killed, but about the stance of faith in the face of the adversity Jesus had just predicted (12:57-59).

24. A mass slaughter by Pilate of Jews protesting his seizure of temple funds to build an aqueduct is reported by Josephus (*Antiquities* 18.3.2); cf. below, p. 91.

25. According to Zahn and Grundmann, the unfruitful fig tree is Jerusalem, the

predicted literally soon after (vv. 33-35). The reason Jesus is intrepid in the knowledge of Herod's threat (vv. 31-32) is that he knows that his fate awaits him at Jerusalem; such a linkage is meaningful only in the perspective of a Jerusalem ministry analogous to the crowd-gathering, order-threatening activity which had disquieted Herod. Herod cannot be seeking to kill Jesus for heresy or prophecy; sedition would be the only possible charge.

But no longer is this crucifixion perspective reserved to Jesus himself. The brief warning "not peace but a sword" is immediately expanded into an extended passage (14:25ff).[26] It is just when "great multitudes were accompanying him" that Jesus speaks his first severe public word of warning:

> "If anyone does not hate father and mother and wife and
> children and brothers and sisters,
> Yea, and even his own life,
> He cannot be my disciple."

Modern psychologizing interpretation of Jesus has been bothered largely with whether the word *hate* here should be taken seriously or not. This is certainly to miss the point of the passage. The point is rather that in a society characterized by very stable, religiously undergirded family ties, Jesus is here calling into being a community of *voluntary* commitment, willing for the sake of its calling to take upon itself the hostility of the given society. The seriousness of the alternative posed before the would-be disciple is underlined by the parables of the builder and the king who too hastily committed themselves to enterprises for the cost of which they were not prepared.[27] Again we could

---

owner impatient to cut it down is John (cf. 3:9), and the vinedresser pleading for one more chance is Jesus.

26. This passage has parallels in all the Gospels. In Mark it is linked with "Thou art the Christ," in Matthew with the sending of the twelve.

27. The standard commentaries support the conjecture that Jesus' hearers clearly heard here the allusion to Herod, who had recently given striking examples of both rash warfare and ambitious unfinished building plans. Thus to allude to the king's foolishness is itself political preaching. Any listener would have caught the mockery in the allusion. In addition to such passages, where the very speaking of the parable implies a political judgment, there are other parables drawn from the political realm. Joachim Jeremias, *The*

modernize the text and be surprised, and perhaps usefully instructed, by the fact that whereas modern churchmanship tries to make membership attractive to the great number, Jesus was here moving away from the crowd. But again the point is not the tactical question, whether Jesus wanted many disciples or a few. What matters is the quality of the life to which the disciple is called. The answer is that to be a disciple is to share in that style of life of which the cross is the culmination.[28]

The same warning is still more clear in the reprimand to the disciples in their concern about privilege in the coming kingdom, which Luke incorporates in the Last Supper account.

> "The kings of this earth lord it over their subjects;
> But it shall not be so among you. . . .
> For I am among you as one who serves." (22:25ff.)[29]

In none of the accounts where this word is reported does Jesus reprimand his disciples for expecting him to establish some new social order, as he would have had to do if the thesis of the only-spiritual kingdom were to prevail. He rather reprimands them for having misunderstood the character of that new social order which he does intend to set up. The novelty of its character is not that it is not social, or not visible, but that it is marked by an alternative to accepted patterns of

---

Parables of Jesus (London: SCM, 2nd ed. 1963), p. 59, suggests that the parable of the nobleman who goes on a journey to claim a kingdom was a reference to Archelaus, who went to Rome to obtain his appointment (Josephus *Wars* 2.80; *Antiquities* 17.9).

28. If we read the text alone, assuming that the word "cross" can only derive its meaning from the later death of Jesus, then its appearance in this text must be an anachronism read back into the story after the crucifixion. This conclusion becomes unnecessary if (Hengel, *Die Zeloten,* p. 266; Brandon, *Jesus and the Zealots,* p. 57, following A. Schlatter) the cross, being the standard punishment for insurrection or for the refusal to confess Caesar's lordship, already had a very clear definition in the listeners' awareness. "Take up the cross" may even have been a standard phrase of Zealot recruiting. The disciples' cross is not a metaphor for self-mortification or even generally for innocent suffering; "if you follow me, your fate will be like mine, the fate of a revolutionary. You cannot follow me without facing that fate."

29. Luke puts Jesus' reference to himself in the context of the Supper; thereby "I am among you as a servant" becomes a parallel to the washing of the disciples' feet in John 13. Matthew brings the same words into the context of Jesus' going to Jerusalem to be crucified (20:17ff.).

leadership. The alternative to how the kings of the earth rule is not "spirituality" but servanthood.

There are thus about the community of disciples those sociological traits most characteristic of those who set about to change society: a visible structured fellowship, a sober decision guaranteeing that the costs of commitment to the fellowship have been consciously accepted, and a clearly defined life-style distinct from that of the crowd. This life-style is different, not because of arbitrary rules separating the believer's behavior from that of "normal people," but because of the exceptionally normal quality of humanness to which the community is committed. The distinctness is not a cultic or ritual separation, but rather a nonconformed quality of ("secular") involvement in the life of the world. It thereby constitutes an unavoidable challenge to the powers that be and the beginning of a new set of social alternatives.

The political import of the formation of a group of disciples is heightened if we take seriously Oscar Cullmann's suggestion that perhaps as many as half of the twelve were recruited from among the ranks of the Zealots.[30] The formation of an inner team comprising both former Zealots and former publicans, the symbolic number twelve, and the first mission of the twelve which is reported to have been the source of Herod's first perplexity about Jesus, are all supporting evidence of this social relevance of the minority.

The Epiphany in the Temple: Luke 19:36-46

The central section of Luke's Gospel beginning with 9:51, "He set his face to go to Jerusalem," reaches a first level of culmination with the event we celebrate on Palm Sunday. "Blessed be the king who comes in the name of the Lord!" This is the first public use of messianic

30. O. Cullmann, *The State in the New Testament,* pp. 8ff. Martin Hengel, *Die Zeloten,* provides throughout a host of analogues to Jesus' ministries. S. G. F. Brandon, *Jesus and the Zealots,* while illuminating at many points, is too conjectural and too interested in proving a thesis to be convincing. Thanks to Hengel's sober objectivity, touching on Jesus only most marginally, the similarity of issues and patterns (withdrawal to the desert, purification of the temple, paying taxes to Caesar, etc.) is all the more striking. Especially the figures Hengel calls "prophets" are like Jesus in some of their behavior.

language in Luke's account. Quite without the incorporation of additional reference to a particular text from Zechariah, which Matthew adds at this point in 21:5, the political meaning of the Lucan account is already sufficiently clear. This language is made all the more striking when the report tells us that the multitude of disciples was rejoicing and "praising God with a loud voice for all the mighty works that they had seen."[31] What were these "mighty works"? The phrase hardly seems to be adequately supported by the preceding chapters of the Gospel; there must be further dimensions of imminent victory in their minds.[32]

The narrative of Matthew moves immediately to the cleansing of the temple.[33] Here we have a kind of fulfillment of the prediction of Malachi; the sudden appearance in the temple of "the Lord whom you seek," coming to "purify the sons of Levi." It is not sufficient to see here a simple expression of prophetic indignation toward the economic

31. After the revolt of A.D. 70 had already been begun by the temple captain Eleazer, son of Ananias, the Zealot leader Menahem entered the city "like a king" in a processional and took over the control of the rebellion (Hengel, *Die Zeloten,* p. 369). William Klassen ("Jesus and the Zealot Option," *Canadian Journal of Theology,* 16/1, 12-21) and W. R. Farmer, *Maccabees, Zealots, and Josephus* (New York: Columbia University Press, 1956), pp. viff. and 198ff., see in the triumphant procession a recurrent symbolic pattern of Zealot political activity.

Ethelbert Stauffer suggests another juxtaposition: "Pilate had just entered Jerusalem at the head of his Roman troops, and Jesus at the head of the pilgrim procession." *Christ and the Caesars* (Philadelphia: Westminster, 1955), p. 120.

A. T. Olmstead, *Jesus in the Light of History* (New York: Scribner, 1942), pp. 210-11 pictures Jesus as preoccupied with not giving a disorderly impression, and all the messianic language of the crowds as a misunderstanding due to the teaching of John the Baptist.

32. The following adjoining events, the "triumphal entry" and the "cleansing of the temple," have caught the imagination of many contemporary advocates of "nonviolent direct action." The parallelism is partially valid. Some of the differences become visible when one asks whether Jesus' "demonstration" was a "success."

33. The most imaginative interpretation of the cleansing of the temple is Ernest F. Scott, *The Crisis in the Life of Jesus* (New York: Scribner, 1952). Like other interpreters from his generation, Scott overdoes the disjunction between the religious and the social dimensions of Jesus' work.

Following Matthew and Luke, our description here underlines the unity of the procession and the temple cleansing. Scott, *Crisis,* pp. 21-22, argues for the greater authenticity of Mark's report, according to which by the time the procession had reached the temple it was already late, so that Jesus simply "looked round at everything" and withdrew to Bethany. While decreasing the dramatic immediacy of the seizure of the temple, such an interpretation accentuates the deliberateness of the act.

exploitation of the temple clientele. Linked as it is in the next sentence with Jesus' initiation of a daily teaching presence, this is a symbolic takeover of the temple precinct by One who claims jurisdiction there.[34] That the "chief priests and the scribes and the principal men of the people sought to destroy him" is linked to the messianic claim acted out in the nonviolent seizure of the holy place, and not simply to the offense against order which might have been involved in his driving out the bulls.[35] In fact, had the cleansing of the temple been in any way disorderly or illegal, this would have provided a clear legal pretext

34. "This is the Lord coming to inspect and take possession of what belongs to Him. . . . He consecrates anew as it were, giving sight to the blind and making the lame to walk — the unmistakable sign of the breaking in of the eschaton." Ernst Lohmeyer, *Lord of the Temple* (Richmond: John Knox, 1962), p. 34.

Scott, *Crisis,* accents the very last words of Jesus' quotation from Isa. 56 (which Matthew and Luke omit) . . . "for all nations." Thus whereas in Matthew and Luke "my house is to be a house of prayer" is directed against the profanation of the temple, according to Mark it is against the exclusion of the Gentiles which is implied when the "court of the Gentiles" is made a marketplace instead of being considered part of the sanctuary. Here as in Luke 4 (above, p. 29n.11) it is risky to make much of the phrases omitted in a citation.

35. All four Gospels connect the cleansing of the temple with a debate on the nature of Jesus' authority. Picking up from a whimsical appreciation of the sensationalistic reconstruction of Joel Carmichael, *The Death of Jesus* (New York: Macmillan, 1962), Etienne Trocmé suggests that there is substantial evidence for ascribing to the episode in the temple a larger, more crucial significance (and perhaps an earlier dating) within the unfolding of Jesus' ministry than the received text makes clear. *RHPR* (1964), pp. 245ff.

This example may stand as another confirmation of the general observation that, if we did seek (as this survey does not) to reach behind the canonical Gospels to "the real historical Jesus," such an effort would surely increase rather than decrease the socio-political dimensions of our picture of his work.

Victor Eppstein seeks to illuminate the temple-cleansing episode by placing it within the context of a struggle between priest and rabbi, temple and Sanhedrin. "The Historicity of the Gospel Account of the Cleansing of the Temple," *ZNW,* 55 (Oct. 1964), 44. The priesthood had just expelled the Sanhedrin from the temple grounds; it settled across the Kidron at Hanuth where the vendors of sacred offerings were. The vendors in the temple yard were not a long-standing institution but an innovation, brought in by Caiaphas to compete with the Hanuth merchants and thereby indirectly to undercut the Sanhedrin. Jesus sides with the Sanhedrin, i.e., with the rabbinic class against the priestly class. Eppstein's conjectures may be too ingenious to be convincing; but they have at least the virtue of seeking to read the story with social-historical realism.

The economic dimension of the event is especially emphasized by Neill Q. Hamilton, "Temple Cleansing and Temple Bank," *JBL,* 88 (Dec. 1964), 865ff.

for action against him, which, however, we are told the adversaries could not find.[36]

Ever since the early Christian centuries, the whip in the temple has been considered the one act in the life of Jesus which could be appealed to as precedent for the Christian's violence. The older versions gave room for such an understanding, as if the whip had been used against the merchants: ". . . he drove them all out of the temple, and the sheep, and the oxen . . ." (AV, following Vulgate). The reader can take "them all" as referring to the money changers and the vendors of animals. Yet, ever since the earliest centuries,[37] careful analysis of the

36. S. G. F. Brandon *(Jesus and the Zealots)* hinges the entire argument of his book on the likelihood that the temple cleansing report is one of the few remaining indices of an original (historically authentic) memory of a violent Jesus, modified later by all the Gospel writers. We agree with Brandon that any historical reconstruction must find a Jesus who was executed for sedition, and who was socially close to the Zealots. We may agree as well that the depoliticizing of the memory of Jesus in early Christianity (though far less of this than he thinks can have taken place within the New Testament canon) was apologetically motivated. But by no means does it follow from this that the revolutionary initiative for which Jesus was executed must have been violent. At this precise point (esp. pp. 311ff.) Brandon's surmising has no critical grounds. The fault we find with Brandon is not that he interprets Jesus as politically relevant, but that he assumes violence is the only model for such relevance.

In his *Jesus and the Politics of Violence* (New York: Harper, 1972), George R. Edwards has brought together the overwhelming scholarly case against Brandon on historical and literary-critical grounds. Edwards (being willing to meet Brandon on that common ground of vocabulary) prefers to use the word "political" in a modern lay sense as including nationalistic violence, and therefore to describe the pacific Jesus as not political.

I have preferred to contest the meaning of the term, insisting that nonviolence and nonnationalism are relevant to the *polis,* i.e., to the structuring of relationships among persons in groups, and therefore are political in their own proper way. My difference with Edwards is in semantic strategy not in substance.

37. To discuss the "whip" we must telescope into our discussion the account of John, which differs significantly. It comes at the beginning of Jesus' ministry. The following anecdote is recounted by Cosmas Indicopleustes (*ca.* 530) concerning Theodore of Mopsuestia (d. 428):

"Rabbula previously showed much friendship toward the famous interpreter (Theodore) and studied his works. Yet when, having gone to Constantinople to attend the Council of the Fathers (381) he was accused of striking priests, and he responded that Our Lord had also struck when he entered the temple, the Interpreter arose and reprimanded him saying, 'Our Lord did not do that; he only spoke to the men, saying "take that away,"

text has excluded this interpretation and supported the trend of the newer translations: ". . . drove all the animals out of the temple, both the sheep and the cattle" (Today's English Version; also Moffatt, Goodspeed, the Zurich Bible, and commentators McGregor, Temple, Plummer, Strachan). The normal sense of the conjunction *te kai* is to initiate a list, not to continue a series beginning with "them all."[38] The "them all" *(pantas)* may with equal grammatical propriety refer to the preceding "sellers and changers" or to the following "sheep and bullocks."[39] The "cast out" *(exebalen)* posits no violence; elsewhere in the New Testament it means simply "send away."[40]

Jesus is now in control of the course of events. It would be but one more step to consolidate that control, riding the crest of the crowd's enthusiasm and profiting from the confusion as the liberated cattle stampede from the court and the traffickers scramble across the cobblestones after their money. The coup d'etat is two-thirds won; all that remains is to storm the Roman fortress next door. But it belongs to the nature of the new order that, though it condemns and displaces the old, it does not do so with the arms of the old. Jesus passes up his golden chance, and withdraws to Bethany. But the city will not be the same again. Now it is clear that he must be killed (19:47; 20:19; 22:2).

Between the triumphal entry and the purification of the temple, Luke (alone among the Evangelists) has inserted a poignant vignette.[41]

---

and turned over the tables. But he drove out the bullocks and the sheep with the blows of his whip.' " Wenda Wolska, *La Topographie de Cosmas Indicopleustes* (Paris: Presses Universitaires Francaises, 1962), p. 91. Cited in Lasserre (n. 38 below), p. 7.

38. Jean Lasserre, "Un Contresens tenace," *CR* (Oct. 1967), pp. 7ff., surveys all the New Testament usages of *te kai.* In 86 cases a rendering comparable to ". . . as well as the sheep and the oxen" would be impossible. In five it would be possible but is not so rendered by the translators. Only in John 2:15 is the particle ever so rendered. English version "A Tenacious Misinterpretation," in Willard Swartley (ed.), Occasional Papers of the Council of Mennonite Seminaries and Institute of Mennonite Studies No. 1 (Elkhart, 1981), pp. 35-47.

39. *Ibid.,* pp. 13ff.

40. Mark 5:40; Matt. 9:38.

41. Scott, *Crisis,* p. 24 and *passim,* makes much of the strategic importance of this event for the Gospel narration. It forms the hinge between the teaching ministry and the passion; it is the point of irruption of the messianic secret, the first outright challenge to the sacerdotal class, and the detonator of the antagonisms that had been building up against him. Jesus himself chooses the time and the shape of the final clash, and precipitates it. "He

Here in a kind of prophetic lament, Jesus at the gate of the city weeps because the city "did not know its time of visitation." There is about the very coming of the King a built-in illustration of that rejection which is already sure. At the point of the city's most uninhibited welcoming of the Messiah, Luke will not let the reader forget that his rejection was already sealed. Despite the joyous crowds, this man on the donkey is beginning his passion.

Every pericope in the section 19:47–22:2 reflects in some way the confrontation of two social systems and Jesus' rejection of the status quo. The trap question about the denarius (20:20-25) is the most openly political, but differs from the others only in that this meaning is more transparent.[42] The challenge to Jesus' authority (20:1-8), the parable of the unfaithful vineyard-keepers cast out by the owner (20:9-18; with the allusion to Ps. 118, also quoted in the triumphal entry), the Davidic sonship of the Messiah (vv. 41-44, with reference to Ps. 110), the scribes who devour widows' houses (vv. 45-47), rich scribes and poor widows (20:45–21:4), tribulation and triumph (21:5-36); all is cast in the mood of impending clash between two regimes.

It is hard to see how the denarius question could have been thought by those who put it to be a serious trap, unless Jesus' repudiation of the Roman occupation were taken for granted, so that he could be expected to give an answer which would enable them to denounce him. Once again, the "spiritualizer's" picture of a Jesus whose only concern about politics was to clarify that he was not concerned for politics is refuted by the very fact that this question could arise. In the context of his answer "the things that are God's" most normally would not mean "spiritual things"; the attribution "to Caesar Caesar's things and to God God's things" points rather to demands or prerogatives which somehow overlap or compete, needing to be disentangled. What

---

thereby decided how his enemies would have to proceed against him. He defined the issue on which they would have to meet him and forced them to accept it" (p. 124).

42. Cf. J. Spencer Kennard, Jr., *Render to God: A Study of the Tribute Passage* (New York: Oxford, 1950); and E. Stauffer, *Christ and the Caesars,* p. 112.

A special depth of analysis of the denarius passage is offered by Stauffer, "The Story of the Tribute Money," ch. 8 in *Christ and the Caesars,* pp. 112ff.; and by Donald D. Kaufman, *What Belongs to Caesar?* (Scottdale, Pa.: Herald, 1969), pp. 35ff.

is Caesar's and what is God's are not on different levels, so as never to clash; they are in the same arena.[43]

The Last Renunciation: Luke 22:24-53

These thirty verses bring together in remarkable density four episodes. Following the institution of the Supper, there is first the dispute about who would be the greatest, in response to which Jesus calls his disciples to be servants rather than lords. This text has its parallels in Mark 10 and Matthew 20, where it comes before the entry into Jerusalem, in response to an overture from Madame Zebedee or her sons. Next comes the warning of Peter's betrayal (where Matthew and Mark predict the falling away of all the twelve). Then the report, unique in Luke, of the reversal of the disciples' earlier traveling orders, instructing them to take a purse and a bag *and a sword,* in order that the Scripture be fulfilled which predicted, "He was reckoned with transgressors."[44] Then comes the prayer for the removal of "this cup" (without the threefold repetition

43. Paul's echo of the criterion, "to each what is due to him" (Rom. 13:7), is likewise not a distinction between two realms, nor a listing of what is due to Caesar, but a guide for dissecting competing claims for loyalty. (Cf. below, pp. 205ff.)

44. Traditional proof-texting debate for and against pacifism has always made much of the "two swords" passage. If Jesus had meant his disciples never to kill why would he now have told them to arm? Is he not preparing them for legitimate defense while on their post-Pentecost missionary travels? But Jesus says he is preparing them for his capture, for the fulfillment of the prediction that he would be found among compromising company. When they respond, "We have two swords," his response, "Enough," cannot mean that two swords would be enough for the legitimate self-defense against bandits of twelve missionaries traveling two by two. He is (in direct parallel to Deut. 3:26, where YHWH tells Moses to change the subject, LXX *hikanon estin*) breaking off the conversation because they don't understand anyway.

According to Hans Werner Bartsch, *Jesus: Prophet und Messias aus Galiläa* (Frankfurt: Stimme-Verlag, 1970), p. 56, the reference to Isa. 53:12 cannot be Luke's insertion, for it is not according to the Septuagint. Luke in any case does not give to the fulfillment of prophecy the recurrent function it has for Matthew. This makes it all the more striking that just here, as in Luke 24:26 (dealing also with the suffering of the Messiah), the theme of fulfillment should be thus accented. In the Matthew account of the sword in the garden (26:54) the reference to fulfillment is in Jesus' own words (rather than, as usual in Matthew, the Evangelist's) and likewise centers upon the sword. Thus the "fulfillment of prophecy" theme has a special link to the garden capture in both Gospels.

and without the concentration on the disciples' drowsiness which are emphasized in Mark and Matthew), followed immediately by the betrayal and capture.

The creation of a literary unit in which two elements are inserted by Luke which were not present in Mark focuses even more clearly the question which most traditional interpretation has avoided. What would it have meant for the petition to be answered, "Let this cup pass from me?" What else could possibly have happened then?

Both pious and scholarly commentary on this crucial choice have uniformly seen it in the light of what did happen later. In the reverence which surrounds Christian interpretation of the story of Gethsemane, the reader and even the professional commentator seldom have indulged the historical curiosity which would ask what it could have meant for "this cup to pass." In what way would it have been possible, in the situation Jesus' offensive behavior in the temple had brought upon him, for him to avoid the ultimate clash and destruction? What was the option with which he was struggling? Was it that he might silently slip away to Qumran until the storm was over? Or could he have reconciled himself to the authorities by retracting some of his more extreme statements? Should he have announced a deescalation, renounced his candidacy for the kingship, and gone into teaching?

The only imaginable real option in terms of historical seriousness, and the only one with even a slim basis in the text, is the hypothesis that Jesus was drawn, at this very last moment of temptation, to think *once again* of the messianic violence with which he had been tempted since the beginning. Now is finally the time for holy war. All four Gospels report Peter's use of the sword in legitimate defense. All but Mark interpret it in such a way as to suggest that the episode is symbolic of a deeper struggle. According to John, Jesus' rebuke to Peter uses the very language of his prayer: "Shall I not drink the cup which the Father has given me?"

The narrative of Matthew interprets the episode of the sword by spelling out at greater length what Jesus might have done. "Do you think that I can not appeal to my Father, and he will at once send me more than twelve legions of angels? But how then should the Scriptures be fulfilled that it must be so?" The themes of an appeal to the Father and the notion of the fulfillment of prediction again place the sword episode in the context of the words of the Prayer. I have little qualification for surmising what it would have looked like for twelve legions of angels — a Roman legion is said to have been 6,000 soldiers — to come into that garden. But what I can imagine is not very much to the point. Matthew's report is clear, and Matthew *could* imagine that this final encounter with Judas and the Jewish and perhaps Roman police would have been just the point at which God would unleash the apocalyptic holy war, where the miraculous power of the angelic hosts, Jesus' disciples as shock troops, and the crowds in Jerusalem with their long-brewing resentment would rise up in one mighty surge of sacred violence and would finally drive the heathen from the land and restore to God's people (as Zechariah had predicted) the possibility to serve JHWH in freedom and without fear.[45]

In the account of Luke the interpretation of Peter's sword is given not after the event but proleptically, in the cryptic instruction to the disciples to have weapons about them, because the Scripture was to be fulfilled according to which the suffering servant would be counted among transgressors. The Matthean account projects a vision of the apocalyptic battle; the Lucan story soberly portrays the formal guilt of attempted armed insurrection into which Jesus was placed by the presence of weapons and by Peter's defense.

This is the third chance. As the tempter has suggested, Jesus once could have taken over the rule by acclamation after the feedings of the multitude. His second chance for a coup d'etat had been at the entry into the temple, with the jubilant crowd at his back, the temple police thrown off guard by the noise and the Roman guards cowed by Jesus' air of moral authority. Both times Jesus had turned away from the challenge to take over.

Here is now the last opportunity. As Satan had come thrice in the

45. The assistance of warrior angels was a regular element of the Zealot hope; Hengel, *Die Zeloten*, pp. 284ff. and 311n.2. The hypothesis is not new that the intention of Judas was not to turn Jesus over to the authorities but rather that by his betrayal he might force Jesus, in order to defend himself, finally at the last minute to precipitate that holy war through which Judas the *sikarios* (Zealot) expected the breakthrough of the Kingdom of God to be achieved. Mark 13:26-27 and Matt. 24:30-31 also see warrior angels in the entourage of the Son of Man. Cf. also W. R. Farmer, *Maccabees, Zealots, and Josephus*, pp. 180, 194.

desert, so the real option of Zealot-like kingship comes the third time in the public ministry. It is not without both literary and theological justification that commentators have pointed to a parallelism between the testing in the desert and the trial in Gethsemane.[46] Once more, now clearly for the last time, the option of the crusade beckons. Once more Jesus sees this option as a real temptation.[47] Once more he rejects it.

Execution and Exaltation: Luke 23–24

Just as the passage from the Lord's Supper to Gethsemane was underlined by Luke with reference to servanthood and to the swords, so now the movement from Pilate's court to Golgotha is interpreted by Luke in language reminiscent of the triumphal entry. A great multitude of lamenting people follow Jesus, who warns them of the disaster yet to come.[48]

Whereas Mark simply names Barabbas, and Matthew calls him simply "a notorious prisoner," Luke tells us twice that he was imprisoned for insurrection and emphasizes the ironic tragedy of the trade:

46. We shall leave to the form critics the question whether Matthew's or Luke's sequence in presenting the three temptations in the desert may have been influenced by the parallel between them and the three political crises of Jesus' later ministry. This allusion opens up a larger question which would perhaps reward the same critics. If it is conceivable on the one hand that either Matthew or Luke modified the sequence of the temptations from the way they stood in the prior common source because of a parallel he perceived between the three temptations and three landmarks of the later ministry, then we must also admit the corollary hypothesis, that the structure of the later narrative may have been seen by the Evangelist as the unfolding of the test already present in "digest" form in the desert. Then the temptation becomes the prologue to the entire public ministry, which is conceived as an unfolding of what was already projected there. This would especially fit in with Luke's concluding report that the devil left Jesus "until the appropriate time" (4:13).

47. Bob W. Brown, in a very lively Lenten devotional article, "He Could Have Saved Himself," *Eternity* (Apr. 1968), pp. 13ff., comes within a hair of recognizing a genuine dimension of social strategic choice in Jesus' acceptance of the cross. Many strands of the historical concreteness of Jesus' career are here discerned in a realistic way. Yet the closed circle of prior assumptions about the nature of atonement ends with the impression after all that while avoiding the cross would have been a concrete human choice, meaningful in the gamut of available social options, accepting it was not.

48. Cf. O. Cullmann, *The State in the New Testament,* p. 48.

"He released the man who had been thrown into prison for insurrection and murder, whom they asked for: but Jesus he delivered up to their will."[49] The story ends with both the inscription on the cross and the mockery of the soldiers focused upon his kingship and his not saving himself. Jesus was thus traded for a Zealot leader and put to death as "King of the Jews."

This is another of those points where spiritualistic-apologetic exegesis has always emphasized that the Jews, or the Romans, or the Zealot-minded disciples, had Jesus all wrong; he never really meant to bother the established order. Then the illegality of the proceedings and the impropriety of the accusation must be demonstrated. Even then it would need to be explained why a Jesus whose main concern is to be apolitical would be misunderstood in just this way instead of some other way, and would not protect everyone against such a radical misperception of his intent. Granted, the trials as recounted are irregular in procedure, and normal due process according to either Jewish or Roman law might have disculpated Jesus by virtue of the lack of *armed* insurgent actions. Still the events in the temple court and the language Jesus used were *not* calculated to avoid any impression of insurrectionary vision. Both Jewish and Roman authorities were defending themselves against a real threat. That the threat was not one of *armed,* violent revolt, and that it nonetheless bothered them to the point of their resorting to irregular procedures to counter it, is a proof of the political relevance of nonviolent tactics, not a proof that Pilate and Caiaphas were exceptionally dull or dishonorable men.

In a sketch of this kind there would be no profit in dealing with the ancient yet constantly recurring discussions of the legality of the condemnation and execution of Jesus by the Romans or by the Jews.[50]

49. Interpreters disagree whether there really existed a settled custom, as this account infers, of releasing a condemned person in the Passover season, and whether Pilate's appeal to it should be understood as a sincere effort to save an innocent man, or else to avoid releasing the more dangerous Barabbas. Paul Winter, *On the Trial of Jesus* (Berlin: De Gruyter, 1961), pp. 91ff., is the most clear in the claim that such a habit of Pilate (Mark 15:6ff.; Matt. 27:39) or such a Jewish custom (John 18:39) never existed.

50. The most careful book-length study of the trial is that of Paul Winter *(On the Trial of Jesus).* Another very thorough effort is that of Israeli Supreme Court Justice Haim H. Cohn, "Reflections on the Trial and Death of Jesus," *Israel Law Review,* 2 (1967), 332ff., also expanded in book form, *Jesus alim,* in Hebrew (1968).

Nor need we catalog the incessant efforts, by combining higher-critical, novelistic, and apologetic techniques in ingenious ways, to reconstruct a brand new picture of "how it really happened" which is much fuller, surer, and less complimentary to the Jews or to the Romans or to Jesus (or to the Gospel writers) than the canonical reports.[51] It is perhaps significant — but to seek to prove even this much would divert us — that *any* such serious effort at hypothetical reconstruction does move toward taking more seriously the economic-political threat Jesus posed to the Romans than does the traditional ecclesiastical interpretation.[52] But for our purposes the *titulon* on the cross is sufficient testimony. Whether the legal procedure was proper or not, whether or not the Jewish authorities shared a portion of responsibility, all that needs to be affirmed to make our point is that Jesus' public career had been such as to make it quite thinkable that he would pose to the Roman Empire an apparent threat serious enough to justify his execution.[53]

51. Joel Carmichael (n. 35 above) and Hugh Schonfield found a wide readership. S. G. F. Brandon *(Jesus and the Zealots)* is incommensurably more careful but still marked by some of the same sweeping overconfidence in his ability to second-guess the sources, and by the assumption that Jesus could have constituted a political threat only by being violent.

52. ". . . The question of the political dimension of Jesus' ministry . . . , though it remains the object of lively debate, has been public property for a good two score years, and is only rarely ignored in scholarly works devoted to the life of Christ." Étienne Trocmé, *RHPR,* pp. 245ff.

53. "There is increasing evidence that the role of Pilate was considerably greater in the execution of Jesus than the tradition and even the Gospels lead us to think. The precise role of the Jewish leaders we cannot assess. The nature of the sources makes it unlikely that we ever will. The crucifixion — a Roman execution — speaks its clear language, indicating that Jesus must have appeared sufficiently messianic, not only in a purely spiritual sense, to constitute a threat to political order according to Roman standards." Krister Stendahl, "Judaism and Christianity — Then and Now," *New Theology No. 2,* p. 158 (*Harvard Divinity Bulletin,* Oct. 1963). According to Nils A. Dahl, *Der Gekreuzigte Messias,* in H. Ristow and K. Matthiae (eds.), *Der historische Jesus und der kerygmatische Christus* (Berlin: Evangelische Verlagsanstalt, 1962), pp. 149ff., it might even have been the inscription on the cross that finally determined that Jesus would come later to be called Messiah in the full, "royal" sense of the title.

This interpretation is supported by J. B. Souček, "Zum Prozess Jesu," *Communio Viatorum,* 6/2 (1963), 201. According to Ferdinand Hahn, *The Titles of Jesus in Christology* (New York: World, 1969), pp. 160-61 and esp. 173ff., the outspoken confession of Jesus as Messiah/Christ/King arose in the church's reflection on the inscription over the cross. Speculative reconstructions of the usages of the very earliest churches must be taken with

"We had hoped that he was the one who would redeem Israel" (24:21) is not just one more testimony to the disciples' obtuse failure to get Jesus' real point; it is an eyewitness report of the way Jesus had been heard. Jesus' rebuke to the unseeing pair on the road to Emmaus was not that they had been looking for a kingdom, and should not have been. Their fault is that, just like Peter at Caesarea Philippi, they were failing to see that the suffering of the Messiah *is* the inauguration of the kingdom. "Was it not necessary that the Messiah should suffer these things and enter into his glory?" "Glory" here cannot mean the ascension, which has not been recounted yet, and in fact is not clearly described in Luke's Gospel at all, although we know from Acts that Luke knew the tradition. Might it not then mean (as with the concept of "exaltation" in John's Gospel) that the cross itself is seen as fulfilling the kingdom promise? Here at the cross is the man who loves his enemies, the man whose righteousness is greater than that of the Pharisees, who being rich became poor, who gives his robe to those who took his cloak, who prays for those who despitefully use him. The cross is not a detour or a hurdle on the way to the kingdom, nor is it even the way to the kingdom; it is the kingdom come.

The preceding account has left major gaps; thoroughness at these points would only have reinforced the impression already accumulated. I have commented on the annunciation but passed rapidly over the birth narratives (the significance of the imperial census, Bethlehem as the city of the King, the angels' cry of "Peace on Earth"; cf. in Matthew the magi and the slaughter of the innocents). I have observed the song of Zechariah at the birth of John, and John's preaching, but given only a paragraph to his career and fate (the political dimension of his denunciation of Herod's remarriage, his emissaries' question and Jesus' answer, Jesus' identification of John's fate with his own). I have not interpreted in depth specifically ethical passages like chapter 6 or the dense "discipleship" texts of 9:57-62.[54] I have not investigated the special complex of probably politically oriented narratives in chapter 13 (Pilate's massacre of the Galileans, the tower of Siloam, the unfruitful

---

great skepticism; yet in any case Hahn's hypothesis underlines the clear meaning of the inscription, and therefore of the crucifixion as a public event.

54. Cf. Otto Glombitza, "Die Christologische Aussage des Lukas in der Gestaltung der drei Nachfolgeworte," *Novum Testamentum,* 13 (1971), 14-23.

fig tree); nor have I surveyed the extended discussion of the tribute money (ch. 20). I have not investigated the cases where Jesus was appealed to to take on the role of judge (Luke 12:13-14; John 8:1ff.).[55]

Without the reinforcement which careful analysis of all this material would have brought, the conclusion is already clear enough to bring the answer to the question with which we began.[56] Jesus was not just a moralist whose teachings had some political implications; he was not primarily a teacher of spirituality whose public ministry unfortunately was seen in a political light; he was not just a sacrificial lamb preparing for his immolation, or a God-Man whose divine status calls us to disregard his humanity. Jesus was, in his divinely mandated (i.e., promised, anointed, messianic) prophethood, priesthood, and kingship, the bearer of a new possibility of human, social, and therefore political relationships. His baptism is the inauguration and his cross is the culmination of that new regime in which his disciples are called to share. Hearers or readers may choose to consider that kingdom as not real, or not relevant, or not possible, or not inviting; but no longer can

55. In John 8, Jesus is challenged to take a stand regarding the condemnation of an adulteress. Often this is understood as a test of his casuistic skill as a rabbi, like Mark 12:13-34 or Luke 10:25ff. (cf. 11:53-54). Joachim Jeremias ("Zur Geschichtlichkeit des Verhörs Jesu . . . ," *ZNW,* 43 [1950/51], 148) sees in it a challenge to participate in (or interfere with) the judicial process, as a "demagogue from Galilee" might want to.

56. In retrospect, one may well ask: If the presence and attraction of the Zealot option was as significant as this analysis has made it seem, why is the presence of a Zealot "party" not more visible in the texts? If, as we argue, the fact that Jesus perceived the Zealot alternative, was tempted by it as by no other, and nonetheless rejected it, is of fundamental significance for our understanding of his ministry, why do the Gospels not say so in so many words? The Gospels report frequently that "the Pharisees" or "the Jews" come to Jesus in an identifiable way: why not "the Zealots"? There are good reasons. (a) The Zealot option was present in the disciples' ranks in a stronger way. It was represented in Peter's rejection of suffering (Matt. 16:22) and in the disciples' speculation about who would have the most power in the kingdom (Luke 22:24 and par.). (b) By its nature as a guerrilla movement, the Zealot group would not appear in public identified as such. (c) After the cross, the line between Christians and Zealots was clear, whereas Pharisaism continued to be a factor in Christian/Jewish conversations and even within the church (Acts 15:5). Even after the fall of Jerusalem, the Pharisees remained within the diaspora Judaism with which the church remained in conversation for several generations. Thus, to the extent to which the wording of the Gospel traditions during the period of oral transmission was influenced by the relevance of current concerns, references to Pharisees could be expected to have been retained and reinforced as still relevant, and references to Zealots to have become veiled.

we come to this choice in the name of systematic theology or honest hermeneutics. *At this one point* there is no difference between the Jesus of *Historie* and the Christ of *Geschichte,* or between Christ as God and Jesus as Man, or between the religion of Jesus and the religion about Jesus (or between the Jesus of the canon and the Jesus of history). No such slicing can avoid his call to an ethic marked by the cross, a cross identified as the punishment of a man who threatens society by creating a new kind of community leading a radically new kind of life.

EPILOGUE

Luke's Biases

There are two ways to read the editorial tendency of the Gospel according to Luke. In the 1950s and '60s (this part of *The Politics of Jesus* goes back to a text first prepared in 1957 for presentation to an ecumenical conference of the "Church and Peace" series),[57] the dominant understanding among exegetes was that Luke's principal editorial intention was "apologetic." Luke's objective was to assure his reader "Theophilus," a man of some status, that the Christian movement was not a threat to the peace and order of the empire. Such an editorial intention can be discerned by asking how Luke differed from Mark and Matthew, as he edited the same material to fit his special purposes. Then the persistence within Luke's collection of elements describing Jesus as a kind of revolutionary, after being filtered through the grid of Luke's assumed apologetic intentions, should be an index of the veracity of those reports. Luke would not have invented or added such accounts, as they would not further his thesis.

57. Cf. above, ch. 1, n. 3 (pp. 2f.). Other papers from the Iserlohn conference of July 29-August 1, 1957, are reproduced in Donald Durnbaugh (ed.), *On Earth Peace* (Elgin, Ill.: Brethren Press, 1978), 146-84. A standard survey, from that time, of the editorial intent of Luke was C. K. Barrett, *Luke the Historian in Recent Study* (Philadelphia: Fortress, 1970).

Yet there is another way to understand the intentions of Luke. Instead of asking how Luke modified older material, one may ask what material he selected and accentuated. Some who follow this line see Luke as especially attentive to underdogs — women, tax collectors, soldiers, the poor, lepers; in short, he gave status to outsiders. This would fit with contrasting Luke's Sermon on the Plain with Matthew's counterpart, or with the foundational importance Luke gave to the Nazareth sermon (4:1ff.), which is not found in the other Gospels. Then Luke was a Social Gospeler.[58] Then my choosing to follow the Lucan story line could have made my task easier.[59]

I do not grant that my original reading was *limited* to the vision of Luke, in such a way that it would not be a coherent witness common to all the Gospels.[60] Since all of the Gospels say enough of the same things to make my point,[61] I have no stake in preferring one school of Gospel criticism to another.

Historical Skepticism and the Jesus of History

There was in my study no intention to offer an original contribution to the debate about "the historical Jesus." This is a deep axiomatic debate, which has been going on in University theology since Reimarus in the 1770s, and in popular literary culture at least since Renan a century later. There is, however, a subliminal awareness of that debate operating in my

58. Cf. Petr Pockorny, "Die Soziale Strategie in den Lukanischen Schriften," *Communio Viatorum,* 34 (1992), 9-19.

59. This critique was first expressed in a review by Donald Dayton in *Christianity Today* (Dec. 21, 1973), p. 361. It was further tested by a deeper analysis, reinforced by a study of Luke's use of the word "peace," by Willard Swartley, "Politics or Peace in Luke's Gospel," in Richard J. Cassidy and Philip J. Scharper (eds.), *Political Issues in Luke-Acts* (Maryknoll, N.Y.: Orbis, 1983), pp. 18-37.

60. In fact most readers see the strongest single statement of the same position in the Matthean "Sermon on the Mount." Cf. my chapter "The Political Axioms of the Sermon on the Mount," in my *The Original Revolution* (Scottdale, Pa.: Herald Press, 1972), pp. 34ff., and "Jesus' Life-Style Sermon and Prayer," in Dieter Hessel (ed.), *Social Themes of the Christian Year: A Commentary on the Lectionary* (Philadelphia: Geneva Press, 1983), pp. 87-96.

61. Fernando Belo, *A Materialist Reading of the Gospel of Mark* (Maryknoll, N.Y.: Orbis, 1981), and Ched Myers, *Binding the Strong Man* (Maryknoll, N.Y.: Orbis, 1988), found a very similar message in Mark.

text. It is noteworthy that within that debate, what is least open to doubt, in all of the Gospel accounts and in all the critical reconstructions, is the historical/political dimension of what Jesus did.[62] It is with regard to the Zealot option, that is, to the prospect of anti-Roman violence, that the Gospel text is closest to the issues of historical conflict.

One point at which the shape of the debate has changed somewhat in the last quarter-century is the awareness that the reading of ancient texts is a creative process. The "original meaning" of a text or of its author will not stand still, as an earlier scholasticism assumed, since every reader does something new with it.[63] The "History" itself "as it really happened" will not stand still either, since the meaning of events is never free from interpretation.[64] These awarenesses of still greater variability stand only to reinforce my thesis; they will never effectively undergird an antipolitical reading of Jesus, now that our sense of incarnation has been let loose.

What I just called a "sense of incarnation" has been developing further at the hands of what some call "sociological exegesis" or "social scientific criticism."[65] I cannot seek to review the substance of these studies;[66] the fact that they take place at all suffices to attest to the acceptance of my formal thesis.

62. Cf. Bultmann's affirmation, p. 102n.9, as well as nn. 51ff. above.

63. The recent scholar most popularly associated with this accent is Paul Ricoeur, but John Knox was saying something similar a generation earlier.

64. Here the name to drop is that of H. Gadamer, although the insight is not as original with him as some would seem to think.

65. E.g., John Elliott's several writings on 1 Peter, beginning with *A Home for the Homeless* (Philadelphia: Fortress, 1981). Other writers associated with the same agenda are Ched Myers (n. 5 above), Norman Gottwald, Bruce Malina, and Richard A. Horsley. This subdiscipline does with far greater expertise and complexity the kind of concrete interpretation which my amateur outline took for granted. It has become so much a "school" that it is now divided by internal debates about how new the approach is, and about what one finds when one pursues it, with Wayne Meeks *(The First Urban Christians: The Social World of the Apostle Paul* [New Haven: Yale University Press, 1983]), and Robert M. Grant, *Early Christianity and Society* [San Francisco: Harper, 1977]) on the other side, and Gerd Theissen (*The Social Setting of Pauline Christianity* [Philadelphia: Fortress, 1982] and *Sociology of Early Palestinian Christianity* [Philadelphia: Fortress, 1978]) in the middle.

66. I certainly sympathize with their concern to correct the way in which university Scripture scholarship has in the past been tilted by the sex and class biases of the mostly gentile, mostly male, mostly North European scholars. Yet some of them propose to correct those biases by adding another layer of methodological preoccupation, further from the text, still elite, and not free of "politically correct" faddism.

From Story to Creed

As a kind of outrigger to the present study, I take note of a related concern upon which my case does not depend. The last quarter-century has seen a new kind of attention given to the Jesus of the Gospel account as the basis for a nontraditional approach to the previously more abstract discipline of "systematic" theology, that is, as an access to traditional themes like "Incarnation" and "Trinity." This occurs both in brief "radical" works of reconception)[67] and in massive mainstream studies[68] under the rubric "Christology from below." It is the claim of some of those studies that the New Testament's narrative reading of Jesus is not only a way to approach the believers' commitment to social righteousness; it is also the best way to retrieve or to reconceive what is valid about the themes which came to prominence in later developments of dogma (divine sonship, kenosis, lordship) which for centuries have been interpreted "from above" as if they had been derived from elsewhere than from the Jesus story.

Was Jesus a Rebel?

Two lines of challenge have been addressed to my description of "the Zealot option" in Jesus' career. One line argues that the *term* "Zealot" is anachronistic, and should not be used, because it was not used by Jesus, or by anyone before Menachem's uprising of the years 66ff. This statement is literally true and substantially trivial. When Luke wrote a generation or two later, he used that noun because it would be meaningful to his readers, whenever that was, to designate the general phenomenon of subversive violence. What the noun *means* was present in the time of Jesus, as was already sweepingly demonstrated by Oscar Cullmann in lectures in Basel in 1950.[69] Since then studies by Richard-

67. E.g., John J. Vincent, *Radical Jesus* (Basingstoke: Marshall and Pickering, 1986); Neill Q. Hamilton, *Jesus for a No God World* (Philadelphia: Westminster, 1969), Albert Nolan, *Jesus before Christianity* (Maryknoll, N.Y.: Orbis, 1976).

68. Cf. the works of Schillebeeckx, Moltmann, and Walter Kasper. Even when one intends to get around to classical themes like the Trinity and the two natures, these authors assume that the study should begin with the earliest texts and the Jesus story.

69. Oscar Cullmann, *The State in the New Testament* (cf. above, p. 36n.22). A wider

son, Hengel, Horsley, and the Bammel collection have enriched and complicated the picture but not essentially changed it.[70]

> What Christ really rejected must therefore have been within the compass of his earthly life. . . . This offer comes mainly from the "freedom party" that zealots and their followers among the crowd, and such a role would then include action against Roman domination. The reality of Jesus' temptation is best understood when we reflect upon the fact that this role stood in fact open to him and that it appealed to him as a chance to establish God's Kingdom.[71]

A different complaint about attention to the Zealot option has been stated by some Marxist-oriented critics. What the actual "Zealots" of history[72] wanted, it appears, was to reinstate the law as a backward-looking social force, with God on the side of the landlords and the managers of the temple, not as a "progressive" power in favor of the proletariat. The Zealots were thus nationalist, reactionary, monarchist, ethnocentric.[73] It

---

review in Cullmann's vein (but differing from him on the meaning of "Iscariot") is J.-Alfred Morin, "Les Deux Derniers des Douze," in *Revue Biblique,* 80 (1973), 332-58.

70. Richard A. Horsley and John S. Hanson, *Bandits, Prophets, and Messiahs: Popular Movements in the Time of Jesus* (Minneapolis: Winston, 1985; Horsley has continued the discussion with numerous additional papers), say very sweepingly that to speak of Jesus' facing a "Zealot option" is to misread the setting of Jesus. The term "Zealot" according to Horsley should be reserved for one group which arose within the great revolt of 66-70. Yet what Horsley denies is only (a) that there existed a single continuous, centrally coordinated movement, and (b) that they called themselves "Zealots." Neither of these oversimplifications is necessary to make credible my interpretation of the choices Jesus faced. As to the substance of Jesus' moral stance, Horsley does not really disagree; cf. his *Jesus and the Spiral of Violence* (San Francisco: Harper, 1987). There were according to Horsley numerous uprisings of the rural poor; some of them "messianic," i.e., led by men making special claims, and some not. Other efforts were not rural (later Horsley adds "longshoremen"), or not poor, or claimed no religious legitimacy. Seán Freyne, "Bandits in Galilee," in Jacob Neusner et al. (eds.), *The Social World of Formative Christianity and Judaism* (Philadelphia: Fortress, 1982), pp. 50-68, demonstrates the difficulty of identifying any one typical class of troublemakers. None of the scholarship circulated since then adds much to the state of the question as summarized in the sources cited on p. 40 above.

71. Piet Schoonenberg, S.J., "The Kenosis or Self-Emptying of Christ," in *Concilium* I/2 (Jan. 1966), 33-34. As the author says, this is a summary, not a daring thesis.

72. These readers are less skeptical than Horsley about finding a true type of Zealot "back there."

73. Morin, "Les Deux Derniers," points out that they attacked not only Romans but also (and earlier) Jews whom they found guilty of apostasy or collaboration with the infidel.

is therefore inappropriate to juxtapose the "Zealot temptation" facing Jesus with the advocacy of a just and "liberating" revolution in our time.

That may be correct, historically, though as long as the anti-Roman forces had no power at all, historians can hardly be sure about distinguishing between visions describing the restoration of something like the rule of David and Solomon and other visions calling for the poor of the earth to have a better deal.

What my narration meant by "the Zealot option" was, however, not the details of some Zealot's or some Zealots' social blueprint, but more simply the principle of violent insurrection as such, which "Zealots" whether on the right or the left held would be justified by a divine mandate and empowered by angelic assistance. The question facing Jesus was not a choice between backward-looking and forward-looking visions of liberation (as socially committed people in the 1980s or 1990s assume we are qualified timelessly to identify "backward" and "forward"), or between socialist and bourgeois understandings of freedom; the issue was whether violence is justified in principle for what one considers to be a very righteous political cause.

Concerning the rest of Jesus' social blueprint, we have plenty of information from the rest of the story. It was different from that of the several types of "Zealots"; and for that matter from that of Marxists. None of Jesus' teachings about love for the enemy or about the wrongness of lordship indicate a basis for discriminating between bourgeois enemies and other enemies, or between socialist lordship and other kinds of lordship, in such a way that the violence which would be forbidden to obtain one could be mandatory to attain the other.

Further Support

Friendly critics have pointed out that the above summary neglects components of the Gospel account which would be very supportive of my thesis, especially Jesus' "teachings" like the Parable of the Good Samaritan, the conversation with the Syrophoenician woman or with the "rich young ruler," or the Sermon on the Plain. My reason for omitting them was not that they would not support my case, but that those are specifically the materials which the traditional arguments for setting Jesus aside as apolitical were calculated to relativize. My last page of text in the 1972 chapter identifies numerous other omissions of yet other strands of the story which would strengthen my case.[74]

74. Probably the most obvious omission was the specific instructions of Jesus transforming the "natural" commandment to love the neighbor into the counter-intuitive imperative of enemy love. This is the only point at which human behavior is called to be like God's (see below, pp. 115f.). This theme has recently been found worthy of book-length treatment by William Klassen *(Love of Enemies: The Way to Peace* [Philadelphia: Fortress, 1984]), and by Willard Swartley (ed.) *(The Love of Enemy and Nonretaliation in the New Testament* [Louisville: Westminster/Knox, 1992]). Cf. also A. L. Harvey, *Strenuous Commands: The Ethic of Jesus* (London/Philadelphia: SCM/Trinity, 1990), pp. 96ff.

CHAPTER 3

The Implications of the Jubilee

A single discourse, that of Nazareth, is not sufficient to prove that Jesus really proclaimed the inauguration of the year of jubilee. Only a more complete reading of the Gospel texts could support or undermine this thesis. Such a reading would push further along some of the following lines.[1]

The jubilee year or the sabbath year included four prescriptions: (1) leaving the soil fallow, (2) the remission of debts, (3) the liberation of slaves, (4) the return to each individual of his family's property. The purpose of the present chapter is to examine whether the Gospels contain any other allusions to these four activities.

The Fallow Year

Jesus does not speak directly of leaving the soil fallow. His silence is not at all surprising because, of all the prescriptions for the sabbath year, only this one had become common usage. It would, therefore, have been pointless to exhort the Jews to practice it. But — somewhat like the case of the fast of the Ramadan, which all Muslims practice but often amid complaint and cheating — it still took great courage for the Jews to leave their fields fallow every seven years, counting on

1. This chapter is adapted freely, with the author's permission, from André Trocmé, *Jésus-Christ et la révolution non-violente* (Geneva, 1961), since published in English as *Jesus and the Nonviolent Revolution* (Scottdale, Pa.: Herald, 1973). The annotation is mine.

God that they would receive from him what they would need! Many worried. Leviticus (25:20-21), expecting such concern, declared: "If you say: 'what will we eat the seventh year, since we will not sow nor harvest?' — I will give you my blessing on the sixth year and it will produce enough for three years."[2]

Now we find Jesus using practically the same words to his disciples. The proclamation of jubilee in A.D. 26 may have troubled them because they had left their fields untilled and left their boats at the lakeshore to follow Jesus:

> "Do not be anxious, and do not say: 'what shall we eat and what shall we drink, with what shall we be clothed' — for all these things the Gentiles seek to obtain, and your heavenly Father knows that you need them. Seek first of all the kingdom and the righteousness of God and all of these things shall be added to you."[3]

Such an exhortation, often poorly understood because it seems to encourage laziness, is understandable without difficulty as soon as it is placed in the framework of the expectation of the Kingdom of God, of which the year of jubilee was one of the precursors. Thus, we should interpret the text in this way:

> "If you work six days (or six years) with all your heart, you can count on God to take care of you and yours. So without fear leave your field untilled. As he does for the birds of heaven which do not sow or harvest or collect into granaries, God will take care of your needs. The Gentiles who pay no attention to the sabbath are not richer than you."

Remission of Debts and Liberation of Slaves

In contrast to the above, the second and third provisions of the jubilee order are not marginal but central in the teaching of Jesus. They are even at the center of his theology.

2. Donald Blosser (see below, p. 73) reviews the evidence of grain scarcity every seven years through the first century, evidence that this rule was respected by some at least.

3. Luke 12:29-31.

The Lord's Prayer, which summarizes the thought of Jesus concerning prayer, includes the following request: "remit us our debts as we ourselves have also remitted them to our debtors" (the verb is *aphiemi*). Those numerous versions are in error which translate: "Forgive us our offenses as we forgive those who have offended us." Accurately, the word *opheilema* of the Greek text signifies precisely a monetary debt, in the most material sense of the term. In the "Our Father," then, Jesus is not simply recommending vaguely that we might pardon those who have bothered us or made us trouble, but tells us purely and simply to erase the debts of those who owe us money; that is to say, practice the jubilee.[4]

It is remarkable that the verb most used by Jesus is *aphiemi,* which means "remit, send away, liberate, forgive a debt" and which is regularly used in connection with the jubilee.[5]

The material meaning of the word "debts" in the Lord's Prayer was so clear that the Evangelist Matthew (or was it Jesus himself?) added a gloss to the "Our Father" in order to explain that the words concerning debts applied here also to offenses in general: "If you pardon others for their offenses" (here the term is *paraptoma,* "transgression"), your heavenly Father will forgive you as well: but if you do not forgive others, your father will not pardon your offenses *(paraptoma)* either" (Matt. 6:14-15).

Thus the "Our Father" is genuinely a jubilary prayer. It means "the time has come for the faithful people to abolish all the debts which bind the poor ones of Israel, for your debts toward God are also wiped away (for that is the gospel, the good news)." Furthermore, this is the way Jesus' listeners understood his prayer. Jesus was establishing a strict equation between the practice of the jubilee and the grace of God. He who was not legalist at any other point, and who was ready without

4. Trocmé's interpretation of "forgive us our debts" is strongly supported, independently, by F. Charles Fensham, "The Legal Background of Mt. vi:16," *NovT,* 4 (1960), 1. It should be noted that *opheilemata* is used in the Matthean version of the Lord's Prayer, not in Luke's. If we were *only* discussing Luke 4 (pp. 28f. above) it could be argued that the reference to Matthew's vocabulary is inappropriate. Trocmé's intention, however, is a synthesis of all the ways in which forgiveness figures in Jesus' message.

5. *Aphesis,* the noun form of the same verb, is the term regularly used by the Septuagint for the jubilee; Lev. 25:28, 54; Deut. 15:1ff.; Isa. 61:2; Jer. 35:8.

hesitation to pardon prostitutes and disreputable people, was nonetheless extremely strict upon one point: "only one who practices grace can receive grace. The *aphesis* of God toward you becomes vain if you do not practice *aphesis* toward each other."

Two parables will help to make more precise Jesus' thinking at this point. The most impressive is certainly the one usually called the parable of the "merciless servant," which states in all its rigor the equation of "Our Father": "no grace for one who is not gracious."[6]

Unfortunately this parable, detached from its sociological background, has too often been considered as a rather pale picture of the forgiveness of sin which is granted by God to those who forgive their brethren or sisters.

As a matter of fact, the sad hero of the parable is a real person, a Galilean peasant whose name the disciples of Jesus probably knew. Benefiting, like all those to whom Jesus addressed himself, from the proclamation of the jubilee, he was the object of an act of grace. All his debts had been wiped away: enormous debts, ten thousand talents. We should not be surprised at that figure. It expressed the total insolvency of the debtor over against the prince.

S. W. Baron in his history of Israel[7] describes how in the age of Jesus the Galilean peasant who had previously been a free property owner had been reduced to the practical equivalent of slavery by way of progressive indebtedness. Herod the Great was the one responsible for this situation. He had crushed the people with heavy taxes and expropriated the recalcitrant property owners.

To escape such appropriation the peasant would borrow from the usurer, who was often in liaison with the king's representative or the tax collector. His property, which he gave as security, soon fell into the hands of the usurer, and the peasant became his sharecropper or servant. But the problem of the peasant was not thereby resolved. His unpaid debts continued to pile up to astronomic levels. Then, in order to regain his funds, the creditor ordered that the sharecropper should be sold with his wife and children and all his possessions in order to cover the debt.

6. Matt. 18:23-35.

7. Salo Wittmayer Baron, *A Social and Religious History of the Jews* (New York: Columbia University Press, 2nd ed. 1952), I, 262ff.

This is exactly the situation into which the "unmerciful servant" of the parable had come. Jesus describes the relationship between the rising indebtedness of the poor peasant, the loss of his properties, and the loss of his liberty which followed directly.

The jubilee year having been proclaimed, the servant now appears before the king, who forgives his debt. The king, the text says, releases him and "remits" (again the verb *aphiemi*) the debt. If our story stopped here it would be encouraging. But Jesus tells it at a time when the majority of his fellow citizens, even the most humble, had already refused him the jubilee. The rest of the story reflects the bitter disappointment felt in the face of this refusal. The slave who has been freed by the jubilee, he says, meets one of his fellow slaves who owes him a modest sum of seventy francs, and refuses him the benefit of the same jubilee forgiveness from which he himself had profited. Instead he seizes him, saying, "Pay me what you owe me."

Denounced by his fellows, the servant was now arrested and led before the king. To this man, without pity and without gratitude, the jubilee is no longer applicable. By order of the king he will be sold for his debts with his wife and children. There is no divine jubilee for those who refuse to apply it on earth.

The frequent remission of debts had a serious inconvenience, already indicated in Deuteronomy 13:7-11: it froze credit. Because of this the rabbis, even the most orthodox like Hillel and Shammai, who had become the champions of the strict application of the law of Moses, hesitated to demand the strict application of the jubilee. The closer the sabbatical year came, the more the wealthy hesitated to lend to the poor for fear of losing their capital. Hereby the economic life of the country was paralyzed. The rabbis sought out a solution to this problem. Adroit commentators of the law, they knew how to make it say the opposite of what it ordered.

It was the most congenial among them, the famous Pharisee Hillel, whom Jesus sometimes quoted, the grandfather of Gamaliel (who was to be in his turn the teacher of Paul), who found a neat solution to the problem.

This solution was called the *prosboul.* This word probably signifies: *pros boule,* which is Greek for "an action formalized before the tribunal." According to the treatise *Gittin* of the Mishnah, Hillel in this way authorized a creditor to transfer to a court the right to recover in his name a debt which the sabbatical year otherwise might have canceled.

The very existence of the *prosboul* proves that, contrary to the statements of some authors, there was at the time of Jesus a strong current favoring the strict application of the provision of the jubilee for periodic remission of debts. Otherwise the institution of this procedure of *prosboul* would have been unnecessary. Thanks to such a subterfuge, lending on interest, which had been forbidden by the law of Moses (Exod. 22:25) and was always limited in time by the return of the sabbatical year, again became possible. The rich, like the Pharisees whom Jesus accused of "devouring the houses of widows" (Mark 12:40; Matt. 23:14), did not miss their chance. This is the form of an act of *prosboul,* the text of which has been preserved in the Mishnah:

> I _____ transmit to you _____, judges at _____ my credit, in order to be able to recover whatever sum is due to me from _____ whatever might be the date when I express the desire.

This declaration was then signed by the judges and witnesses. Jesus was decidedly an adversary of the *prosboul.*

At this point an important observation can be made. Generally we are given the picture of Jesus as an adversary of the sabbath laws, whereas in the present case the contrary applies. As soon as it was a matter of accentuating the humanitarian prescriptions of the law of Moses, Jesus became more radical than the Pharisees. His constant controversies with them would lose all meaning if they had had to do with the form religious practices should take. In reality, the conflict was much more serious: it had to do with the very nature of the moral law. "What is the good?" the Pharisees asked, and they answered by applying the detailed prescriptions in the midst of which they lost the essential. "What is the good?" asked Jesus; and neglecting details, he went directly to the essential which he found in Moses without passing by the detour of the tradition of the scribes.

This radicalism of Jesus was quite different from latitudinarianism. When he said, "God made the sabbath for humankind" (Mark 2:27), he meant that God had liberated the Jews by taking them out of Egypt. The sabbatical year, like the day of sabbath, must be practiced. They are both meant to liberate people and not to enslave them. This is why the *prosboul,* like all the other human traditions, which were added to the law in order to attenuate its revolutionary and liberating character, called forth Jesus' indignation.

But how can one avoid the freezing of credit if one rejects the bait of profit? In the Sermon on the Plain Jesus gives the answer. The rich man should be generous, rejecting the fear of not being repaid, because God will take care of him. "If you lend to those from whom you hope to receive, what thank have ye? Sinners also lend to sinners in order to receive the same. But . . . lend without expecting anything or even despairing; and your reward shall be great, and you shall be sons of the most high, because he is good to the ungrateful and the evil. . . . Absolve and you shall be absolved; *give and it will be given to you;* there shall be poured into your lap a good measure, pressed and shaken down and running over."[8]

The honesty of the debtor should correspond to the generosity of the lender. The debtor should not hide himself behind the protection of the law of the sabbath to avoid keeping his commitments. The Sermon on the Mount contains two striking paragraphs where Jesus indicated how the problems over which Hillel and the Pharisees stumbled could be resolved.

Hillel said to the worried creditor: "Transfer your credit to the tribunal, which will collect for you." Jesus says to the negligent debtor: "Don't wait until you fall into the hands of the court to reimburse the debt. If your creditor wants to take you to court by way of the *prosboul* to take away your tunic (which he keeps as security for the debt which you have not been able to pay him), let him (again the verb *aphiemi*) take your coat too."[9] Earlier: "Hasten to make your peace with the adversary as long as you are on the road with him, for fear that your adversary (using the *prosboul*) might turn you over to the judge, and the judge to the guard, and you might be thrown in prison, from which you will not get out until you have paid the last penny."[10]

Luke, in the parallel to the text quoted, places in the mouth of

8. Luke 6:33 (my italics).
9. Matt. 5:40ff.
10. Matt. 5:25.

Jesus, in the form of the question, a very interesting thought: "Why do ye not yourself judge what is right?"[11] Thus his disciples are to be free from litigation. They should not have recourse to the tribunals to know whether it was just or not to pay their debts.

Now we move on to another parable which also contains a jubilee teaching: that of the unfaithful steward.[12] Like that of the unmerciful servant, it takes its point of departure from the situation of the peasant at the time of Jesus.

We recall what was said above. As a result of the demands of King Herod and his sons and the Roman occupant, most of the former rural property owners had lost their independence. Obliged to mortgage their goods in order to pay the tax, they were thereby reduced to half-slavery. The obligations in kind, in oil and wheat, which they paid to their masters often amounted to half or more of their harvests.

The peasant situation in Israel was aggravated by still another plague: the absenteeism of the owners. A hierarchy of intermediate functionaries contracted for the collecting of debts. They extorted from the sharecroppers arbitrary sums which widely exceeded the rent and debt and taxes which were really due. But the poor were always wrong. They had no recourse because the collectors presented fraudulent accounts to their masters, which permitted them to accumulate in very few years what Jesus called "unrighteous wealth." It was by pursuing without cease the possession of this kind of wealth that the collectors lost the real wealth, namely the friendship and respect of their fellow citizens.

Now our parable tells how an owner one day discovered the dishonesty of his steward. Not content to despoil his sharecroppers, this steward was also stealing from his employer to whom he presented falsified records. Now that his cheating was discovered, the steward felt a guilty conscience. He understood that he would never be able to pay back to his employer the amount of his embezzlement. But he decided that at least he would not demand from the sharecroppers the big sums by which he had increased their obligations. He therefore restored to his debtors the unjust excess of the debt which they were supposed to

11. Luke 12:59.
12. Luke 16:1ff.

owe him. Jesus pictures him convening his debtors and with a stroke of the pen lowering their debts to the right amount: fifty measures of oil instead of a hundred, eighty measures of wheat instead of a hundred, etc.

Certainly such a decision would only aggravate the insolvency of the steward. It would reduce him to poverty. But in acting this way he acquired genuine wealth, namely the gratitude and the friendship of his former victims. Now poor among the poor, man among men, he shall be received as a brother in their home and this hospitality will continue into eternity. This is what Jesus calls the joy of the Kingdom of God. "Make yourselves friends with unrighteous wealth,"[13] he declares in conclusion. "Practice the jubilee which I am announcing. By liberating others from their debts to you, liberate yourself from the bonds which keep you from being ready for the kingdom of God."

What is most remarkable in this parable is the praise which Jesus places in the mouth of the employer who is the representative of God: "Here is an intelligent man," says God, far "more intelligent than the average of those who want to be my disciples."

In the parable of the merciless servant it was God who had taken the initiative. God had first remitted the debt to the man and expected the man to do the same. In the parable of the dishonest steward it is the man who takes the initiative. It is he who first, obeying the messianic appeal, practices the jubilee by remitting the debts of those who are at the same time debtors to God and to him. Consequently God praises that intelligent man who before he was even being touched by grace practices the redistribution of wealth. This man was able to read the signs of the Kingdom of God and to understand that the reign of unrighteous mammon is of the past.

The two parables of the merciless servant and the unfaithful steward thus confirm what the Nazareth discourse, the Lord's Prayer, and the Sermon on the Mount had already given us to understand. It is really a jubilee, conformed to the sabbatical instructions of Moses, that Jesus proclaimed in A.D. 26: a jubilee able to resolve the social problem in Israel, by abolishing debts and liberating debtors whose insolvency had reduced them to slavery. The practice of such a jubilee was not optional. It

13. Luke 16:9.

belonged to the precursors of the kingdom. Those who would refuse to enter this path could not enter into the Kingdom of God.

Fourth Jubilee Prescription: The Redistribution of Capital

Before the invention of the machine, the only wealth of a people was constituted by the soil and the flocks. This is what today would be called capital. Evidently Jesus accepted voluntary poverty for the sake of the kingdom and he ordered his disciples to practice the jubilary redistribution of their capital: "all of these things, it is the Gentiles of the world who seek them. Your Father knows that you need them. Seek rather the kingdom of God and all these things will be added to you. Do not fear, little flock, because your Father has chosen to give you the kingdom; sell all that you have and give it as alms."[14] No one doubts that he said this. All that has been debated is whether this redistribution of capital was commanded by Jesus for all Christians at all times and in all places or whether it was just a "counsel of perfection" directed to the saints.

Traditionally the church has chosen the second solution, the easy one. Only the person, the church says, who is the object of a very special vocation, for instance the monk or the nun, is called upon to abandon all property. The ordinary believer can be satisfied with "doing charity," i.e., distributing as alms a part of his income.

Such a position would be completely justifiable if Jesus had not been so severe precisely toward those who in his time considered it adequate to practice charity, namely the Pharisees. They did give the tithe of all income and that was not so bad. How few are the people who do as much today!

But Jesus considered the tithe insufficient: "Woe to you, hypocritical scribes and Pharisees, who pay the tithe of mint and anise and cummin [that is, product of the soil] after having neglected the most important points of the law: righteousness, goodness, good faith. This you should have practiced without neglecting that."[15]

14. Luke 12:30-33.
15. Luke 11:42.

Such a word confirms what we were saying about the radicalism of Jesus. He did not wish to abolish tithes. He wished only to go beyond the level of easy fulfillment and easy moral self-satisfaction which could be had by giving the tithe, and to call people to reach the level of "righteousness, goodness, and good faith."

But what was meant by these last three phrases? We have reason to believe that they mean the gratuitous act whereby the disciple, seeking to provide for his or her own comfort, gives away what was personally needed, namely capital: if your righteousness does not go beyond that of the scribes and Pharisees you will not enter the Kingdom of God.

Comparing one day the generosity of the wealthy, who ostentatiously were throwing large offerings in the temple treasury, with that of the poor widow, Jesus exclaimed, "This poor widow has put in more than all of them. They put in from their overflow but she from her poverty has given all that she had to live!"

In modern language we can translate: "The quantity of money that one gives is of little importance. What is important is what one gives. If it only is a part of one's income, then this is not yet righteousness, goodness, and good faith. If it is capital that one gives, then everything is in order."

Still it is not our belief that Jesus prescribed Christian communism. If he had done this he would have left to his disciples either monastic rules comparable to those of the Essenes, or some kind of constitution for a Jewish collective state. This he did not do. Collectivism was contrary to the spirit of Moses.

So when Jesus formulated the celebrated commandment, "Sell what you possess and give it as alms" (a better translation would be, "sell what you possess and put in practice compassion"), this was not a "counsel of perfection," but neither was it a constitutional law to found a utopian state of Israel. It was a jubilee ordinance which was to be put into practice here and now, once, in A.D. 26, as a "refreshment," prefiguring the "reestablishment of all things."

Such a redistribution of capital, accomplished every fifty years by faithfulness to the righteous will of God and in the expectation of the kingdom, would today be nothing utopian. Many bloody revolutions would have been avoided if the Christian church had shown herself more respectful than Israel was of the jubilee dispositions contained in the law of Moses.

EPILOGUE

Oversimple Relevance

In 1976 I received a letter which drew my attention to a possible interpretation of the jubilee message which I had not foreseen. A devoted Christian, writing on behalf of a local body of believers, asked whether, since André Trocmé had cited (p. 61 above), the year A.D. 26 as the scholars' best guess for the date of the beginning of Jesus' public ministry and therefore for the Nazareth sermon, it would then be in 1976 (after 39 × 50 years) that the jubilee should fall again.

It had not occurred to me that Jesus' use of jubilee language to describe the imminence of the kingdom could have been construed as continuing or reinstating literally the fifty-year pattern of the Mosaic legislation, so that his followers should continue the same literal application through the centuries.[16]

The more normal line of interpretation, in response to this sincere question, was so normal that it did not occur to Trocmé or to me to say so. It would be that the fundamental notion of periodic leveling would have been lifted, as Jesus appropriated it out of the Hebrew heritage, from the level of some practices implemented every seven years or every forty-nine years. It would have become in Jesus' teaching a permanently defining trait of the new order. That would have been parallel to what Jesus did with other elements of the Jewish heritage. It would fit with what actually turned out to be practiced in the community he created.

16. Since the cycle would be 49 years, not 50, 1976 would have been wrong anyway.

Further Critical Scholarship

More important is the question whether Trocmé's hypothesis, which I characterized in 1972 (p. 30 above) as "ingenious," at a time when professional Bible scholars were ignoring his book, does in fact make sense as contributing to a serious interpretation of the Nazareth sermon. Such further study has since in fact been forthcoming.[17]

In 1977 the Theology Faculty of the University of Basel awarded its doctorate *insigne cum laude* to Robert B. Sloan, Jr. for his dissertation *"The Favorable Year of the Lord": A Study of Jubilary Theology in the Gospel of Luke.*[18] Sloan's primary interest is not in the sermon's impact on social ethics. His concern is, as his title says, with "theology," and even more narrowly with Luke's eschatology. The themes which the Nazareth sermon picks up from the Old Testament are as much prophetic as they are legislative. Luke's editorial intention is to introduce his Gospel with the proclamation of the beginning of a new age. For Sloan to make that argument, however, presupposes that he must concede some degree of accuracy in Trocmé's original point, namely that the phrase "the acceptable year of the Lord" (whether or not in the original intent of the Isaiah passage, at least to readers in Jesus' age) meant the jubilee in the first place.

Sloan strengthens the case for that meaning's being evident by showing the presence of the jubilee concept within the eschatology of the Dead Sea communities. Sloan also shows that the language and the tone of the Nazareth Sermon cast a special light across the rest of the Gospel. Luke's continuing use of the terms *euangelizein* (proclaiming good news) and *aphesis* (release, pardon) in the remaining account projects the jubilee language through the rest of Jesus' teaching.

Sharon Ringe, now teaching at the Methodist Theological School in Ohio, was awarded her doctorate in 1981 by Union Theological Seminary for *The Jubilee Proclamation in the Ministry and Teaching of Jesus: A Tradition-Critical Study in the Synoptic Gospels and Acts.*[19] Ringe's

17. I am pursuing here only the basic question. On some of the surface matters, I would not support Trocmé's too simple views, notably in the way he characterizes "the Pharisees" and in his description of the *prosboul.*

18. Printed by Schola Press, Austin, Texas.

19. Thoroughly reworked in *Jesus, Liberation, and the Biblical Jubilee* (Philadelphia: Fortress, 1985).

focus on "tradition criticism" indicates less concern than others might have for what can be known or surmised about Jesus' actual public ministry. Ringe's interest is in how sets of thoughts and sets of phrases, motifs, and images were correlated with one another as the language of the early Christians was passed on from Jesus to the point where our extant Gospel texts were redacted. Like Sloan she is more interested in jubilee proclamation as a component of Jesus' kingdom language, that is, in knowing how clusters of metaphors work, than for narrative realism about Jesus' movement.

As Sloan did for Luke, Ringe shows how language derived from the jubilee complex ("good news," "forgiveness," "return") is present even in parts of the New Testament where the concrete jubilee meaning (i.e., freeing slaves and reclaiming land) is no longer implied. This would seem to confirm the derivation of these terms from Jesus' own usage, rather than indicating that they were the contributions of later authors. This is also reinforced by the fact that some of the juxtapositions of jubilee-related words make sense only in Aramaic or Hebrew, not in Greek. To Sloan's interest in the Hebrew prophets Ringe adds the awareness that in ancient Israel to proclaim "release" or "amnesty" was a royal prerogative, not the role of a scribe, a priest, or even a prophet.

Donald W. Blosser's dissertation *Jesus and the Jubilee: The Year of Jubilee and Its Significance in the Gospel of Luke* was accepted by St. Mary's College of the University of Saint Andrews in 1979. In contrast with the other two dissertations, whose concerns were with specific questions of hermeneutical method, Blosser reviewed in an encyclopedic way the entire scriptural corpus, also reaching beyond the canon to the Mishnah, Qumran, Philo, and Josephus.

Blosser's historical conclusion is that the entire body of jubilee prescriptions, all the way to land redistribution, was never regularly practiced, yet nonetheless remained alive in the mind and culture of Jews. As the centuries passed, the accent changed from a command to be obeyed to a dimension of the promise about what God would do in the age to come. Yet the elements of debt release and leaving some land fallow were practiced often enough that they were in people's minds and often enough to make an economic difference (e.g., there are clear records of decreased agricultural productivity every seven years).

Blosser then turns to a very broad survey of all the commentary literature on Luke 4, and a dozen other Lucan texts with analogous themes. He sees the proclamation of jubilee as central to Jesus' message according to Luke's thought. Luke probably moved the Nazareth event from a later time, where it was found in his sources, to where we find it in his chapter 4, because it mattered for him to use this account as a programmatic "platform statement" for the beginning of the public ministry, and to make that beginning fall on a jubilee year. Blosser takes seriously the ethical pertinence of jubilee as the background to other teaching (treasures in heaven, the rich ruler, Zacchaeus) and refutes Sloan's overdone "eschatological" or metaphorical spiritualization.

> The Jubilee is not simply a theological concept providing insight into the nature of God; it is a guide for living which is to be observed in normal daily practice among believers. . . . These Jubilee acts are not simply to be expected in the future, they are to be given concrete expression among the people of God in the present . . . what had been expected in the future can now be experienced in the present because we are now living in the new age, . . . characterized by Jubilee activity among the believers. (p. 297)

Along the way Blosser expertly investigates numerous prickly problems of chronology and of source criticism, and enriches his account with recent practical and pastoral literature.[20]

Other interpreters who affirm the jubilee dimension in Luke are Marshall,[21] Tiede,[22] and Danker.[23]

The simplest strong challenge to Trocmé's thesis is another dissertation, accepted in 1978 by the Toronto School of Theology. *The Beginning of Jesus' Ministry in the Gospel of Luke* by Jacob Elias examines in great detail the single Nazareth passage, Luke 4:16-30. Elias uses the tools of redaction criticism, setting aside the matters of context that were given more weight by Strobel[24] and Trocmé, whom he cites

20. *Sojourners,* Don Kraybill, Mar Paulus Gregorious.

21. I. H. Marshall, *Luke* (Grand Rapids: Eerdmans, 1978), pp. 184ff., with reservations as to the chronology in Luke.

22. D. L. Tiede, *Luke* (Minneapolis: Augsburg, 1988), p. 107.

23. F. W. Danker, *Jesus and the New Age* (Philadelphia: Fortress, 1988), p. 107.

24. A. Strobel, *Jesus in Nazareth* (Berlin: W. de Gruyter, 1972).

(pp. 147, 198), and Blosser, whose work Elias of course could not cite. Elias looks at one verse, one line at a time, asking first with every phrase the question of Luke's redactional intent. Elias sees no case for considering "the year of the Lord's favor" in 4:19 (= Isa. 61:2) as referring to the jubilee.

One component of the tradition to which the Trocmé text could have given more attention was the way in which jubilee language was part of prophetic images of the return to the land of Israel after the exile. Distributing land is part of regaining the land:

> "In the hour of my favor I answered you,
> I helped you on the day of deliverance;
> putting the land to rights,
> sharing out afresh its desolate fields.
> I said to the prisoners, 'go free!'
> and to those in darkness 'come out and be seen!' " (Isa. 49:8ff., NEB)

This is one of the "servant songs"; the similarity to the language of chapter 61 is evident.

Pastoral Appropriation

The metaphor of "jubilee" continues to encounter wide resonance in our culture. "Jubilee housing" is a ministry of the Church of the Savior in Washington, D.C. "Jubilee partners" is a voluntary agency serving captives of the U.S. prison system and of the Immigration and Naturalization Service. Popes frequently proclaim "jubilee" as a special time for pilgrims to visit Rome.

CHAPTER 4

God Will Fight for Us

When modern Christians approach the Old Testament with the question of war in mind, our attitude tends to be a legalistic one and the questions we ask tend to generalize. We ask, "Can a Christian who rejects all war reconcile his position with the Old Testament story?" If the generalization that "war is always contrary to the will of God" can be juxtaposed with the wars in the Old Testament, which are reported as having been according to the will of God, the generalization is destroyed.

This approach hides from us the realization that for the believing Israelite the Scriptures would not have been read with this kind of question in mind. Rather than reading with the modern question in mind, whether it confirms certain moral generalizations or not, the Israelite read it as his or her own story, as the account of his or her own past throwing light on who he or she was. A story may include a moral implication or presuppose moral judgments, but it does not necessarily begin at that point.

One of the traits of the Old Testament story, sometimes linked with bloody battles but also sometimes notably free of violence, is the identification of YHWH as the God who saves his people without their needing to act. When we seek to test a modern moral statement, we are struck by the parts of the story that do not fit our modern pattern; but the Israelite reading the story was more likely struck by the other cases, where Israel was saved by the mighty deeds of God on their behalf.

We cannot undertake here even a capsule enumeration of the

strands of Hebrew history which are taken up and woven into Jesus' story. We are glancing back at the story of ancient Israel, the reader will remember, not for its own sake or for scholarly curiosity, but as a test of modern ethical hermeneutics. We are asking how Jesus and his listeners were likely to conceive of the action of God, against the background of their people's way of telling their history.

The Exodus

> "Fear not, stand firm,
> And see the salvation of the LORD,
> which he will work for you today;
> For the Egyptians whom you see today,
> you shall never see again.
> The LORD will fight for you,
> and you have only to be still."
>
> (Exod. 14:13)

Every portion of the Exodus account, difficult to interpret at other points, is clear in the report that the Israelites did nothing to bring about the destruction of the Egyptians. The only call to them was to believe and obey. When they did so, the seemingly inevitable menace hanging over them disappeared.

This emphasis of the Exodus story is not reversed by the reporter in chapter 17 of the battle against the Amalekites. It is striking, in comparison to the rest of the narrative in this portion of Exodus, that the decision of Moses and Joshua to undertake a war against Amalek is not reported as having been commanded by YHWH, even though such commands are quite frequent elsewhere. It is rather the culmination of a period of Moses' being frustrated by the people's bitterness and their asking for a test of the Lord's presence. This time Moses and Joshua respond in their own way to the Amalekites' attack; they fight their own battle. Yet the battle goes against them when Moses' tiring arms lower the symbolic "rod of God," and they prevail only as the rod is again held aloft. Thus even when Israel uses the sword, in a most fearful and destructive way, the victory is credited not to the prowess of the swordsmen or the wisdom of the generals, but to the help of

YHWH.[1] This remains the main point of the accounts throughout the books of Joshua and Judges.[2]

It is a general rule of proper textual interpretation that a text should be read for what its author meant to say and what its first readers or hearers would have heard it say. Whether the taking of human life is morally permissible or forbidden under all circumstances was not a culturally conceivable question in the age of Abraham or that of Joshua. It is therefore illegitimate to read the story of the planned sacrifice of Isaac[3] or of the Joshuanic wars as documents on the issue of the morality of killing. Although the narrative of the conquest of Canaan is full of bloodshed,[4]

1. The name recent scholars have chosen to render as "Yahweh" is the *proper* name of the God of Israel, as distinguishable from the generic appellations "god" or "lord," which applied to other deities as well. I prefer to omit the vowels as the Hebrews did. The vocalization is a modern non-Jewish surmise. One of his earliest appellations is "YHWH of Hosts," i.e., "of the armies" — another index of the place of these deliverances in Israel's earliest understanding of God.

2. The institution of "holy war" is only one expression of this providential protection. Its importance as perhaps the most fundamental social institution of earliest Israel has been pointed up by G. von Rad, *Der heilige Krieg im alten Israel* (Göttingen: Vandenhoeck & Ruprecht, 1951; concerning a new translation see below, p. 88n.15). The nonmartial deliverances, which for the Israelite were part of the same picture, have been given less scholarly attention.

3. The command to Abraham to sacrifice his son has been made a test case for casuistic ethics by modern Protestant ethical theory, because to the modern reader it seems so evidently to present the spectacle of God ordering a creature to break God's own rules. Such a reading, however, ignores the cultural context. In the age of Abraham, or even in the age when the account in Gen. 22 was written, the sacrifice of the firstborn was a common cultic custom. It was no more ethically scandalous or viscerally disturbing than the killing of the villain in a western film is to most watchers today. It was not conceived of as coming under the prohibition of murder, for it was a ritual act. The test for Abraham's faith lay not in the command to sacrifice one he tenderly loved, nor in the command to break the moral law, but rather in that the command put in jeopardy the promise of God that Abraham's posterity should prosper. Even when the sacrificing of human victims later came under the prophets' condemnation, this was at first more because it was idolatrous than because it was murder.

4. This bloodshed as well must be understood in its cultural context, i.e., cultically. Before a battle the enemy army or city would be "devoted to the lord"; i.e. it was declared to be *ḥerem* or *qādōsh,* set apart, holy, taboo; it henceforth belonged to YHWH like the animal on the altar. This is why no booty was taken; neither slaves, nor cattle, nor gold. The killing was not *instrumental,* contributing in a practical way to a political goal; it was *sacrificial.*

Our purpose here is only to clarify the background for an understanding of what

what the pious reader will have been most struck by in later centuries was the general promise according to which, if Israel would believe and obey, the occupants of the land would be driven out little by little (Exod. 23:29-30) by "the angel" (23:23) or the "terror" (v. 27) or the "hornets" (v. 28) of God,[5] or the most striking victories of Joshua over Jericho (Josh. 6), or Gideon's defeat of the Midianites (Judg. 7) after most of the volunteers had been sent home and the remaining few armed with torches in order (7:2) not to let Israel think military strength or numbers had brought the victory: To "believe" meant, most specifically and concretely in the cultural context of Israel's birth as a nation, to trust God for their survival as a people. This theme then entered into the theologically oriented view of history which we find most clearly stated in the books of Chronicles.

The Kingdoms

> "O LORD, there is none like thee to help
> Between the mighty and the weak.
> Help us, O LORD our God, for we rely on thee,
> And in thy name we have come against this multitude."
>
> (2 Chron. 14:11)

---

the holy war heritage meant and did not mean in Jesus' time. More study would be needed to exposit its meaning for Christian ethics today. The comments made here are further expanded in my *The Original Revolution* (Scottdale, Pa.: Herald, 1972), pp. 91ff.

5. Some interpreters have held that if Israel had been fully faithful, the other peoples in Canaan would have withdrawn without violence in line with this promise. Von Rad (*Der heilige Krieg,* pp. 14ff.) reconstructs the history on the grounds of his critical understanding and comes to the conclusion that the original pattern of "holy war" was only defensive. In this earliest form an Israelite tribe, already infiltrated among the other Canaanite peoples, was attacked by them and defended itself according to the holy war pattern. Only later was this pattern spread out by the historians over the Joshua narratives as if the entire territory had been seized in one aggressive campaign. We are not qualified to evaluate such a critical sifting of the sources and hypothetical historical reconstruction; nonetheless it may be significant that such an effort does not heighten the impression that the holy wars "really" were more aggressive, imperialistic, and self-righteous than the texts indicate.

In any case, it is clear that not all the Canaanite centers were destroyed in the age of Joshua; for generations later they were still there.

Yet the thrust of our present argument is not dependent on a reconstruction like von Rad's.

This was the prayer with which Asa son of Abijah went out to meet an Ethiopian army four times as strong as his own. The result was that "the Lord defeated the Ethiopians before Asa and before Judah, and the Ethiopians fled."

Their flight was not brought about by a simple miracle, and the pursuit by the army of Judah was most destructive. Yet what was retained in the memory of Judah was not a record of exceptional prowess in battle or brutal mopping-up, but rather a victory brought about by the Lord himself. This is evident in the next story.

2 Chronicles 16 recounts the formation of an alliance between Asa of Judah and Benhadad of Damascus against the Northern Kingdom. Whether it is the alliance itself or the attack against the sister kingdom which brought forth the word of condemnation by the prophet Hanani, one cannot say for sure. In any case, what the prophet's words condemn specifically is the reliance upon politico-military resources:

> "Because you relied on the king of Syria,
> And did not rely on the LORD your God,
> The army of the king of Syria has escaped you.
> Were not the Ethiopians and the Libyans a huge army
> With exceedingly many chariots and horsemen?
> Yet because you relied on the LORD,
> He gave them into your hand.
> For the eyes of the LORD run to and fro
> Throughout the whole earth,
> To show his might in behalf of those
> Whose heart is blameless toward him.
> You have done foolishly in this;
> For from now on you will have wars."

This vision, for which King Asa was quick to punish the prophet, is one of the leitmotifs of this part of Chronicles. Wars are the outworking of the unwillingness of Israel, especially of the kings, to trust YHWH.

> "You will not need to fight in this battle;
> Take your position, stand still,

And see the victory of the LORD on your behalf,
O Judah and Jerusalem.
Fear not, and be not dismayed;
Tomorrow go out against them,
And the LORD will be with you."

(2 Chron. 20:17)

The crowning example of this theme of Chronicles is chapter 20, recording the response of Jehoshaphat to a massive attack from the neighboring tribes to the south. The whole population of Judah, led by the prophet Jahaziel, paraded out to meet the enemy, with the temple singers, the Kohathites and the Korahites, groups of Levitical musicians, leading the total people in songs of praise.[6] As the singing procession advanced they discovered that the enemies had come to blows among themselves and destroyed one another before they even got to Judah.

And the fear of God came on all the kingdoms of the countries
When they heard that the LORD had fought against the enemies of Israel. (20:29)

A second most striking example of this kind of preservation is found in chapter 32, recording the deliverance of Hezekiah and his people from Sennacherib.

"Do not be afraid or dismayed before the king of Assyria and all the horde that is with him; for there is one greater with us than with him. With him is an arm of flesh; but with us is the LORD our God, to help us and to fight our battles." (v. 8)

The same story is told at great length in 2 Kings 18–19. The enemy army after all its impressive threats was decimated by "the angel of the Lord" in one night.

In some of these cases there is no way to picture for the modern imagination just what might have happened. In other cases, the Israelite militia[7] or the "judge" is actively involved, without making the

6. The cultic form of the event is important. The ceremonial procession is an act of collective worship, just as the sacrificial slaughter of the victim of the holy war had been.

7. We have already noted that the holy war is more a miracle than a calculating

events any less miraculous.[8] Nor is Israel's part, when active, always violent. This is most striking in the story of Elisha's nonviolent misdirection of the Syrians (2 Kings 6:11ff.). Those with prophetic vision could see that "the mountain was full of horses and chariots of fire about Elisha," but the prophet did not leave it to the horses and chariots to solve the problem; he led the enemy armies together and ordered a banquet of reconciliation.

In the next chapter Elisha's strategy is the opposite; the prophet has to protect himself against his own king, but the enemy army is driven to flight by a noise they hear.

After the Exile

The outworking of this history, as it continued to bear fruit in the minds of pious Israelites, is exemplified in the story of Ezra as he set out from Babylon to return to Jerusalem with the authorization of Artaxerxes.

> Then I proclaimed a fast there, at the river Ahava,
> That we might humble ourselves before our God,
> To seek from him a straight way . . .
> For I was ashamed to ask the king for men,
> Soldiers and horsemen to protect us against the enemy on our way;
> Since we had told the king,
> "The hand of our God is for good upon all that seek him,
> And the power of his wrath is against all that forsake him."

---

instrument of politics. Still another characteristic that sets it apart from any comparison to modern war was the absence of any professional soldiers. The combatants were a volunteer militia gathered by a trumpet blast from their daily occupations, not professionals paid and drilled for military effectiveness. Once Saul and David had made the transition to an organized state with a standing army, there were no more holy wars of the classic "Joshua" type.

8. By "miraculous" here is meant only what the root meaning of the word accents; that it is cause for wonderment. We are not concerned here for philosophical meditations about the laws of nature, breaking the laws of nature, what miracles prove, or what is meant by miracle stories if they cannot have happened the way it says.

So we fasted and besought our God for this,
And he listened to our entreaty.

(Ezra 8:21ff.)

It had thus become a part of the standard devotional ritual of Israel to look over the nation's history as one of miraculous preservation. Sometimes this preservation had included the Israelites' military activity; at other times no weapons at all were used. In both kinds of case, however, the point was the same: confidence in YHWH is an alternative to the self-determining use of Israel's own military resources in the defense of their existence as God's people.

Our purpose in summarizing this story here is not to seek to reconstruct in just what way whatever happened did happen when YHWH saved Israel, or whether in each case any of the Israelites used weapons or not. Our present concern is rather with what it meant for Jesus and his contemporaries and his disciples to read this kind of story in their Bible.

We must conclude that the faith of the pious Israelite was nourished by a body of what the cultural anthropologists will call "legend,"[9] the central themes of which were that God himself will take care of his people —

"The LORD will cause your enemies
who rise against you
to be defeated before you;
They shall come out against you one way,
and flee before you seven ways."

(Deut. 28:7)

— and that therefore the Israelites' preoccupation with their own power as the instrument of their own surviving or prevailing is misdirected.

9. The term "legend" designates a cultural usage, not a judgment of historicity. The "legend" is that which in a given community is *legendum,* an account to be told over and over, which forms the identity and the values and the self-awareness of that community through the much telling. To identify these stories as Israel's legendarium, as the body of story-telling that made Israel remember what it meant to be Israel, implies no judgment on the historicity of the accounts.

"He will guard the feet of his faithful ones;
For not by might does one prevail."

(1 Sam. 2:9)

The reasonableness of this stance was reinforced by the stories of Abraham's relinquishing the best lands to his greedy nephew (Gen. 13:8ff.), of Isaac's relinquishing his pastures and wells to Abimelech at Gerar (26:16ff.), of Joseph's and Daniel's rising to prominence by way of exile and prison. What the stories told by example, the prophets made into precept.

"Not by might, nor by power,
but by my Spirit, says the LORD of Hosts."[10]

Now whatever be the "actual historical shape" of the events lying behind the story, we can be assured that, in the atmosphere of heightened apocalyptic sensitivity into which Jesus came, it was at least *possible* if not *normal* for those who were "waiting for the consolation of Israel" to see in these miraculous deliverances of the Old Testament story a paradigm of the way God would save his people now. When, therefore, Jesus used the language of liberation and revolution, announcing a restoration of "kingdom" community and a new pattern of life, without predicting or authorizing particular violent techniques for achieving his good ends, he need not have seemed to his listeners to be a dreamer; he could very easily have been understood as updating the faith of Jehoshaphat and Hezekiah, a faith whereby a believing people would be saved despite their weakness, on condition that they "be still and wait to see the salvation of the LORD."

10. Zech. 4:6. Millard Lind in several studies has exposited at length the underlying meanings of this prophetic view of YHWH's working to save Israel. The prophets remolded the holy war heritage in the use they made of it in recalling Israel to trust in God. Here our concern is much more limited. We are asking not about the prophets' theology but about the Jews' piety, about the sense of reality and the understanding of God's intervention that were common among Jesus' hearers. Gerhard von Rad, *Old Testament Theology* (London: Oliver & Boyd, 1962), I, 347ff., characterizes the history of Chronicles as lacking in theological clarity and unity. Von Rad might consider this theme, "God will take care of his people," as insufficient to meet his criteria of clarity and coherence; nonetheless it is a major theme on the face of the text, and one to which von Rad does not refer explicitly. Cf. Millard Lind, "The Concept of Political Power in Ancient Israel," *ASTI,* 7 (1970), 4ff.

To take into account the permeation of pious Jewish hope with such a body of national legend has serious implications for the meaning of such "Kingdom Inaugural" discourses of Jesus as the Platform statement at Nazareth or the Sermon on the Plain.

(a) The modern reader is struck by the improbability, indeed the seeming impossibility, of any such saving event as a generalized jubilee or an adversary leaving. Since he or she assumes Jesus could hardly have meant what he said, the reader's mind is sent to meander down the sidetracks of paradoxical or symbolic reinterpretations. For Jesus' listeners, on the other hand, as believing Jews, the question of possibility was not allowed to get in the way of hearing the promise. They therefore did not prejudice their sense of what might happen by knowing ahead of time what Jesus could not mean.

(b) In correlation with our sense of impossibility we tend to think of "apocalyptic" promises as pointing "off the map" of human experience, off the scale of time, in that they announce an end to history. But the past deliverances of Israel had been recounted as having taken place within their own history and on their own Palestinian soil. The whole body of hermeneutic prejudices linked with the concept of the "interim ethic," as if what Jesus was predicting was an end to time and space, gets us off the track right at this point.[11] Jesus' proclamation of the kingdom was unacceptable to most of his listeners *not* because they thought it could not happen but because they feared it might, and that it would bring down judgment on them.

If, with the cultural empathy that is the elementary requisite for honestly understanding any ancient documents, we measure Jesus' meaning not by what *we* can possibly conceive of as happening but by what his listeners can have understood, then we are forbidden to filter his message through our modern sense of reality, of the uniformity of nature and the inconceivability of the extraordinary. "Miracles don't happen" is the one assumption we dare not impose from outside on Jesus or his listeners.

11. In an earlier section I already argued that the haste with which recent scholars have discounted the realism of Jesus' intentions was the result of a particular negative philosophical prejudice extraneous to the texts (pp. 5ff., 15ff.); here we observe that Jesus' listeners might well have heard him with a particular affirmative predisposition concerning an intervening God, intrinsic to their faith and culture.

Our modern sense of what may and may not reasonably be expected to happen in our age and in our world will, of course, not avoid coming to terms with the deterministic worldview that surrounds us. We may even be driven by the commitment we make to this contemporary view to project it backward as a judgment as to what can really have happened in the time of Hezekiah, or of Jesus. That is a problem of modern theological self-understanding which the present study does not mean to resolve, nor to pass off lightly. But here our topic is much more modest and much more precise. We are testing whether *what Jesus meant* is properly to be determined under the shadow of our assumption that for him, or for his listeners, or for the Gospel writers and readers, concrete divine intervention was no option, or if conceivable at all, would have meant the end of time and of social-historical process. The evidence is abundant that such a dilemma not only was not self-evident, but was unthinkable. The mighty acts of God in Israel's history had been neither the end of history, nor off the scale of human events. We have every reason to assume that the inauguration of the jubilee was understood by Jesus' hearers with the same concreteness as the Exodus story or the deliverance of Jehoshaphat had for them.

EPILOGUE

Ever since Marcion, the picture of the God of the ancient Israelites as a God of war has been an occasion for caricature and embarrassment for Christians. That is one of the reasons why both Christians and Jews have developed ways to read those stories that might avoid ascribing to God qualities that we do not praise in men and women. The above chapter did not address that embarrassment, since its concern was not our modern reading of the holy war heritage but how that heritage made sense in the first century, as background to Jesus' and his contemporaries' thought about God's possible intervention in history.

Older interpretations of how Christians should understand the wars of YHWH most often sought simply to set them aside. Some have sought to resolve this on the grounds of a "new dispensation" after the model of Jesus' repeated "but I say to you" in Matthew 5. This was done by the Czech Brethren of the fifteenth-century "First Reformation," by "Anabaptist"-type pacifists since then, and by Tolstoy. Jesus being God's qualified envoy, inaugurating a new age, he had every right to change the rules.

In a different form of the same logic, the wars of the early Hebrews can be set aside on the more general grounds of the post-Enlightenment notion that we moderns are qualified, by the mere fact of our modernity, to rule on which elements of an ancient culture we choose to find usable. Thus it is we, in place of Jesus, who have the right to declare "ancient good uncouth."

Both of these postures are still very much alive among us; their simplicity makes them more accessible than the more careful historical-anthropological angle which I here have assumed.

The above chapter interprets only one dimension of the legacy of the Hebrew story of YHWH/God helping Israel in war: namely the difference which that heritage, remembered as Jews in the age of Jesus must have remembered it, should make for our interpreting the setting of Jesus' decisions. Yet there is much more to say about how the Old Testament story of YHWH as warrior should be taken in its own right.

Almost simultaneously with the first publication of *The Politics of Jesus,* my more analytical chapter, "If Abraham Is Our Father,"[12] addressed the challenge of how the Christian can own the Israelite history, in such a way as to see the gospel as an organic prolongation of the original early Israelite experience and vision, rather than as a rejection or reversal.

In 1980 Millard C. Lind's *Yahweh Is a Warrior*[13] exposited with much greater scholarly depth the same perspective. I have sought once more to capsule this message briefly in " 'To your tents, O Israel'; The Legacy of Israel's Experience with Holy War."[14]

12. In *The Original Revolution* (Scottdale, Pa.: Herald, 1972), pp. 85-104.

13. (Scottdale, Pa.: Herald, 1980); I already cited Lind in n. 10 above. An excellent popularization of the same perspective is Lois Barrett's *The Way God Fights: War and Peace in the Old Testament* (Scottdale, Pa.: Herald Press, 1987). Further papers on the same theme by Lind are gathered in his collected essays *Monotheism, Power, Justice* (Elkhart, Ind.: Institute of Mennonite Studies, 1990), esp. pp. 171-96.

14. *Studies in Religion/Sciences Religieuses,* 18 (Summer 1989), 345-62. Cf. also my

The general theme of how Christians can understand the wars of YHWH has since continued to draw widespread attention.[15] Other studies have built upon the Hebrew understandings of faith, power, and nationhood, reaching beyond the issue of war itself; among these are dissertations on the Hebrew Scriptures by Gerbrandt and Ollenburger[16] and on Ephesians 6 by Thomas Yoder Neufeld.[17]

The numerous works of Walter Brueggemann[18] and Norman Gottwald[19] support in a broader way the above chapter's concern for letting the ancient texts themselves dictate how we should discern the unity of the canonical corpus as a witness for justice. They also find in the Hebrew story, when empathetically and critically read, values compatible with rather than contradictory to the New Testament.

"Texts That Serve or Texts That Summon," in *Journal of Religious Ethics,* 20/2 (Fall 1992), 229ff., responding to a modernizing effort of Michael Walzer.

15. The landmark study in the field, Gerhard von Rad's *Holy War in Ancient Israel,* was published in English translation only in 1991 (Grand Rapids: Eerdmans, translation edited by Marva J. Dawn). A literature survey by Ben C. Ollenburger and a topically analyzed and annotated bibliography by Judith E. Sanderson in the same volume offer the best general introduction to the subject. To the Sanderson bibliography we might add: Sa-Moon Kang, *Divine War in the Old Testament and in the Ancient Near East* (Berlin: de Gruyter, 1989); Anton van der Lingen, *Les Guerres de Yahvé* (Paris: Cerf, 1990).

16. Gerald E. Gerbrandt, *Kingship according to the Deuteronomic History* (Th.D. diss., Richmond, Va.: Union Theological Seminary, 1979); Benjamin C. Ollenburger, *Zion, City of the Great King* (Sheffield: JSOT Press, 1987).

17. Thomas R. Yoder Neufeld, *God and Saints at War: The Transformation and Democratization of the Divine Warrior* (Th.D. diss., Harvard University, 1989).

18. Brueggemann's writings are too numerous to try to sort out here; all of them fit the above characterization.

19. Especially *The Tribes of Yahweh* (Maryknoll, N.Y.: Orbis, 1979).

CHAPTER 5

The Possibility of Nonviolent Resistance

Readers of the Gospel story, we have noted, have had difficulty conceiving of Jesus' public ministry as involving any genuine options for social change. This difficulty is reinforced not only by the factors we have thus far been dealing with,[1] but also by the assumption that in his time there were clearly no other ways to resist the Romans than those which the Zealots advocated. We have been giving increased attention to the Zealot option; but thereby we have risked reinforcing this misconception. We have spoken of the pious Israelite's ability to believe in divine intervention[2] but without suggesting how, in the thought of a devout Jew, such an intervention might take place.

To dispel some of this air of irrealism we should therefore be reminded that effective nonviolent resistance was not at all unknown in recent Jewish experience.[3] Just before his brief reference to Jesus, the historian Josephus reports this singular episode:[4]

1. The logical axioms leading to the claim that the gospel is apolitical are identified especially above, pp. 5ff.

2. Above, ch. 4, pp. 76ff.

3. The following exposition parallels and expands a segment of André Trocmé's *Jésus-Christ et la révolution non-violente*, pp. 103ff. The same account is reviewed in a wider context by Milton R. Konvitz, "Conscience and Civil Disobedience in the Jewish Tradition," in his *Judaism and Human Rights* (New York: Viking, 1972), pp. 164ff., reprinted in Menachem Marc Kellner, *Contemporary Jewish Ethics* (New York: Sanhedrin Press, 1978), pp. 239ff.

4. Quoted here from Josephus *Antiquities* 18.3; a briefer parallel report is found as well in his *Wars* 2.9. The latter source adds that the sit-in lasted five days and nights.

> But now Pilate, the procurator of Judea, removed the army from Caesarea to Jerusalem, to take their winter quarters there, in order to abolish the Jewish laws. So he introduced Caesar's effigies, which were upon the ensigns, and brought them into the city; whereas our law forbids us the very making of images; on which account the former procurators were wont to make their entry into the city with such ensigns as had not those ornaments.[5] Pilate was the first who brought those images to Jerusalem, and set them up there; which was done without the knowledge of the people, because it was done in the nighttime; but as soon as they knew it, they came in multitudes to Caesarea and interceded with Pilate many days, that he would remove the images; and when he would not grant their requests, because it would tend to the injury of Caesar, while yet they persevered in their request, on the sixth day he ordered his soldiers to have their weapons privately, while he came and sat upon his judgment seat, which seat was so prepared in the open place of the city, that it concealed the army that lay ready to oppress them; and when the Jews petitioned him again, he gave a signal to the soldiers to encompass them round, and threatened that their punishment should be no less than immediate death, unless they would leave off disturbing him, and go their ways home. But they threw themselves upon the ground and laid their necks bare and said they would take their death very willingly rather than that the wisdom of their law should be transgressed; upon which Pilate was deeply affected with their firm resolution to keep their laws inviolable, and presently commanded the images to be carried back from Jerusalem to Caesarea.

This was evidently not a planned campaign to achieve a set goal, but rather a spontaneous common response, effective perhaps partly

5. Carl H. Kraeling, "The Episode of the Roman Standards at Jerusalem," *HTR,* 35 (1942), 263ff., tries to spell out something of the fuller meaning of these events: What kinds of standards were so offensive? What kind of army unit bore them? If this happened in A.D. 26, as Kraeling and others surmise, then 1,290 days, which according to Dan. 12:11 were to separate "the setting up of the abomination of desolation" from the beginning of the end, would have run from then just about to the time of Jesus' public ministry. Kraeling suggests that apocalyptic calculations in this vein might have contributed to an especially tense expectancy in the situation into which John and Jesus came.

because it surprised Pilate. It did not set up a repeatable pattern. The next effort of protest, this time against Pilate's confiscation of the consecrated temple treasure to build an aqueduct, was put down bloodily. The situation in that latter case was quite parallel, and the Jews' massing unarmed for protest was the same; but this time Pilate gave them no summons to withdraw, and thus avoided giving them a signal to throw themselves on his mercy.[6]

Not much later another threat called forth a concerted act of resistance which this time had all the marks of a Gandhian campaign.[7] Gaius Caligula, the first of the Caesars to demand formal worship of himself, was incensed at the Jews' refusal to obey, and ordered Petronius, Roman legate of Syria, to install a statue of Caligula in the temple at Jerusalem. This would have been to repeat the "abomination of desolation," the profanation of the temple itself by idolatry, which had been perpetrated once before by Antiochus Epiphanes and had triggered the Maccabean wars. This time, however, the response was a general strike. Fields were left untilled in the sowing season, and by the tens of thousands the Jews gathered to entreat Petronius, at Ptolemais and then at Tiberias, for over a month.[8] The unity of the people could not be broken; the leaders when summoned privately by Petronius took the same position as the multitudes. Even the heads of the Romanizing royal house, King Agrippa at Rome, and his brother Aristobulus, supported the petition. Disavowing any desire to war against Caesar, the Jews all together could not be moved from the promise to give their lives and those of their wives and children, before permitting the threatened sacrilege. Petronius was finally moved to risk his own

6. This second episode is reported in both Josephus sources, in the immediately following paragraph. This juxtaposition might indicate more than time sequence; it might suggest a conscious repetition of the same strategy by the Jews. Some have conjectured that this latter massacre might be the same as the event mentioned in Luke 13:1-2 (above, pp. 36f.), where it is said that Pilate "mingled with that of their sacrifices" the blood of certain Galileans. But neither the reference to Galilee nor that to sacrifice seems to fit with Josephus's account.

7. *Antiquities* 18.8; *Wars* 2.10.

8. The *Antiquities* account reports forty days, the *Wars* fifty. The economic loss from crop failure seems to have been part of the conscious threat, a threat under which the Jews themselves of course stood to suffer as much as the Romans.

standing before Caligula, and became himself the advocate of the Jews' scruples.[9]

Thus collective nonviolent resistance by the Jewry of Palestine was successful against the Roman forces twice within a decade. Called forth by a threat pointed at the heart of the people's religious identity, the reaction founds its own forms of leadership and interpenetration, despite the total absence of any prior training or planning, and without the support of an ethical commitment excluding all violence. This does not suffice to verify the strained hypothesis that if Jesus' message had been accepted by the multitudes he would have led them in such campaigns. It does suffice nonetheless to negate the sweeping assumption that in rejecting the Zealot option Jesus' only other conceivable alternative would have been the end of the world or a retreat to the desert; in other words, to reject the responsible sword is to withdraw from history.

9. Josephus clearly intends to report that these events included providential intervention. Just after Petronius's decision there came a late, hard rain which made late seeding possible without loss of crops. Caligula, who had first been moved by Agrippa's pleading to withdraw the threat, was nonetheless angered by Petronius's taking the side of the Jews and ordered him to commit suicide. But then Caligula died, and the news of his death reached Petronius before the messengers bearing the order to kill himself (which had been delayed providentially by bad weather on the Mediterranean, thus rewarding him with his life for his sympathy to the Jews).

CHAPTER 6

Trial Balance

The reader who has followed us thus far may be ready to grant that, by watching closely the details and the context of the Gospel narrative, we can see reported the work of an ethical-social Jesus whose words and work, life and death, consistently project and make real a particular pattern of presence in the world. But if the reader grants this, and grants as well, hypothetically, that Jesus may have tried to get others to share in that new kingdom reality, does such an argument suffice to reach the present? Did it even reach into the other parts of the New Testament? Did it even survive the translation into the cultural idiom of the early non-Jewish churches?

A sustained, systematic argument would soon become repetitive. We can, however, substantially support our claim in a more episodic or selective way. For our purposes it need not be air-tightly demonstrated that every section of the early church, or of the New Testament, extends in full clarity and fidelity the social stance of Jesus; it suffices to find that at several points, in varied languages and contexts, in more than one style and kind of literature, something of the same posture is found again. The fragmentary essays in the chapters that follow are selected with a view to the variety of semantic and cultural styles into which the Jesus kind of life was transposed, with special attention to those points where it has often been argued or assumed that we are farthest from his influence, or that his influence is of the least concrete kind. As before, no original textual insight will be argued here; I shall merely summarize scholarly trends whose relevance, or whose unity, has hitherto not been exploited for social-ethical thought. To facilitate the testing of how the "Jesus kind of life was transposed" I first devote this chapter to a schematic summary.

From Luke to Paul

Assuming that the Jesus of the earliest tradition was something like the Jesus of Luke, we move to the next question, that of post-Pentecost ethics, with a certain momentum. The motif of the disciples' cross is carried over directly from Luke 14 to the epistles. The place the epistles give to sharing in the sufferings of Christ, as a key concept in piety and in ethics, has been widely analyzed in recent study.[1]

Paul can speak of his own ministry as a sharing in the dying and rising of Jesus (most pointedly in 2 Cor. 4:10-11, "I carry about in the body the dying of Jesus . . ."; cf. Col. 1:24: "I will fill out what is lacking in the afflictions of Christ for his body the church").

Or he can draw the parallel to the sufferings of all believers (Phil. 1:29, "To you is given not only to believe in Christ but also to suffer for him"). Christ's self-giving can be made paradigmatic for the love between spouses (Eph. 5:25) or for the disposition that enables unity in the church (Phil. 2:1-5).[2] 1 Peter speaks of the cross as an example finding concrete imitation when a slave obeys a cruel master; Hebrews 12 describes Jesus as the author and finisher of that faith whose expression in believers may yet reach to the shedding of blood. 1 John 3 makes the polarity Cain/Christ, hate/love, killing/laying down one's life, typical of all the meaning of obedience.[3]

1. This "imitation" theme is expanded in ch. 7 below. Here we sketch only enough to lead into a summary of the conclusions to draw from the Gospels. It might be asked why in this survey we do not follow Luke's narrative on into Acts. (a) The epistles are earlier than either the Acts or the Gospels, and thereby constitute a corroboration from a source more independent of Luke; (b) our concern is not for Luke's own editorial or theological contribution (which would lead us to seek its continuation in Acts) but for the common primitive Jesus story which shows through his narrative despite his particular editorial concerns.

2. By thus moving to the epistles we do of course leave untouched some questions which our reading of Luke would lead us to put to Acts: Is the eschatology of the discourses of Acts different from that of the Gospels? What has come of the at-hand-ness of the kingdom after Pentecost?

3. A sample of recently renewed scholarly awareness of the centrality of the theme

Before drawing any affirmative conclusions let us first note the absence of the concept of imitation as a *general* pastoral or moral guideline. There is in the New Testament no Franciscan glorification of barefoot itinerancy. Even when Paul argues the case for celibacy, it does not occur to him to appeal to the example of Jesus. Even when Paul explains his own predilection for self-support there is no appeal to Jesus' years as a village artisan. Even when the apostle argues strongly the case for his teaching authority, there is no appeal to the rabbinic ministry of Jesus. Jesus' trade as a carpenter, his association with fishermen, and his choice of illustrations from the life of the sower and the shepherd have throughout Christian history given momentum to the romantic glorification of the handcrafts and the rural life; but there is none of this in the New Testament. It testifies throughout to the life and mission of a church going intentionally into the cities in full knowledge of the conflicts which awaited believers there. That the concept of imitation is *not* applied by the New Testament at some of those points where Franciscan and romantic devotion has tried most piously to apply it, is all the more powerfully a demonstration of how fundamental the thought of participation in the suffering of Christ is when the New Testament church sees it as guiding and explaining her attitude to the powers of the world. Only at one point, only on one subject — but then consistently, universally — is Jesus our example: in his cross.

This much could have been said without special attention to our learnings from Luke. But all of this language of imitation and participation, all the pious and pastoral meditation on the believer's cross,

---

of "sharing in the sufferings of Christ" is seen in Edvin Larsson's *Christus als Vorbild* (Lund: Gleerup, 1964). The theme "What is lacking in the sufferings of Christ" is exposited by Henry Gustafson, *BR,* 8 (1963), 28ff. Our observation that Paul saw himself and his church living on in the line of the sufferings of Jesus, and perhaps as fulfilling in his flesh some "Words of the Lord" to that effect, would only make more concrete the other dimensions of corporate personality, eschatological tribulation, and participation in faithful witness which are Gustafson's leitmotifs.

C. H. Dodd suggests that one of the principles of selection operative in the writing of the Gospels may well have been the concern to gather examples that could throw light on Christians' moral choices. "It is probable that the idea of the *imitatio Christi* had more to say than is commonly recognized . . . in the selection of incidents from the life of Jesus for record in the Gospels" (Moffatt commentary on 1 John, p. 85).

takes on a new dimension if we take the measure of the social character of Jesus' cross.

The believer's cross is no longer any and every kind of suffering, sickness, or tension, the bearing of which is demanded. The believer's cross is, like that of Jesus, the price of social nonconformity. It is not, like sickness or catastrophe, an inexplicable, unpredictable suffering; it is the end of a path freely chosen after counting the cost.[4] It is not, like Luther's or Thomas Müntzer's or Zinzendorf's or Kierkegaard's cross or *Anfechtung,* an inward wrestling of the sensitive soul with self and sin; it is the social reality of representing in an unwilling world the Order to come. The Word:

> "The servant is not greater than his master.
> If they persecuted me they will persecute you."
>
> (John 15:20)

is not a pastoral counsel to help with the ambiguities of life; it is a normative statement about the relation of our social obedience to the messianity of Jesus. Representing as he did the divine order now at hand, accessible; renouncing as he did the legitimate use of violence and the accrediting of the existing authorities; renouncing as well the ritual purity of noninvolvement, his people will encounter in ways analogous to his own the hostility of the old order.

Being human, Jesus must have been subject somehow or other to the testings of pride, envy, anger, sloth, avarice, gluttony, and lust; but it does not enter into the concerns of the Gospel writer to give us any information about any struggles he may have had with their attraction. The one temptation the man Jesus faced — and faced again and again — as a constitutive element of his public ministry, was the temptation to exercise social responsibility, in the interest of justified revolution, through the use of available violent methods. Social withdrawal was no temptation to him; that option (which most Christians take part of the

4. John J. Vincent, "Discipleship and Synoptic Studies," *TZ,* 16 (1960), 456ff., argues cogently the value of the Synoptic concept of discipleship as foundation for a theologically valid reconception of ethics; what Vincent argues on formal grounds is here worked through in a concrete application. Vincent, however, does not give to the issue of kingship and cross the central place it seems to have in the Synoptic discipleship sayings.

time) was excluded at the outset. Any alliance with the Sadducean establishment in the exercise of *conservative* social responsibility (which most Christians choose the rest of the time) was likewise excluded at the outset. We understand Jesus only if we can empathize with this threefold rejection: the self-evident, axiomatic, sweeping rejection of both quietism and establishment responsibility, and the difficult, constantly reopened, genuinely attractive option of the crusade.

The statement of the problem with which we began was drawn not from Luke but from the present. Because Jesus is not meant to be taken as normative for political ethics, it is said, we must obviously, consciously, properly get our ethics elsewhere, from a "responsible" calculation of our chances and our duty to make events come out as well as possible. This substitution of nature or history for Jesus as the locus of revelation was justified by the claim that Jesus had nothing to say on this subject. But now we see that he did have something to say; in fact that he said little that was not somehow on this subject. The Gospel record refuses to let the modern social ethicist off the hook. It is quite possible to refuse to accept Jesus as normative; but it is not possible on the basis of the record to declare him irrelevant.

Back to the Present

The fruit of this sketchy survey can be only a global impression, but it is a consistent one. It leaves no room for the prevalent tradition of discounting Jesus' ethic as socially irrelevant either because Jesus' intentions were only on some other level or because the issues he faced were radically different from our own. According to the record, as gathered by witnesses who have never been accused of warping the report to make this point,[5] what Jesus announced was a new stance to

5. If there is any critical consensus on the particular concerns present in Luke's compilation and editing, it is that he meant to give an impression opposed to the one we have been finding here. A resume of the critical conjecture that *all* the Gospel writers slanted their materials so as to weaken the impression that Jesus' ministry was any threat to society is offered by Ellis E. Jensen, "The First Century Controversy over Jesus as a Revolutionary Figure," *JBL*, 60 (1941), 261ff. S. G. F. Brandon, *Jesus and the Zealots*, and

be taken by repentant hearers in the midst of the world: his vocabulary and his picture of what must come to pass were much more "political" than they were "existential" or cultic. His disavowal of Peter's well-intentioned effort to defend him cannot be taken out of the realm of ethics by the explanation that he had to get himself immolated in order to satisfy the requirements of some metaphysically motivated doctrine of the atonement; it was because God's will for God's servant in this world is that he should renounce legitimate defense. When Jesus wrestled repeatedly with the tempter, from the desert at the beginning to the garden at the end, this was not a clumsily contrived morality play meaning to teach us that kingship was no temptation; it was because God's servant in this world was facing, and rejecting, the claim that the exercise of social responsibility through the use of self-evidently necessary means is a moral duty.

At the outset of our study we noted the kinds of arguments with which the exemplarity of Jesus' work and the relevance of his teachings are often set aside. They may not unfairly be characterized as seeing Jesus through ebionitic eyes, that is, limiting his relevance to that which one chooses to attribute to his human status as a radical rabbi. We have observed in the main body of our study that as a radical rabbi Jesus was far more of a political figure than the ebionitic view had been ready to concede; and now we have seen, though only briefly, and shall spell out further, that the early apostolic church made that political human-

---

Neill Q. Hamilton, *Jesus for a No-God World* (Philadelphia: Westminster, 1969), pp. 43-120, make the same sweeping assumption.

The last few years have seen an accumulation of journalistic-type references to "Jesus as a radical," seeking to catch the mood of an age when "revolution" is an "in" word. With much of what I am saying here, the stance suggested in such texts (e.g., Stephen Rose, "Agitating Jesus," *Renewal* [Oct. 1967]; Sebastian Moore, *No Exit* [Paramus, N.J.: Newman, 1968]) can be fruitfully compared. Yet the differences are significant. By skipping over the challenge of the collision with traditional interpretations, such claims tend to discredit themselves for novelty-mongering. Often as well (e.g., Willis E. Elliott, "No Alternative to Violence," in *Renewal* [Oct. 1968]) they fail to discern the particular place that the temptation of the sword and his rejection of it has in the *form* and the *substance* of Jesus' social proclamation and impact. They thereby call on Jesus to legitimate their own contemporary revolutionary visions rather than perceiving the uniqueness of his vision. Thereby the risk is great of missing the very core of his originality, namely his rejection (sympathetic, but a clear rejection nonetheless) of the Zealot option.

ness normative for their life. We could support this consideration further if we were to follow the developments which Christian doctrine underwent. When the later, more "theological" New Testament writings formulated the claim to preexistence and cosmic preeminence for the divine Son or Word (John 1:1-4; Col. 1:15ff.; Heb. 1:2ff.) the intent of this language was not to consecrate beside Jesus some other way of perceiving the eternal Word, through reason or history or nature, but rather to affirm the exclusivity of the revelation claim they were making for Jesus. The same must be said of the later development of the classic ideas of the Trinity and the Incarnation. "Incarnation" does not originally mean (as it tends to today in some theologies of history, and in some kinds of Anglican theology) that God took all of human nature as it was, put his seal of approval on it, and thereby ratified nature as revelation. The point is just the opposite; that God broke through the borders of our standard definition of what is human, and gave a new, formative definition in Jesus. "Trinity" did not originally mean, as it does for some later, that there are three kinds of revelation, the Father speaking through creation and the Spirit through experience, by which the words and example of the Son must be corrected; it meant rather that language must be found and definitions created so that Christians, who believe in only one God, can affirm that that God is most adequately and bindingly known in Jesus.

I did not at the beginning of the paper identify in the same way the other set of alternatives, that is, the docetic ways of avoiding the political Jesus. These approaches concede unique authority to Jesus, but do so by divorcing him from our humanity.

(a) According to all orthodox doctrines of salvation, Jesus had to die for the sins of human beings. This was predicted in the prophecies of the Old Testament so that Jesus and Paul could speak of his death as having happened "according to scripture." It was also necessary because of the meaning of human lostness and the demands of the holiness of God. Jesus had to die — as a ransom to purchase humanity's liberty from bondage, or as an expiatory sacrifice to purge the stain of sin, or as a substitutionary penalty to pay the price of broken law. Whatever be the imagery, Jesus knew he had to die, for reasons unrelated to his social humanity. Therefore the social humanity of how that necessity came to be carried out is unimportant. The reason he refused to be king or to defend himself was not that there was anything wrong with kingship or self-defense; he just could not have met his destined cross that way.

(b) It is possible to claim that within the space of a generation the concern of the early Christians had moved from the human Jesus of the Gospels to the cosmic Jesus of the letter to the Colossians. In the name of this cosmic Christ the church proclaimed a general acceptance by God of the nature and structures of this world, from which there must flow an ethic of world-affirmation and of creativity. The whole cosmos must be taken as the ultimate revelation of the dimensions of humankind: the Jesus of the Gospel stories is merely a bridge from the cultural isolation of Judaism to the world-encompassing acceptance of the givenness of history and humankind in the deutero-Pauline proclamation.

There was a time earlier in this century when such a contrast between the Jesus of the Gospels and the Christ of Paul was so understood as to prefer the former to the latter. Today, in the most widely publicized thinking on the mission of the church, in the popularization of which Joseph Sittler's 1961 New Delhi poem-sermon[6] and Harvey Cox's 1967 interpretation of "Church and Society"[7] were two landmarks, the current has moved clearly in the other direction. One makes majestic, orthodox-sounding statements about the cosmic significance of Christ; but the effect of this language — just the opposite of what it has for Paul — is to move farther from the claims that could be made for the Palestinian Jesus. The hidden workings of the cosmic Christ throughout the fabric of present history, they assume, will give us more guidance than a bygone Jesus.

(c) The other frequent way of making almost the same point is the appeal to the dogma of the Trinity, most sweepingly and structurally stated in the analysis of H. Richard Niebuhr.[8] An ethic of the Son,

6. Joseph Sittler, "Called to Unity," *Ecumenical Review,* 14/2 (Jan. 1962), 177ff.

7. Harvey Cox, "The Biblical Basis of the Geneva Conference," *CC* (Apr. 5, 1967), p. 435.

8. Initially projected in his *Christ and Culture* (New York: Harper, 1951), pp. 80-81, 114, 131, this analysis is extended in "The Doctrine of the Trinity and the Unity of the Church," *TT,* 3/3 (Oct. 1946), 371ff.; reprinted in *TT,* 40 (July 1983), 150ff. under the sharpened title: "Theological Unitarianism."

guided by either the teachings or the example of Jesus of Nazareth, needs to be completed or even corrected by two other kinds of resource. We first of all need an ethic of the Father, in whose name the structures of the created world must be affirmed. What traditionally was called an ethic of the orders of creation is therefore founded in the will of the Father. Perhaps he might as well be appealed to as the authority underlying the moral teaching of the Old Testament.

Probably still more significant in Niebuhr's intent is the completion or correction which needs to be brought from the perspective of the Holy Spirit. By this is not meant — at least not primarily, not in the thinking of Niebuhr himself — any ecstatic or prophetic insight, mystical or pentecostal, but rather the whole body of decisions and precedents, arrangements and adaptations which have been made between Christ and culture throughout the history of Christendom. These decisions have been made by the churches and may be presumed to have been the work of the Holy Spirit. They have by and large led away from an ethic of the Son.

It is quite evident that, caught between the universality and the validity of the orders of creation on the one hand and the historical continuity and present relevance of the accumulation of Christian tradition on the other, whatever substantial originality there may have been in the ethic of Jesus is no longer of determining significance. If it still enjoys some kind of symbolic centrality, the gem is nevertheless almost lost within the size of the setting.

(d) Still one other kind of cavil must be recognized. We have been admonished for the past three-quarters of a century to be clear in distinguishing between *Historie* and *Geschichte*. Is there not a difference between the historic and the historical Jesus? Can we bypass either the literary questions or the philosophical ones with which our colleagues have been entertaining us since it began to be recognized that the Gospel sources are not neutral chronicles but witnesses of the faith?

As distinct from some of the other questions above, this is one that cannot be resolved simply by reading the sources, since it reflects the modern reader's judgment on the character and authority of the sources. Neither can it be resolved from traditional perspectives, since it reflects a conception of the novelty and authority of the modern mind for which study of any binding heritage becomes irrelevant. But fortunately for our purposes, this is a question we need not answer in a general, methodological way, since it just happens — or *is* it just happenstance? — that the particular Gospel materials we have been looking at are generally conceded to be those points at which the historic and the historical most nearly coincide. These are the points where there is the least distinction between what the critic thinks must actually have happened and what the believing witnesses reported.[9] There is widespread debate about the sense in which the resurrection reports can be called "history," or about how much the sayings and parables have evolved when we find them in their Synoptic settings. The doubts have not the same depth or breadth when we turn to the narrative skeleton of the Gospels, according to which Jesus gathered disciples, proclaimed the imminence of the kingdom, and was executed accused of insurrection.

To deal with the many ways, ebionitic and docetic, of avoiding the normativeness of Jesus would call for a different kind of study from the present one. Such questions are of a dogmatic, not exegetical character, and would need to be encountered on that level. From the perspective of our reading of Luke and our brief glance at the epistles, all that can be said is that these texts themselves provide no demand for such redefinitions and raise no need for them. If we were to carry on that other, traditionally doctrinal kind of debate, I would seek simply to demonstrate that the view of Jesus being proposed here is more radically Nicene and Chalcedonian than other views. I do not here advocate an unheard-of modern understanding of Jesus. I ask rather that the implications of what the church has always said about Jesus as Word of the Father, as true God and true Human, be taken more seriously, as relevant to our social problems, than ever before.

But then relevance must be redefined. If it is not enough to say with the Reformation traditions that Jesus purges our will and dampens our pride, sending us back to follow the dictates of our "office" or

9. Rudolf Bultmann's most basic statement on "the relationship of the primitive Christian proclamation of Christ to the historical Jesus," *Das Verhältnis der urchristlichen Christusbotschaft zum historischen Jesus* (Heidelberg: Carl Winter, 3rd ed. 1962), considers as fully *certain* only that Jesus died the death of a political criminal (p. 12) and as *probable* that he cast out demons, broke the sabbath law, favored the social outcasts, and gathered a small circle of disciples (p. 11).

"station" with greater modesty and thoroughness; if it is not enough to say with the Puritan traditions that we derive from Josiah and Theodosius the vision of a holy commonwealth constantly being reformed to approach increasingly the theocratic ideal; if it is not enough with the "natural law" to find our instructions in the givenness of the fallen world; if it is not enough with the quietist and sectarian traditions to let someone else take care of the world out there, what can then be the shape of a reformulated social responsibility illuminated by the confession that it is Jesus who is the Messiah and Lord? Where are we called to an ethicist's repentance, that is, to a reformulation of the thought patterns that underlie moral choice? I suggest that this reformulation must take five lines:

1. Recent systematic tradition tells us that we must *choose between the Jesus of history and the Jesus of dogma.*

If Jesus is the divine Word incarnate, then what we will be concerned about is the metaphysical transactions by means of which he saved humanity by entering into it. We will then leap like the creed from the birth of Jesus to the cross. His teachings and his social and political involvement will be of little interest and not binding for us.

If, on the other hand, we seek to understand the "Jesus of history" in his human context, as this is reconstructed by the historical disciplines, this will be in order to find a man like any other, a reforming rabbi fully within the limits attainable by our human explanations, who is sometimes mistaken, especially about the future, and whose authority over us will depend on what we ourselves can consent to grant to his teachings.

The nineteenth century chose the Jesus of history, until Albert Schweitzer showed us that Jesus "as he really was" really did take himself to be an apocalyptic figure and his age to be the one just before the New Order begins. Then the systematic tradition veered back to metaphysics, using literary criticism to demonstrate how the Gospel documents project onto Jesus the existential self-awareness of the young church — an awareness closely tied to the name of Jesus but not to his historical reality, so that if he hadn't really been who he was it wouldn't jeopardize anything of his "meaning for us."

If we confess Jesus as Messiah we must refuse this choice.

The Jesus of history is the Christ of faith. It is in hearing the revolutionary rabbi that we understand the existential freedom which is asked of the church. As we look closer at the Jesus whom Albert Schweitzer rediscovered, in all his eschatological realism, we find an utterly precise and practicable ethical instruction, practicable because in him the kingdom has actually come within reach. In him the sovereignty of YHWH has become human history.

2. The systematic tradition tells us that we are obligated to *choose between the prophet and the institution.*

The prophet condemns and crushes us under God's demand for perfection. The prophet is right, ultimately, both in convincing us of our sinfulness and in pointing us toward the ideal which, although unattainable, must remain our goal. But as far as that social order is concerned which it is up to us to administer today and tomorrow, those demands are without immediate relevance. Love, self-sacrifice, and nonviolence provide no basis for taking responsibility in this world. Dependent upon the grace of God alone, one cannot act in history. Those who are called to assure the survival and the administration of institutions will therefore accept violence in order, one day, to diminish or eliminate it. They will accept inequality and exploitation with the goal of progressively combating them. This is a very modest task and one in which one dirties oneself, but an indispensable task if something worse is to be prevented. While respecting the prophet, the rest of us will choose the institution.

The new regime instituted by Jesus as Messiah forbids us to make this choice.

The jubilee which Jesus proclaims is not the end of time, pure event without duration, unconnected to either yesterday or tomorrow. The jubilee is precisely an *institution* whose functioning within history will have a precise, practicable, limited impact. It is not a perpetual social earthquake rendering impossible any continuity of temporal effort, but a periodic revision permitting new beginnings.

3. The systematic tradition tells us that we must *conceive of the Reign of God either as external and catastrophic or as subjective, inward.*

Jesus announced the imminent certain end of history as an event which could happen tomorrow or which was, at the latest, sure to come soon after his death. The apostles maintained this intensity of expectation for a few decades, but finally it had to be admitted that there had been a mistake about the date, or perhaps about what they were looking for so soon.

The other option begins by assuming that Jesus could not have been wrong. It must then be concluded that he was speaking of the Kingdom of God and its coming only in order to teach, by means of the mythical language which was current in his time, about an inner, spiritual, existential kingdom, whose reality properly will always remain hidden to the eyes of the unbeliever and of the historian.

Once again if Jesus is the Christ we must refuse this choice.

The Kingdom of God is a social order and not a hidden one. It is not a universal catastrophe independent of the will of human beings; it is that concrete jubilary obedience, in pardon and repentance, the possibility of which is proclaimed beginning right now, opening up the real accessibility of a new order in which grace and justice are linked, which people have only to accept. It does not assume that time will end tomorrow; it reveals why it is meaningful that history should go on at all.

That the hearers would refuse this offer and promise, pushing away the kingdom that had come close to them, this Jesus had also predicted. He was not mistaken.[10]

4. The systematic tradition tells us we must *choose between the political and the sectarian.*

In the tradition of Ernst Troeltsch, Western theological ethics assumes that the choice of options is fixed in logic and for all times and places by the way the Constantinian heritage dealt with the question. Either one accepts, without serious qualification, the responsibility of politics, that is, of governing, with whatever means that takes, or one chooses a withdrawn position of either personal-monastic-vocational or sectarian character which is "apolitical."[11] If you choose

10. André Trocmé's book *(Jesus and the Nonviolent Revolution)* includes a chapter, "Was Jesus Mistaken about the Date?" which points to what might be a whole new, specifically biblical grasp of the relation of present and future in moral thought. For further comment on the non-coming of the kingdom, cf. the epilogue to this chapter, below, pp. 109ff.

11. Troeltsch has obtained a wide following in American thought through the brothers Niebuhr; it is very difficult for an American Protestant ethicist even to conceive that questions might be posed in other terms. H. Richard Niebuhr's classic *Christ and*

to share fully in the duties and the guilt of government, you are exercising responsibility and are politically relevant; if you choose not to, it is because you think politics is either unimportant or impure, and are more concerned for other matters, such as your own salvation. In so doing you would have Jesus on your side,[12] but having Jesus on your side is not enough, for there are issues to which Jesus does not speak (here this view overlaps with and appeals to the other three already sketched). We must therefore supplement and in effect correct what we learn from him, by adding information on the nature and the goodness of the specifically "political" which we gain from other sources.[13]

If Jesus is confessed as Messiah, this disjunction is illegitimate. To say that any position is "apolitical" is to deny the powerful (sometimes conservative, sometimes revolutionary) impact on society of the creation of an alternative social group. It is to overrate both the power and the manageability of those particular social structures identified as "political." To assume that "being politically relevant" is itself a univocal option so that in saying "yes" to it one knows where one is going, is to overestimate the capacity of "the nature of politics" to dictate its own direction.

Because Jesus' particular way of rejecting the sword and at the same time condemning those who wielded it *was* politically relevant,

---

Culture presupposes it, reinforces it with the trinitarian language we have already noted, and has propagated it widely. Paul Ramsey's *Basic Christian Ethics* uses this formulation of the problem to provide his outline. If we had space for a wider excursion in the byways of hermeneutic theology, we might link this dichotomy (or that of Cavil 2 above) with those others which often separate history from meaning, *Historie* from *Geschichte,* the course of world events from the concern of religion, "revelation" from "fact," or "faith" from "science."

12. The strongest statement of the concession that Jesus is really on the other side from one's own is in Reinhold Niebuhr's writings, beginning with his *Interpretation of Christian Ethics,* where this problem of the sword is the basic one. Niebuhr does not deal in this book with work, or sex, or truth-telling, or education; the problem of faithfulness and compromise in dealing with power in politics and economics, as best portrayed by what we do with the Sermon on the Mount, is for him the central ethical issue (as it was for Jesus). Paul Ramsey (*Basic Christian Ethics,* esp. pp. 35ff.: "In What Way, Then, Are the Teachings of Jesus Valid?") makes the same admission.

13. See above, pp. 8ff. and 15ff., concerning the "other sources." Cf. also my *Original Revolution,* pp. 132ff. with reference to "other lights."

both the Sanhedrin and the Procurator had to deny him the right to live, in the name of both of their forms of political responsibility. His alternative was so relevant, so much a threat, that Pilate could afford to free, in exchange for Jesus, the ordinary Guevara-type insurrectionist Barabbas. Jesus' way is not less but more relevant to the question of how society moves than is the struggle for possession of the levers of command; to this Pilate and Caiaphas testify by their judgment on him.[14]

One can sympathize with those who think that problems of substance can be swept away by semantic conventions. Some would say there is such a difference of character between what Jesus represents and what the whole world considers as politically relevant that we should grant the definition of the "political" as best represented by what Jesus rejects. Then Jesus would be after all "apolitical," taking for himself and his disciples a withdrawn stance. After thus agreeing on definitions, we could then go on to argue the moral justification, and perhaps also the political relevance on some other level, of the apolitical stance;[15] but at least we would not need to stumble over diversities of definition. But Jesus chose not only to stumble over diversities of definition but to be crucified on them. He refused to concede that those in power represent an ideal, a logically proper, or even an empirically acceptable definition of what it means to be political. He did not say (as some sectarian pacifists or some pietists might), "you can have your politics and I shall do something else more important"; he said, "your definition of *polis,* of the social, of the wholeness of being human socially is perverted."

14. "This denial that the human exercise of violent power is necessary to existence was not a withdrawal from political concerns. . . . Yahweh's leadership in history had to do with political order, both for the community's external and internal relationships." Millard Lind, "The Concept of Political Power," *ASTI,* VII, 4ff.

15. Reinhold Niebuhr himself devoted half a chapter of his *Interpretation of Christian Ethics* to affirming the "relevance of an impossible ideal." There is the relevance of the ideal's indiscriminate criticism, which by condemning all human achievements as insufficient takes us off the scale of ethical options and drives us to repentance; there is also the discriminate criticism whereby the ideal, impossible in itself, still helps to determine which of the real options is preferable. There is the prophetic relevance of the minority whose vocation it is to represent that double critique by withdrawing from the political realm. Yet all of this relevance can only be had at the cost of admitting first that Jesus' way is not *really* for here and now.

5. The tradition tells us that we must *choose between the individual and the social.*

The "ethics of the Sermon on the Mount" is for face-to-face personal encounters; for social structures an ethic of the "secular vocation" is needed. Faith will restore the individual's soul, and Jesus' strong language about love for neighbor will help with this; but then how a restored person should act will be decided on grounds to which the radical personalism of Jesus does not speak.

But Jesus doesn't know anything about radical personalism. The personhood which he proclaims as a healing, forgiving call to all is integrated into the social novelty of the healing community.[16] This is clear from the Lucan text we have read; it would be even more clear if we could read the Jesus story with a stronger sense of the Jewishness of his context and with Amos ringing in our ears. The more we learn about the Jewishness of Jesus (from archeology and the new textual finds, as well as from growing respect for rabbinical studies on the part of Christian theologians), the more evident it becomes that he could not have been perceived by his contemporaries otherwise than as we here have portrayed him. In fact, to be fully honest we must turn the point around: the idea of Jesus as an individualist or a teacher of radical personalism could arise only in the (Protestant, post-Pietist, rationalist) context that it did; that is, in a context which, if not intentionally

16. A few steps in the direction of our concern are made by George S. Hendry in his *The Gospel of the Incarnation* (Philadelphia: Westminster, 1958). Hendry seeks to move beyond the older polarizations of Christology around Bethlehem, the cross, Easter, and Pentecost, finding the center of them all and the rootage of a renewed two-natures doctrine in a vision of the Christ of Galilee. If our contemporaries now perceive reality as personhood-in-relation, then it is in that form that we must cast our vision of the divine originality of Jesus. Jesus is the other-centered man *par excellence,* servant of human beings and of God. The kernel of this double other-centeredness is Jesus' action in forgiving humans, not so much in providing the metaphysical prerequisites for forgiveness as in telling specific people, now, personally, convincingly, that they are freed.

Fully in key with this approach, I need only suggest that if Hendry's question: "If we survey the human life of Christ as a whole, what is the chief characteristic it exhibits?" had been asked with a fuller cultural realism, then the resulting view of Jesus could not have been limited to his one-to-one forgiving relationships, but would have had to englobe as well the social-institutional community-creating aspect of Jesus' ministry. The forgiveness of sins is not, for Jesus, a mere assuaging of personal guiltiness or of interpersonal estrangement; it is the sign of the new age and the presupposition of a new possibility of community.

anti-Semitic, was at least sweepingly a-Semitic, stranger to the Jewish Jesus.

We could extend the list of traditional antinomies of which we must repent if we are to understand. Tradition tells us to choose between respect for persons and participation in the movement of history; Jesus refuses because the movement of history is personal. Between the absolute *agape* which lets itself be crucified and effectiveness (which it is assumed will usually need to be violent), the resurrection forbids us to choose, for in the light of resurrection crucified agape is not folly (as it seems to the Hellenizers to be) and weakness (as the Judaizers believe) but the wisdom and power of God (1 Cor. 1:22-25).

EPILOGUE

As I noted above under the heading (3) "catastrophic or inner kingdom?", the modern notion that the early Christians must have been profoundly shaken by the non-arrival of the Messiah is open to challenge. A. Strobel[17] makes a careful study of this "problem" from the standpoint of Jewish understanding of Habakkuk 2. The not-having-come and the having-come of the Rule of God were both present in the faith of each biblical epoch. The concept of a purely future coming, so firmly dated that at a certain time its failure to arrive becomes a clear disappointment, is foreign to the biblical mind. Thus the concept that the specific character of Jesus' ethic was conditioned upon the imminence for him of a purely future end of human history is likewise unthinkable. This study confirms that the problem of the delay of the parousia is one that scholars have imported into the New Testament. It is certainly one that did not trouble the early church to any degree, to say nothing of providing motive for theological redefinition in the next century, as especially the school of Martin Werner[18] would claim.

17. *Untersuchungen zum eschatologischen Verzögerungsproblem* (Leiden: Brill, 1961).
18. *The Formation of Christian Dogma* (New York: Harper, 1957). Similar argument

Graydon F. Snyder pursued the same theme further in his "Sayings on the Delay of the End,"[19] "This concept of the adjustment to the kingdom's nonarrival is inept also in its unspoken assumption about the development of New Testament literature. Reading through the New Testament in narrative sequence, we find first the human-social Jesus, who calls men to follow him about in a real community in a real Palestine; then we move on to Paul's cosmic Christ, whose risen glory transfigures the cross and dispenses with the earthly career. It is then thinkable that in this movement there was a necessary dehistoricizing, de-Judaizing process, indispensable if the church was to spread beyond Palestine into the Hellenistic world. But this is to forget that Paul wrote before, not after, the Gospel writers. *First* there was the bare resurrection message; *then* there was the lordship proclamation; *then* it was filled out with the body of memories of the words and works of Jesus of Nazareth. The movement in the formation of the New Testament literature was toward, not away from, filling out the picture of Jesus' humanity.[20] This consideration applies to the point at issue in our present study. The sources that make most clear the social-apocalyptic realism of Jesus' claims are those whose authors or editors had had the most time to know that the end of history had not yet come. Fittingly, Titus lifts up the Servanthood episode of John 13 as expressive of the concretization of glorification-Christology with human history.

Of the respected senior scholars in the New Testament field, it is perhaps Amos Wilder who comes closest to holding the door open for the concern of this study. His *Eschatology and Ethics in the Teaching of Jesus*[21] competently dissects the Schweitzerian argument that the radicality of Jesus' call can be understood only if one posits a very brief

---

is made by Ethelbert Stauffer, *Jesus and His Story*, p. 59, and in greater exegetical depth by Hans Werner Bartsch, "Zum Problem der Parusierverzögerung bei den Synoptikern," *EvT*, 19 (1959), 116ff. ". . . The problem of the delay of the parousia is a problem only in so far as the early community misunderstood and literalized the apocalyptic form." Graydon F. Snyder, "The Literalization of the Apocalyptic Form in the New Testament Church," *BR*, 14 (1969), 7.

19. *BR*, 20 (1975), 19-35.

20. This point is made helpfully by Eric Lane Titus, "The Fourth Gospel and the Historical Jesus," in F. T. Trotter (ed.), *Jesus and the Historian* (Philadelphia: Westminster, 1968), pp. 98ff.

21. New York: Harper, 2nd ed. 1950.

"interim" before the parousia. Yet Wilder does not finish his sketch of a coherent alternative. He retains a conceptual division in Jesus' teachings between those of general validity and others characterized as "extraordinary," "drastic," "desperate," or "hasty" — that is, as limited to a *kairos* or a crisis of the "exigencies of his work." Sometimes this distinction seems to suggest after all the legitimacy of a lower-voltage discipleship for run-of-the-mill believers in noneschatological times or places. If this line of thought were carried through we would have once again what Schweitzer meant by his "interim ethic" concept, namely the priority in our noneschatological context of a nonheroic and nonchristological standard for "normal" Christian ethics.[22]

The theme of the end's not having come, noted here as background to the teachings of Jesus in the Gospels, has grown in significance for some modern readers, in the light of the increasing scholarly attention being given to apocalypse as a literary genre and as a worldview. To this we shall return in chapter 12 below.

22. John Knox deals with the "interim" theme under the fitting label "Ways of Escape," in his *The Ethics of Jesus in the Teaching of the Church* (Nashville: Abingdon, 1961), esp. pp. 45ff.

CHAPTER 7

The Disciple of Christ and the Way of Jesus

The question with which our study began was whether Jesus' teaching or example can have been of such character as to provide the substance of guidance in social ethics. We concluded, according to the Gospel accounts and counter to the prior assumptions of many modern interpreters, that his deeds show a coherent, conscious social-political character and direction, and that his words are inseparable therefrom.

But that is not yet the whole story. The traditional axioms can be rephrased so as to place between Jesus and the early church the gap that previously was posited between Jesus and social ethics. Jesus, the reformulated argument may now run, may after all have conceived his ministry as a socially relevant messianity; and the Gospels are accurate enough not fully to have hidden this fact. But still, it is possible to argue, early Christianity turned out to be a far cry from the kingdom he had announced. There must be a hiatus somewhere between the human Jesus' proclaimed kingdom at Jerusalem and the worship of the heavenly Christ in the Gentile churches of Greece and Asia Minor.

The second phase of our study turns therefore to several strands of the apostolic ethical tradition. The thesis we have just posited shall find its response not in detailed debate on its own terms (it is no longer being argued thus simply by New Testament scholars)[1] but by independent induction from the texts. Looking one by one at several distinct

1. It was stated and challenged most clearly by E. C. Hoskyns, *The Riddle of the New Testament* (London: Faber, 1947).

themes of apostolic ethics, each for itself, we shall ask how each related to the Jesus to whom we have seen the Gospels testifying.

One very pervasive such theme, perhaps the most widespread, is the one we here may call participation or "correspondence," in which the believer's behavior or attitude is said to "correspond to" or reflect or "partake of" the same quality or nature as that of the lord. A more careful analysis than we can here undertake[2] would discern great varieties of shading and substance within this one theme, yet without any substantive contradiction.

In addition to numerous expressions where the concept of correspondence/participation appears with no fixed technical label, there are two distinguishable sets of firm images or verbal traditions visible in the traditions. One which we might call "discipleship" centers upon the noun "disciple" and the verb "follow after" or "learn." The image is spatial: the Israelites "following after" the pillar of cloud; a prophet or a rabbi or Jesus being followed around Palestine by his pupils.[3]

The other tradition might be called "imitation." Its imagery is more structural or perhaps mystical; it affirms an inner or formal parallelism of character or intent beneath the similar behavior. Such a concept is found in many religions; it is present in the Old Testament despite its warnings against conceiving of God as comparable to his creatures. The idea, not specifically Christian, that the human being somehow corresponds to or reflects the nature of God, or should seek to do so, was quite current in the Old Testament.[4] However we under-

2. The most thorough studies of the theme are Hans Dieter Betz, *Nachfolge und Nachahmung Jesu Christi im Neuen Testament* (Tübingen: Mohr, 1967), and Anselm Schulz, *Nachfolgen und Nachahmen* (Munich: Loesel, 1967). Both Schulz and Betz survey and digest a very wide field of detailed studies. An earlier exposition of the core concepts was Eduard Schweizer, *Lordship and Discipleship,* SBT, 28 (1960). A more systematic statement is that of E. J. Tinsley, *The Imitation of God in Christ* (Philadelphia: Westminster, 1960).

3. Despite the identity of language, when Dietrich Bonhoeffer uses the term "discipleship" it carries a different shade of meaning. The accent falls less on sharing the Master's way or nature, and more on the unquestioning willingness to obey.

4. Walther Eichrodt in his *Theology of the Old Testament* (Philadelphia: Westminster, 1967), II, 373, characterizes as the basic theme of the holiness code, "The forming of human nature after the pattern of the divine." Edmond Jacob in his *Theology of the Old Testament* (New York: Harper, 1958) designates the imitation of God as "the principle of the moral and spiritual life" (pp. 173ff.). We cannot deal here with the numerous analogous concepts in nonbiblical faiths, or how they differ.

stand the statement that humanity was created "after the image of God," in any case it says at least this much: that in that which they are and that which they should do or become, human beings correspond somehow to God's own being. This status of "image of God" is not questioned. The Old Testament neither preaches nor teaches it, but simply presupposes it universally.[5] The founding of the sabbath law in the reminder of God's resting after creation (Exod. 20) or through reference to how "humane" God was to free Israel from slavery (Deut. 5) is meaningful only if we presuppose some sort of correspondence between God and the creature. "Be holy, for I am holy" (Lev. 19:2) might initially have pointed more to a ritual than to a moral sanctity; nevertheless there begins with this text a tradition of "following God" which stretches through the prophets and through Judaism all the way to Martin Buber.[6] What in the Hebrew Scriptures is a universally presupposed fundamental concept becomes in the New Testament a new reality with the gift of the Holy Spirit. The two metaphors of "discipleship" and "imitation" overlap sufficiently in substance that we properly treat them here together.[7]

5. Johann Jakob Stamm, *Die Gottebenbildlichkeit des Menschen im Alten Testament,* ThSt 54 (1959).

6. Martin Buber, "Nachahmung Gottes," in *Der Morgen,* I (1925), 368ff.; cf. S. Schechter, *Aspects of Rabbinic Theology* (London, 1909; New York: Schocken, 1961), ch. 14, pp. 199ff. David S. Shapiro, "The Doctrine of the Image of God and *Imitatio Dei,*" in Menachem Marc Kellner (ed.), *Contemporary Jewish Ethics* (New York: Sanhedrin Press, 1978), pp. 127ff.; cf. also Deut. 13:4: "The Lord your God you shall follow. . . ."

7. Both Betz and Schulz, after having carefully disentangled the same two strands of thought and analyzed each independently, come to the conclusion that the substantial meaning of the two is parallel. Edvin Larsson, *Christus als Vorbild,* pursues this theme by way of a very thorough study of the Pauline texts dealing with baptism and with the word *eikon* (image). He is driven to challenge the neat distinction between "following" and "imitation" which had long held sway in Lutheran theology.

I. The Disciple/Participant and the Love of God

A. Sharing the divine nature as the definition of Christian existence

God is light, and in him there is no darkness at all. . . . If we walk in the light as he himself is in the light, then we share together a common life. . . . (1 John 1:5-7)

We were called God's children, and such we are. . . . What we shall be has not been disclosed, but we know that when it is disclosed we shall be like him, because we shall see him as he is. Everyone who has this hope before him purifies himself as he[8] is pure. (1 John 3:1-3)

As the One who called you is holy, be holy in all your behavior, because Scripture says, "You shall be holy, for I am holy." (1 Pet. 1:15-16, citing Lev. 19:2)

Even in this world we are as he is. (1 John 4:17)

You have discarded the old nature with its deeds and have put on the new nature, which is being constantly renewed in the image of its Creator. . . . (Col. 3:9; cf. Eph. 4:24)[9]

B. Forgive as God has forgiven you

Be generous to one another, tender-hearted, forgiving one another as God in Christ forgave you. (Eph. 4:32)

Be forbearing with one another, and forgiving, where any of you has cause for complaint: you must forgive as the Lord forgave you. (Col. 3:13, NEB)[10]

8. The context (cf. 2:23-24) would suggest that "he" here points not only to the Father but also to the Son. NEB translates: ". . . as Christ is pure."

9. The concept of transformation *(metamorphosis)* is one of the shadings of meaning which could be pursued further: 2 Cor. 3:18; Rom. 12:2; 8:24; Phil. 3:21; 1 Cor. 15:49. Still other expressions of the same concept are "image" (2 Cor. 4:14; Col. 1:15) and "firstborn" (Col. 1:15, 18).

10. The reference here to "the Lord" would in predominant Pauline usage refer

> Forgive us the wrong we have done, as we have forgiven those who wronged us. (Matt. 6:12; cf. Luke 11:4)

> For if you forgive others . . . your heavenly Father will also forgive you; but if you do not forgive others, then the wrongs you have done will not be forgiven by your Father. (Matt. 6:14-15)

> I remitted the whole of your debt when you appealed to me; were you not bound to show your fellow servant the same pity as I showed to you? (Matt. 18:32-33)

C. Love indiscriminately as God does

> If you love only those who love you, what credit is that to you. . . ? But you must love your enemies, and do good and lend without expecting return; . . . you will be children of the Most High, for he himself is kind to the ungrateful and wicked. Be compassionate as your Father is compassionate. (Luke 6:32-36)

> Love your enemies and pray for your persecutors; only so can you be children of your heavenly Father, who makes the sun rise on good and bad alike, and sends the rain on the honest and dishonest. . . . You must therefore be all goodness, just as your heavenly Father is all good. (Matt. 5:43-48, NEB)[11]

The AV rendering of verse 48: "be perfect as your Father is perfect," has for years been made the key to the whole Sermon on the Mount. Perfectionist preachers saw there the promise of an accessible sinlessness; mainstream ethicists turned it around as the proof that the Sermon's intent is not at all to be obeyed but to prepare people for grace by crushing them under the demand of an unattainable Godlikeness.[12]

---

specifically to Jesus as the one who had forgiven. Thus to be as precise as possible this usage could have been entered as well below under II.

11. We need not enter the scholarly debate about which of these roughly parallel texts more faithfully reflects the original words of Jesus. Both state the same imperative and both root it in the Father/child resemblance.

12. Cf. my fuller analysis of "The Political Axioms of the Sermon on the Mount," in *The Original Revolution,* pp. 34ff.

Both extremes are wrong in that they import a modern concept of "perfection" where it has no place. "All goodness" (NEB) does not make the point quite clear either. The parallel in Matthew 5:45 and in Luke makes it clear that "perfect" here means "indiscriminate" or "unconditional" — a quite conceivable, even attainable imperative. Modern (or Hellenistic or medieval) concepts of "perfection" as meaning that which transcends limitations, as being flawless or living up perfectly to every demand of the law, or having a nature devoid of temptation or self-concern, are brought into this text by those who want to use it to prove a point of their own. All such side meanings distract from the simplicity of the gospel demand, which is no more (and no less) than that because God does not discriminate, his disciples are called upon likewise not to discriminate in choosing the objects of their love.

> Everyone who loves is a child of God and knows God. . . . The love I speak of is not our love for God, but the love he showed to us in sending his Son[13] as the remedy for the defilement of our sins. If God *thus* loved us . . . we in turn are bound to love one another. . . . God himself dwells in us if we love one another; his love is brought to *perfection* within us. (1 John 4:7-12, NEB; emphasis mine)

II. The Disciple/Participant and the Life of Christ

A. Being in Christ as the definition of Christian existence

> Here is the test by which we can make sure that we are in him: whoever claims to be dwelling in him, binds himself to live as Christ himself lived. (1 John 2:6)

B. Having died with Christ and sharing his risen life

> The person we once were has been crucified with Christ, for the destruction of the sinful self. . . . We shall also come to life with him. . . . In dying as he died, he died to sin . . . and in living as he lives, he lives to God. In the same way you must regard yourselves

13. Cf. II/C below.

as dead to sin and alive to God, in union with Christ Jesus. (Rom. 6:6-11, NEB)

If the Spirit of him who raised Jesus from the dead dwells within you, then the God who raised Jesus Christ from the dead will also give new life to your mortal bodies. . . . (Rom. 8:11)

I have been crucified with Christ: the life I now live is not my life, but the life which Christ lives in me. . . . (Gal. 2:20; cf. 5:24)

But that is not how you learned Christ.[14] For were you not told . . . that, leaving your former way of life, you must lay aside that old human nature which . . . is sinking toward death. You must be made new in mind and spirit, and put on the new humanity of God's creating. (Eph. 4:20-24)

In your baptism you were buried with him, in baptizing also you were raised to life with him through your faith in the active power of God. . . . Did you not die with Christ and pass beyond the reach of the elemental spirits of the world. . . ? Were you not raised to life with Christ? Then aspire to the realm above. . . . (Col. 2:12–3:1)

C. Loving as Christ loved, giving himself

I give you a new commandment: love one another. As I have loved you, so you are to love one another. (John 13:34)

This is my commandment: love one another as I have loved you. There is no greater love than this, to lay down one's life for one's friends. (John 15:12)

The message you have heard from the beginning is this: that we should love one another; unlike Cain, who was a child of the evil one and murdered his brother. . . . It is by that that we know what love is: that Christ laid down his life for us. And we ought to lay down our lives for one another. (1 John 3:11-16; cf. 4:7-10, cited above)

14. We note that the concept of "learning" is still present in the writings of Paul. This indicates that the "discipleship" terminology, i.e., the language of learning and following, still is vestigially present, continuing to overlap the imagery of transformation.

It is often mistakenly held that the key concept of Jesus' ethic is the "Golden Rule": "do to others as you would have them do to you." This is stated by Jesus, however, not as the sum of his own teaching but as the center of the law (Mark 12:28-29; Matt. 22:40, citing Lev. 19:15).[15] But Jesus' own "fulfillment" of this thrust of the law, which thereby becomes through his own work a "new commandment" (John 13:34, cited above; 15:12; cf. 1 John 2:18), is different, "Do as I have done to you" or "do as the Father did in sending his Son."[16] It is striking how great is the mass of writings on religious ethics seeking to deal specifically with whether the teaching of Jesus is any different from that of the rabbis (or of Confucius), which still fails to note this very evident structural change.

D. Serving others as he served

> If I, your Lord and Master, have washed your feet, you also ought to wash one another's feet. . . . Servant are not greater than their master, nor are messengers greater than the one who sent them. (John 13:1-17)

> Those of us who have a robust conscience must accept as our own burden the tender scruples of the weak: and not please ourselves. Let each of us please our neighbor . . . for Christ did not please himself. . . . Welcome one another, as Christ has welcomed you. (Rom. 15:1-7)

> His purpose in dying for all was that those who live should cease to live for themselves and should live for him who for their sake died and was raised to life. (2 Cor. 5:14ff.)

> Surely you should show yourselves equally lavish in this generous service. . . . For you know how generous our Lord Jesus Christ has been: he was rich, yet for our sake he became poor, that through his poverty you might become rich. (2 Cor. 8:7-9)[17]

15. That "love thy neighbor as thyself" is the heart of *the law* is said as well in Matt. 19:19; Luke 10:27; Rom. 13:9; Gal. 5:14; and James 2:8.

16. T. W. Manson, *Ethics and Gospel* (London: SCM, 1960), pp. 60ff.

17. This is but one of the places where Phil. 2:1-11 might be cited. That Christ "became poor" is not unrelated to the actual economic practice of Jesus among his disciples; yet that "he was rich" indicates a wider, even a cosmic reference, in the condescension of the Lord, parallel to the "form of God" or the "equality with God" of Phil. 2:6.

> Husbands, love your wives, as Christ also loved the church and gave himself up for it. . . . In the same way men also are bound to love their own wives. (Eph. 5:25-28)

E. Subordination

This last citation, carrying Christ's model of servanthood into the concreteness of family life, links us to another body of apostolic thought which is dealt with at greater length in a separate chapter (cf. below, pp. 162ff.). All the substance of that chapter could well have been digested here as well.

III. The Disciple/Participant and the Death of Christ

A. Suffering with Christ as the definition of apostolic existence[18]

> All I care for is to know Christ, to experience the power of his resurrection, and to share his sufferings, in growing conformity with his death, if only I may arrive at the resurrection from the dead. (Phil. 3:10-11)

> Wherever we go we carry death with us in our body, the death that Jesus died, that in this body also life may reveal itself, the life that Jesus lives . . . for continually . . . we are being surrendered into the hands of death, for Jesus' sake, so that the life of Christ may also be revealed in this mortal body of ours. (2 Cor. 4:10)[19]

18. Cf. Erhardt Güttgemanns, *Der Leidende Apostel und sein Herr* (Göttingen: Vandenhoeck & Ruprecht, 1966). A constant theme of Güttgemanns's work is what he calls "christological distance," i.e., the objectivity of the reference to the earthly Jesus, as over against tendencies (both in the early church and in modern scholarship) to redefine Christ in some more "contemporary" meaning, less dependent on just who the crucified Jesus was.

19. Paul almost always uses "Christ" as a proper name; the usage here of the name Jesus standing alone is a significant pointer. Either Paul is echoing a distinct usage prior to his own adoption of the tradition, or his own free use of the name Jesus must be understood as placing special emphasis on the historical career of the Man of Nazareth, as contrasted to the more general functional title "Christ."

> As we share abundantly in Christ's sufferings, so through Christ we share abundantly in comfort too. (2 Cor. 1:5)

> It is my happiness to suffer for you. This is my way of helping to complete in my poor human flesh the full tale of Christ's afflictions,[20] still to be endured. (Col. 1:24)[21]

Only the artifice of our classification separates the apostle's self-interpretation from what he considers binding on other Christians. He is merely an exemplary follower of the true example.[22]

> For my part, I always try to meet everyone halfway, regarding not[23] my own good but the good of many. . . . Follow my example, as I follow Christ's. (1 Cor. 10:33-34)

> You, in your turn, followed the example set by us and by the Lord; the welcome you gave the message meant grave suffering for you, yet you rejoiced in the Holy Spirit. (1 Thess. 1:6)

B. Sharing in divine condescension

> Rivalry and personal vanity should have no place among you, but you should humbly reckon others better than yourselves. . . . Let your bearing toward one another rise out of your life in Christ. For

20. It should be noted that Paul does not distinguish between the sufferings of Christ and those of the apostles; it is the suffering of Christ, namely in his body the church, that the apostle bears.

21. Literally: "what is lacking in the sufferings of Christ."

22. Cf. again Güttgemanns, *Der Leidende Apostel.* One of the omissions of this outline is the thought of Jesus about his own suffering; we have picked up from the Gospel accounts only a few of Jesus' words about the disciples' cross. In view, however, of the intimate linkage which Paul here affirms, careful analysis should also move farther back. Eduard Lohse, *Maertyrer und Gottesknecht* (Göttingen: Vandenhoeck & Ruprecht, 2nd ed. 1963), and Nils Dahl, *Volk Gottes,* p. 251, suggest that the fusion of the images of the Suffering Servant as community and as messianic figure would not have been possible in the standard Jewish exegesis of Isa. 53, and must have been Jesus' own creative reinterpretation. Paul also speaks of himself as example in 1 Cor. 4:16; Phil. 3:17; 2 Thess. 3:7ff.; and Heb. 6:12 speaks as well of other human models. Victor Paul Furnish, *Theology and Ethics in Paul* (Nashville: Abingdon, 1968), pp. 218ff., discusses especially those passages where the imitation of the apostle illuminates the imitation of Christ.

23. The "regarding" is parallel to the "considering" which was underlined in II/D.

the divine nature was his from the first; yet he . . . made himself nothing, assuming the nature of a slave. . . . (Phil. 2:3-14)

This passage, by widespread scholarly consensus,[24] is built around a pre-Pauline hymn of praise to the condescension of the divine Son. The initial humiliation praised in the hymn was not that of the cross but of abandoning the prerogatives of "the divine nature."[25] Yet in Paul's application the image takes on new dimensions.[26] The reference to humiliation becomes not simply "human form" but "the form of a servant," and this even to the extremity of death on a cross.[27] By its insertion in the larger context of the exhortation addressed to the Philippians, this already doubled meaning of humiliation/exaltation takes on yet a third level of meaning: the self-denial which fosters the unity of the church.

Donald G. Dawe[28] interprets the Philippians hymn at some length, but his understanding of the "kenotic motif" is focused upon the metaphysics of incarnation and how this can be updated. Dawe ignores the possibility that Jesus' renouncing the seizure of Sonship might also have meant concretely his decision in the desert, as well as the possibility that the call to unity of Philippians 2:1-4 might throw light back upon the motive of the example being appealed to.

24. Archibald M. Hunter, *Paul and His Predecessors* (Philadelphia: Westminster, 1962), p. 36; R. P. Martin, *Carmen Christi* (Cambridge University Press, 1967).

25. The thought of "seizing equality with God" may be in contrast to the example of Lucifer or of Adam. In the very earliest stages of christological thinking the concept of "grasping equality with God" might not have presupposed the preexistence of the Son; cf. above, II/D, n. 14, and the temptation narrative above, pp. 24f. It may originally have referred to his renunciation of Zealot kingship.

26. Betz, *Nachfolge und Nachahmung*, says that the imitation imagery is "ethicized" in Paul's application of it to the problem at Philippi. Protestant interpretation has generally sought to ward off the idea that "having the mind of Christ" would be in any way a reflection of the human posture of Jesus. Protestant interpreters have generally preferred more complicated concepts like "having the kind of attitude which befits one who is in Christ," so as to undermine any possibility of moralism. As Schulz points out, however, the simpler conception of imitation is dictated by the context.

27. The Phillips translation is not literal, but renders well the sense of offense or scandal that belongs here, with the paraphrase, "the death of a common criminal." It is widely supposed, following Lohmeyer, that this phrase "even the death on the cross" was an insertion by Paul in the extant hymn text. The reader acquainted with the original hymn would have been more struck by the insertion than we are.

28. *The Form of a Servant* (Philadelphia: Westminster, 1968).

C. Give your life as he did

> As God's dear children, try to be like him, and live in love as Christ loved you, and gave himself up on your behalf. . . . (Eph. 5:1-2; cf. 1 John 3:16, cited above, II/C)

D. Suffering servanthood in place of dominion[29]

> In the world the recognized rulers lord it over their subjects, and their great men make them feel the weight of authority. That is not the way with you; among you, whoever wants to be great must be your servant. . . . For even the Son of Man did not come to be served but to serve, and to surrender his life as a ransom for many. (Mark 10:42-45; Matt. 20:25-28)

In the accounts of Matthew and Mark this word was provoked when, just after Jesus' most detailed prediction of his coming passion, two of his disciples (or their mother) expressed their desire for a place of privilege in his kingdom. Luke records an almost identical statement in the midst of the Last Supper conversations, thus making it in effect a parallel to John 13:1-13 (cited above, II/C). The content differs in two details in Luke's report. Luke adds (22:25), "those in authority are called 'benefactors'" — a recognition, perhaps ironic, of government's claim to moral accreditation. The imperative is founded not in the Son of Man's imminent sacrifice of his life (as in Mark and Matthew) but in Jesus' present posture: "Here I am among you as a servant" (22:27).[30]

Only at two points, here and in III/F, do we include materials from the Synoptic Gospels as testimony to the mind of the apostolic

29. This section is very similar to IID. It differs in that: (a) the specific alternative to servanthood, namely lordship, is looked at and rejected; and (b) the servanthood goes all the way to death.

30. Although the several Gospel accounts vary in the way they place this text, all of them relate it to the mandate Jesus is giving to his church. Most commentators fail to note the anti-Zealot and anti-Roman thrust of the text. Jesus is not simply telling his disciples to be servants. He is pointedly contrasting this command with any way of being "lord" which his listeners are assumed to have in mind. The contrast is meaningful only if the desire for lordship is assumed to be real, as it was in the request of James and John to which he is responding.

church. Both words are somewhat independent of any particular point in the Gospel narrative and are spoken to the continuing career of the church beyond Pentecost. It is thus not improper to draw them into our summary on the thought of the church.

E. Accept innocent suffering without complaint as he did

> When you have behaved well and suffer for it, your fortitude is a fine thing in the sight of God. To that you were called, because Christ suffered on your behalf, and thereby left you an example. It is for you to follow in his steps. (1 Pet. 2:20-21, NEB)

> It is better to suffer in well-doing . . . than for doing wrong. For Christ also died for our sins. . . . He, the just, suffered for the unjust. . . . (3:14-18)

> Do not be bewildered by the fiery ordeal that is upon you. . . . It gives you a share in Christ's sufferings, and that is cause for joy. (4:12-16)

F. Suffer with or like Christ the hostility of the world, as bearers of the kingdom cause.

> No one who does not carry his cross and come with me can be a disciple of mine. (Luke 14:27-33)

Luke's statement of the call to the cross is preceded by the call to forsake family loyalties and is followed by the warning against making a commitment to Jesus' cause without counting the cost. In Matthew (10:37ff.) the setting is the sending of the twelve. In Mark (8:34ff.; also 10:39-40) it follows Peter's confession "You are the Messiah" and the first prediction of the passion. Each setting makes it a foundational statement. Each is in a wider context emphasizing the social suffering of rejection by one's family. It points not to a special elite moral vocation for Jesus or for a spiritual elite, but to a condition for salvation. This is one of the places where the "Disciple/follow" and the "Imitate/partake" language complexes overlap. To follow after Christ is not simply to learn from him, but also to share his destiny.

> Slaves are not greater than their master. As they persecuted me, they will persecute you. (John 15:20-21)
>
> Persecution will come to all who want to live a godly life as Christians. (2 Tim. 3:12)
>
> You have been granted the privilege not only of believing in Christ but of suffering for him. (Phil. 1:29)
>
> You share in Christ's sufferings, and that is cause for joy. (1 Pet. 4:13)

Christian thought is accustomed to conceiving of "persecution" as a ritual or "religious" matter independent of any immediate ethical import. Christians are made to suffer because they worship the true God; what has this to do with our study's concern with an attitude to government, to violence, war, conflict? Is not being persecuted for the faith quite independent of social ethics?

Such a dichotomy between the religious and the social must be imported into the texts; it cannot be found there. The "cross" of Jesus was a political punishment; and when Christians are made to suffer by government it is usually because of the practical import of their faith, and the doubt they cast upon the rulers' claim to be "Benefactor."

We cannot quote in full the text of Hebrews 11:1–12:5, which forms a coherent series of examples or "witnesses" of fidelity, from Abel through to the prophets. "Faith" or "fidelity" in each case meant the readiness to obey amid suffering, trusting God for a not yet discernible vindication.[31] The culmination of this series ("Pioneer and Perfecter," or "Author and Finisher") is Jesus, "who for the sake of the joy that lay ahead of him endured the cross" and whose disciples should be ready to resist to the point of shedding their blood (12:2-4).

31. When the author defines "faith" as assurance of the hoped-for and conviction of the unseen, the "hoped-for" and "unseen" realities are not some otherwise unknown truth, proposition, or prediction but the concrete vindication of obedience. "Faith" is obeying when it is not "visible" that it "pays" or "works."

G. Death is liberation from the power of sin

Since therefore Christ suffered in the flesh, arm yourself with the same thought, for whoever has suffered in the flesh has ceased from sin. . . . (1 Pet. 4:1-2; cf. II/B above)

Those who belong to Christ Jesus have crucified the flesh with its passions and desires. (Gal. 5:24)

H. Death is the fate of the prophets; Jesus, whom we follow, was already following them

"Concerning Jesus of Nazareth, who was a prophet mighty in deed and word before God and all the people, and how our chief priests and rulers delivered him up to be condemned to death, and crucified him." (Luke 24:19-20; cf. Mark 12:5-8)

"Let all the house of Israel therefore know assuredly that God has made him both Lord and Christ, this Jesus whom you crucified." (Acts 2:36; cf. Acts 4:10; 7:52)

. . . who killed both the Lord Jesus and the prophets, and drove us out, they displease God and oppose everyone by hindering us. (1 Thess. 2:15)

I. Death is victory

On the cross he discarded the cosmic power and authorities like a garment; he made a public spectacle of them and led them in his triumphal procession. (Col. 2:15)[32]

Jews call for miracles, Greeks look for wisdom; but we proclaim Christ — yes, Christ nailed to the cross; and though this is a stumbling block to Jews and folly to Greeks, yet to those who have heard this call, Jews and Greeks alike, he is the power of God and the wisdom of God. (1 Cor. 1:22-24)

32. The imagery of the triumphant procession may be interpreted as placing Christians either in the position of captives (God's former enemies) or of soldiers. If like Eph. 4:8 this is an echo of Ps. 68, the former would be more likely.

> This is the hour of victory for our God, the hour of his sovereignty and power, when his Christ comes to his rightful rule. . . . By the sacrifice of the Lamb they have conquered him . . . for they did not hold their lives too dear to lay them down. (Rev. 12:10-11; cf. 5:9ff.)
>
> They [ten kings] will wage war upon the Lamb, but the Lamb will defeat them . . . and his victory will be shared by his followers. . . . (17:14)

Summing Up

What can be said of the total impact of this great bulk of textual evidence? Our pigeonholes are not neat. The subcategories used here do not separate really distinct thoughts; they rather spread out before us a rich variety of shadings and emphases within one pervasive thought pattern. In some expressions the reference to the earthly ministry, especially the death of Jesus, is definite; in others the "descending and ascending" Christ is portrayed in less concrete, more Hellenistic images. In some the element of suffering is not spoken of, in some it is focused upon the cost of ministering to one's brethren, but more often it centers upon the renunciation of lordship, the abandonment of earthly security, the threat which the Suffering Servant poses to the powers of this world, and the antagonism of the world's response. Thus the epistles repeat the Gospel narratives' center points of Mark 8:34 ("let him take up his cross and follow me") and 10:42 ("but let it not be so among you").

As long as readers could stay unaware of the political/social dimension of Jesus' ministry (which most of Christendom seems to have done quite successfully), then it was also possible to perceive the "in Christ" language of the epistles as mystical or the "dying with Christ" as psychologically morbid. But if we may posit — as after the preceding pages we must — that the apostles had and taught at least a core memory of their Lord's earthly ministry in its blunt historicity, then this centering of the apostolic ethic upon the disciple's cross evidences a substantial, binding, and sometimes costly social stance. There have perhaps been times when the issues of power, violence, and peoplehood were not at the center of ethical preoccupations; but in the waning twentieth century they certainly are. The rediscovery of this ethic of "responsibility" or of "power" can no longer at the same time claim to be Christian and bypass the judgment or the promise of the Suffering Servant's exemplarity.

Yet this affirmation encloses some serious negatives. Seldom has the exemplary quality of Jesus' social humanity been perceived as a model for our social ethics;[33] yet the large body of New Testament traditions represented by the texts we have analyzed has not gone unnoticed. It has been perceived, but interpreted differently. To these other interpretations we must now turn.[34]

33. Carl F. H. Henry, in a chapter "Jesus as the Ideal of Christian Ethics," in *Christian Personal Ethics* (Grand Rapids: Eerdmans, 1957), pp. 398ff., gathers a wealth of material to reaffirm an orthodox loyalty to the exemplarity of Jesus. Yet the description of Jesus is strikingly selective. It centers upon motivational virtues (unselfishness, compassion, resisting temptation, meekness, obedience) rather than on ethical specifics. There is no reference to the specific temptation of the Zealot option, and it is expressly denied that Jesus' poverty or celibacy might have any exemplary value (p. 411). Henry's later *Aspects of Christian Social Ethics* (Eerdmans, 1964) makes no use of this theme. Henry thus represents faithfully the tradition that has been able to appropriate much of the New Testament idiom without catching its central historical thrust.

34. In his article "Von der Imitatio Dei zur Nachfolge Christi" (*Aus Frühchristlicher Zeit* [Tübingen, 1950], pp. 286ff.), Hans-Joachim Schoeps supports this chapter's understanding of the meaning of discipleship with analysis of the term's backgrounds. He emphasizes that Jesus' call to "follow me" (Mark 2:14) is a messianic claim; that the invitation to discipleship is founded in Jesus' own claim to be following the Father. Although John's Gospel states this identity with the Father in Greek substantial terms, and although the apostle Paul chooses another set of terminology, that of *mimesis,* they are still all basically within this Jewish framework. Schoeps is concerned to point out that later interpretation of the imitation of Christ took on quite foreign meanings. It could focus upon an ecstatic experience (stigmatization); upon a symbolic repetition of details of the earthly life of Jesus (barefoot itinerancy); or it can claim to partake of the deification of humankind of which the incarnation is the beginning. It is characteristic of all these deviations that they move away from the realm of personal and social conflict within which Jesus originally gave the phrase its meaning.

The "Cross" in Protestant Pastoral Care

One universal demand which the church as an agency of counsel and consolation must meet is the need of men and women of all ages for help in facing suffering: illness and accidents, loneliness and defeat. What more fitting resource could there be than the biblical language which makes suffering bearable, meaningful within God's purposes, even meritorious in that "bearing one's cross" is a synonym for discipleship? Hosts of sincere people in hospitals or in conflict-ridden situations have been helped by this thought to bear the strain of their destiny with a sense of divine presence and purpose.

Yet our respect for the quality of these lives and the validity of this pastoral concern must not blind us to the abuse of language and misuse of Scripture they entail. The cross of Christ was not an inexplicable or chance event, which happened to strike him, like illness or accident. To accept the cross as his destiny, to move toward it and even to provoke it, when he could well have done otherwise, was Jesus' constantly reiterated free choice. He warns his disciples lest their embarking on the same path be less conscious of its costs (Luke 14:25-33). The cross of Calvary was not a difficult family situation, not a frustration of visions of personal fulfillment, a crushing debt, or a nagging in-law; it was the political, legally-to-be-expected result of a moral clash with the powers ruling his society. Already the early Christians had to be warned against claiming merit for any and all suffering; only if their suffering be innocent, and a result of the evil will of their adversaries, may it be understood as meaningful before God (1 Pet. 2:18-21; 3:14-18; 4:1, 13-16; 5:9; James 4:10).

Another transposition makes the cross an inward experience of the self. This is found in Thomas Müntzer, in Zinzendorf, in revivalism, and in Christian existentialism. An excellent modern statement is that by Carl Michalson, "How Our Lives Carry Christ's Death and Manifest His Resurrection."[35]

The other direction in which "cross" language can evolve is that of subjective brokenness, the renunciation of pride and self-will. Bon-

35. *Encounter* (organ of Christian Theological Seminary, Indianapolis), 20/4 (Autumn 1959), 410ff.

hoeffer's *Life Together*[36] speaks of "breaking through to the cross" as occurring in confession. "In confession we affirm and accept our cross." Our sharing in Christ's death, he continues, is the "shameful death of the sinner in confession." A similar thrust is typical of the Keswick family of renewal movements in Anglo-Saxon Protestantism. We may agree that the humility of confession may be quite desirable for mental health, for group processes, and for the creation of community; but this should not keep us from realizing that "cross" is not the word for that in the New Testament.

Kierkegaard is another thinker who makes incisive use of the "cross" and "imitation" motifs; I am less sure than my friend Vernard Eller[37] that this includes the concreteness of enablement for discipleship.

Imitation and Renunciation

A long history of interpretation and application which we might designate as "mendicant" has centered its attention upon the outward form of Jesus' life; his forsaking domicile and property, his celibacy or his barefoot itinerancy. Again, without disrespect for the nobility of the monastic tradition and its needed critique of comfortable religion, we must be aware that it centers the renunciation at another point than the New Testament. Both the few who seek thus to follow Jesus in a formal mimicking of his life-style and the many who use this distortion to argue Jesus' irrelevance, have failed to note a striking gap in the New Testament material we have read.

As we noted before more briefly: there is no *general* concept of living like Jesus in the New Testament. According to universal tradition, Jesus was not married; yet when the apostle Paul, advocate *par excellence* of the life "in Christ," argues at length for celibacy or for a widow's not remarrying (1 Cor. 7), it never occurs to him to appeal to Jesus' example, even as one of many arguments. Jesus is thought in his earlier

36. New York: Harper, 1954, p. 113.

37. *Kierkegaard and Radical Discipleship* (Princeton University Press, 1968), especially the chapter "Christ as Savior and Pattern."

life to have worked as a carpenter; yet never, even when he explains at length why he earns his own way as an artisan (1 Cor. 9), does it come to Paul's mind that he is imitating Jesus. Jesus' association with villagers, his drawing his illustrations from the life of the peasants and the fishermen, his leading his disciples to desert places and mountaintops, have often been appealed to as examples by the advocates of rural life and church camping; but not in the New Testament. His formation of a small circle of disciples whom he taught through months of close contact has been claimed as a model pastoral method; his teaching in parables has been made a model of graphic communication; there have been efforts to imitate his prayer life or his forty days in the desert: but not in the New Testament.

There is thus but one realm in which the concept of imitation holds — but there it holds in every strand of the New Testament literature and all the more strikingly by virtue of the absence of parallels in other realms. This is at the point of the concrete social meaning of the cross in its relation to enmity and power. Servanthood replaces dominion, forgiveness absorbs hostility. Thus — and only thus — are we bound by New Testament thought to "be like Jesus."

EPILOGUE

A very helpful recent study is *The Paradox of the Cross in the Thought of St. Paul* by Anthony Tyrell Hanson.[38] By researches both broad and deep, Hanson demonstrates that the Pauline theme cited above (especially III/A) is far more widely present and more important for Paul and his successors than is usually discerned. Hanson brings to bear powerful erudition in three directions: the power of paradox as not merely a literary form but a theological value; a deep review of Paul's scriptural citations and allusions; and a review of the overlap between Paul and the Gospels. In the light of this it is clear that both Paul and

38. Sheffield: JSOT Press, 1987.

his fellow believers saw themselves as continuing the work of the cross, in the way which the texts cited above state most simply.

In his chapter "Go Thou and Do Likewise" A. E. Harvey[39] reviews some of the nuances surrounding the notion of "doing as Jesus did." He argues that where that imperative is stated most simply (e.g., 1 John 2:6, listed II/a above) what is meant is not any literal conforming of the disciples' lives to that of Jesus but the broad pattern of self-giving love. Harvey agrees with Harnack[40] that the notion of following Jesus' example was absent from Christian thought until the age of Francis.

The Franciscan theologian Bonaventure cited as coming from Gregory or even Augustine the phrase *omnis Christi actio nostra est instructio;* every deed of Christ teaches us. Yet Bonaventure's intent in the citation is to distinguish between "instruction," which is like "the broad pattern of self-giving love," which is binding, and "imitation," which disciples are not called to. He distinguishes six ways in which perfection "shines forth" in Christ; only one of the six is exemplary for believers. He describes it in six traits: poverty, virginity, obedience, praying through the night, praying for his enemies, and offering himself to die for his enemies.[41] To fall short of perfection (thus defined as equal to the monastic state) by marrying, using property soberly, sleeping through the night, and serving one's prince in war, is not sin and requires no forgiveness.[42]

None of these writers, contemporary or classic, seems to have been attending to the quite evident distinction between a naïve outward ("franciscan") replicating of the shape of Jesus' life (barefoot itinerancy, celibacy, and manual labor), which never arises in the apostolic writings, and vulnerable enemy love and renunciation of dominion in the real world,[43]

39. Pp. 169ff. in his *Strenuous Commands: The Ethic of Jesus* (Philadelphia/London: Trinity/SCM, 1990).

40. *History of Dogma* (n.p., 1894), p. 67n.1.

41. In his *Defense of the Mendicants (Apologia Pauperum), The Works of Bonaventure* (Paterson: St. Anthony Guild Press, 1966), vol. 4, esp. ch. II/13, p. 13. Bonaventure is defending the notion of "perfection" against anti-Franciscan polemics. He also wrote the parallel text: *Quaestiones Disputatae de Perfectione Evangelica.*

42. *Ibid.,* p. 34. Bonaventure quotes Jerome: ". . . mediocre actions are tolerated, perfect actions are counseled."

43. Bonaventure does list praying for and dying for one's enemies, but by linking them to the mendicant celibate life he makes clear that they are not a live political alternative to the ethos of Caesar.

which is omnipresent. The latter is far more concrete than "a broad pattern of self-giving love," and the former is a red herring. Thus mainstream interpreters, even when intending to take seriously the originality and radicality of Jesus' teaching in the original setting (as Harvey certainly does at the outset) wind up eviscerating or platonizing the concreteness of the ethic of gospel.

CHAPTER 8

Christ and Power

One of the strands in the argument against the normative claims made by or for Jesus has always been that his radical personalism is not relevant to problems of power and structure. Sometimes this ground for rejection has been covered over by more evident arguments such as the "interim" theme, which says that the ethic of Jesus is disqualified because he expected history not to continue very long. Other times it is shoved aside by the "elenchtic" theme, that the high demands of the ethic of Jesus are meant not to be obeyed but to bring us to sorrow for our sin. Yet often this broader negation on the grounds of personalism shows through as well in the argument. In line with the personal appeal which has been so central in Protestant faith since Luther, even more since Pietism, and especially since the merging of Protestant existentialism with modern secular personalism — and even more especially since Freud and Jung imposed upon everyone in our culture the vision of the person as a self-centered reacting organism — it has seemed quite evident that the primary message of Jesus was a call most properly perceived by an individual, asking the hearer for something that can be done most genuinely by an individual standing alone. Whether this "something that one can do standing alone" be a rare heroic ethical performance like loving one's enemies, or a response more accessible to the ordinary person, like sorrow for his or her sins, it is a response each individual can make only for himself. It has nothing to do with the structures of society.[1]

1. One of the classic modern expressions of this understanding is that of Rudolf

When then in the fourth century Christians found themselves in positions of social responsibility, so the argument continues, they had to go for their ethical insight to other sources than Jesus. This should not surprise us. This happened not only because the writers and readers of the New Testament were culturally naive people without much conception of social institutions and power, although this was also the case and reinforces this consideration. It occurred not only because Christians in the first century were so few in number and so unimportant in terms of social class that they could very well live their lives without paying attention to such issues, although this as well was true and likewise had a reinforcing effect. The real reason we should not be surprised that the church at the age of Constantine had to resort to other models for the construction of a social ethic in Christendom was that, quite simply and

---

Bultmann: "unlike the prophets' preaching, His preaching is directed not primarily to the people as a whole, but to individuals. . . . Thus Jesus in His thought of God — and of man in the light of this thought — 'dehistoricized' God and man." *Theology of the New Testament* (New York: Scribner, 1951), p. 25. Bultmann goes on to say that Jesus "released the relation between God and man from its previous ties to history."

The assumption that biblical language is not immediately socially relevant is by no means made only by those who do not care about social issues. Also among those who are quite committed to "relevance," the assumption can still be made that this is not a properly biblical concern but must be approached somehow indirectly through the generalities of a philosophy of history or a concept of Christian vocation. In the editorial preface to a collection of "biblical passages on power and its use," a part of the special number of the *Student World* on the Problem of Power (57 [1964]), the unnamed editor commented (p. 169): "Our subject is part of a contemporary discussion, and is therefore brought to the Bible rather than lifted from it. . . . The opposite is true of dogmatic questions, which come to us from the records of God's revelation; we would not ask them if it were not for the Biblical text."

I suggest that what have traditionally been thought of as "dogmatic questions" are more foreign to the import of the original texts in many cases than is the problem of power. We have the record of Jesus' dealing explicitly with whether he should be king or whether we should love our enemies, and with what we should do with wealth; only very indirectly can we get from his teachings any help on the metaphysics of incarnation.

A very representative, more recent statement of this same view is the contribution of Roger Mehl, "The Basis of Christian Social Ethics," in John C. Bennett (ed.), *Christian Social Ethics in a Changing World.* Mehl's purpose is to lay the base for an understanding of social ethics, but he does it by setting the New Testament's concern uniquely on a personal level so that the problematic of social ethics is how to get there from Jesus. A major part of the answer will be trying to apply individual categories ("personalization," "responsibility") to social structures.

logically, Jesus had nothing much to say on the subject. And if, perchance, Jesus might be said to have spoken in this area, due to vestiges of the prophetic tradition which he took up only to transmute them into something more existential, then at least it is clear that by the time of the Pauline churches any such dimension was lost.

We have already spoken to the *substance* of this portrayal, by reading again the Gospel story. There we have found a view of Jesus that refutes the whole line of argument. Yet we have not spoken as precisely to its *form,* by asking whether one actually does find in the biblical literature some equivalents of the concepts of "power" or "structure," in the sense in which these terms are used by modern thinkers in the social and political sciences. Does not the preoccupation with the transcendent and with the soul, with justification, revelation, and reconciliation, center our attention so powerfully upon the inner structures of the unique, the individual, that no bridge is possible to that other realm?

Even though the interdisciplinary agenda has not been able to make much of it, it happens to be the case that biblical scholarship in the last generation has come to a rather striking degree of clarity at this point. A body of exegetical literature has been building up, slim in quantity but impressive in the consistency with which several different readers come to basically similar results. Stated most systematically and concisely by Hendrikus Berkhof and G. B. Caird, supported in detailed studies or incidentally by G. H. C. MacGregor and Markus Barth, this renewed understanding has the sympathy of a whole generation of scholars working in the mood of "biblical realism," but its idiom is not yet understood across the borders of the disciplines. The effort of this chapter must therefore be devoted not to explicating the Pauline doctrine of the powers — for this exposition is by now widely understood and accepted by scholars in the field — but to illuminating the way in which this doctrine meshes with modern understandings and questions.

The Clarity and Ambiguity of the Language of Power

It is quite evident in contemporary conversation that one can very well agree on the nature or location of a problem without being sure just how to "get hold of" it. When in modern social analysis such terms as "power" and "structure" are used, everyone knows just about what is meant; but still a logician would have little trouble in demonstrating that not everyone means exactly all the same things and nothing else. Sometimes the term "power" is clearly distinguished from "authority," including in the latter term a special reference to some kind of legitimacy or validation of the exercise of power; other times the two are merged. Sometimes "power" is distinguished from "force" as being somehow more general or more justified or less overt; again they are sometimes identified. The concern for precision and the concern to observe generalities and commonalities constantly cross over and overlap, with the linkages being different within every school of thought and every language.

Something of the same stimulating confusion is present in the thought of the apostle Paul as he applies some of the same thought patterns to different challenges in different contexts. He speaks of "principalities and powers," and of "thrones and dominions," thus using language of political color. But he can also use cosmological language like "angels and archangels," "elements," "heights and depths." Or the language can be religious: "law," "knowledge." Sometimes the reader perceives a parallelism in all these concepts, sometimes not.[2]

The most fruitful illustration of the complexity of this language for the modern reader would probably be a meditation on the variety of meanings of the word "structure" as it is currently widely used in American English. Sometimes it refers to a particular network of persons and agencies able to make decisions or exert pressure, as in the phrase "power structure." When this term is used it may refer to a group of

2. Berkhof (*Christ and the Powers* [Scottdale, Pa.: Herald, 1962]) suggests that probably for Paul each of these several terms had its own very precise and technical meaning; that they are not simply synonyms standing parallel. Still the best we can do today is to come to some understanding about the general trend of meaning which the total body of thought has for us. We may quite agree with Berkhof that Paul probably had such a very precise understanding in mind; but it could be well pointed out that it would hardly matter if he had not. A contemporary sociologist or psychologist can very well use such phrases as "power" or "structure" in different ways when dealing with different audiences or different topics and yet be no less clear or systematic in dealing with his thought. To use several terms with roughly synonymous meaning or to use one term with different meanings and different contexts is not necessarily a sign of unclear thinking.

persons who are known or can be found. A civil rights worker may, for example, use the phrase to refer to the editor of the local newspaper, the banker, the sheriff, the chairman of the school board, and the owner of the largest department store in a Southern town. Other times the "power structure" is not so visible but one is no less sure that it is there, as when Marxists speak of "Wall Street" to symbolize a phenomenon that is no less real for being difficult to localize with exactitude.

Yet other times, "structure" is present only in the mind of the one analyzing it. When a psychologist speaks of the "structure of the personality" or the "structure of a response," he or she does not mean to point our attention most precisely to a certain set of nerve endings and connections. There is rather a pattern in reactions and perceptions which has its character as "structure" quite independently of our knowledge of the actual chemistry and electro-mechanics of the nerve network. Yet again, for the architect, "structure" means the physical artifact. The structure of a language is its grammar and syntax and logic, the way words function following unwritten laws located somewhere in the common mental process of the race.

In all of these many ways and more we could add, the concept "structure" functions to point to the patterns or regularities that transcend or precede or condition the individual phenomena we can immediately perceive. The bridge is more than the cables and girders that compose it; the psychic "complex" or "syndrome" is much more than the thoughts and reflexes it organizes; the "class" is much more than the individual persons who make it up; a "religion" is much more than a bagful of assorted practices. It is this patternedness that the word "structure" tries to enable us to perceive within all the varieties of its appearance. Similarly, "power" points in all its modulations to some kind of capacity to make things happen.

We have already identified a body of vocabulary, especially in the thought of the apostle Paul,[3] that deals with power and structure. What does he say with this vocabulary? And are the things he says translatable into the concepts of modern social science?

3. Perhaps I should write "Paul." It is not crucial for present purposes whether the same person who wrote to the Romans also wrote to the Ephesians and the Colossians.

Christ and the Powers in Contemporary Theology

One of the significant advances of theological understanding in the last generation has been the juxtaposition of a gap in theological ethics with a puzzle in New Testament interpretation. Since the onset of critical New Testament studies it has practically been taken for granted that when the apostle speaks about angels or demons or powers this is a dispensable remainder of an antique worldview, needing not even to be interpreted or translated, but simply to be dropped without discussion. And on the other hand, as we have just observed, under the shadow of Protestant individualism it was assumed that the apostle did not deal with structural problems. What we now behold is that the unmanageable imagery has the same shape as the missing piece in the ethical puzzle. Driven by the events that shook Europe between 1930 and 1950, Protestant theology sought a more adequate theological understanding of the power of evil which had been seen breaking through the crust of the most civilized of societies. No longer can it be taken for granted that human intelligence and institutions can solve all our problems. Theologians began anew to ask what their faith in Jesus Christ could say to a society in disarray.

At the same time the techniques of contemporary erudition had given to theologians a greater capacity to conceive the meaning of scriptural thought within its own original cultural context, a capacity for cultural empathy probably greater than has obtained at any time since the end of the Apostolic Age. So we became able to take up more successfully the task of understanding those New Testament passages which hitherto had been the least "interesting." Instead of asking what those texts mean in the modern world, scholars learned to ask first, more carefully, what the writers, speaking to their own age in its own language, were seeking to say *then,* by means of concepts not immediately understandable to us. This new question and the new technique for putting such a question to the biblical text coincided in such a way as to fit the Pauline answer into the ethical puzzle. The part of the gospel worldview which we had been unable to read was found to speak precisely to those questions which we had earlier been taught the gospel did not speak to.[4]

4. The positive emphasis of this present discussion on the relevance of the apostle's

The present portrayal of this teaching leans gratefully and heavily on the way Paul is interpreted by Hendrikus Berkhof, one of the creative thinkers responsible for this analysis. His statement is, however, only the most transparent and accessible of several whose major thrusts are mutually reinforcing.[5]

The Origin of the Powers in the Creative Purpose of God

> He is the image of the invisible God, the firstborn of all creation. For in him were created all things, those in heaven and those on earth, visible and invisible; whether thrones or dominions or principalities or powers; all was created through him and by him. And he is before all things, and all things subsist in him. (Col. 1:15-17)

The word translated "subsist" in verse 17 has the same root as the modern word "system." The apostle Paul says that this is the share of

---

powers language to the institutions and ideologies of our times need not imply the rejection of all the more literal meanings which the language of the demonic and of bondage can also have (occultism, astrology, possession, exorcism). That these two areas or two kinds of definitions of "the demonic" are quite distinct from one another would probably have been much less evident to Paul than it seems to be to some moderns.

5. Berkhof, *Christ and the Powers.* Next to the Berkhof text, which we are here reflecting extensively, the most helpful other studies, all of them substantially parallel in their interpretation, are the following: G. B. Caird, *Principalities and Powers* (Oxford: Clarendon, 1956); G. H. C. MacGregor, "Principalities and Powers: The Cosmic Background of Paul's Thought," *NTS,* 1 (1954), 17-28; also in H. McArthur (ed.), *New Testament Sidelights* (Hartford, 1960), p. 101; E. Gordon Rupp, *Principalities and Powers: Studies in the Christian Conflict in History* (London: Epworth, 1952); W. A. Visser 't Hooft, *The Kingship of Christ* (New York: Harper, 1948), pp. 186ff.; D. E. H. Whiteley, *The Theology of Saint Paul* (Oxford: Blackwell, 1964), ch. 2, pp. 18-80; Amos N. Wilder, *Kerygma, Eschatology and Social Ethics* (Philadelphia: Fortress, 1966).

Supportive comments are also provided by: James S. Stewart, "On a Neglected Emphasis in New Testament Theology," *SJT,* 4 (1951), 292; and Anders Nygren, "Christ and the Forces of Destruction," *SJT,* 4, 366. The related studies of Clinton Morrison and Heinrich Schlier deal less directly with the possibility of contemporary "translations" of the Pauline concepts. Cf. n. 20 below for an ethics text in the Pauline idiom. Graydon F. Snyder ("The Literalization of the Apocalyptic Form," pp. 8-9) suggests that the use of the "powers" language to describe the origin and the defeat of evil is rooted in what he calls the "watcher myth." Markus Barth surveys recent scholarship concerning the Powers in his *Acquittal by Resurrection* (New York: Holt, 1964), p. 159n.21.

Christ (John would have spoken of the preexisting Word) in creation; namely, in him everything "systematizes," everything holds together. This "everything" that Christ maintains united is the world powers. It is the reign of order among creatures, order which in its original intention is a divine gift.

Most of the references to the "Powers" in the New Testament consider them as fallen. It is important therefore to begin with the reminder that they were part of the good creation of God. Society and history, even nature, would be impossible without regularity, system, order — and God has provided for this need. The universe is not sustained arbitrarily, immediately, and erratically by an unbroken succession of new divine interventions. It was made in an ordered form and "it was good." The creative power worked in a mediated form, by means of the Powers that regularized all visible reality.

The Fallen Powers in the Providence of God

Unfortunately, however, we have no access to the good creation of God. The creature and the world are fallen, and in this the powers have their own share. They are no longer active only as mediators of the saving creative purpose of God; now we find them seeking to separate us from the love of God (Rom. 8:38); we find them ruling over the lives of those who live far from the love of God (Eph. 2:2); we find them holding us in servitude to their rules (Col. 2:20); we find them holding us under their tutelage (Gal. 4:3). These structures which were supposed to be our servants have become our masters and our guardians.

Yet even in this fallen and rebellious state the working of the Powers is not simply something limitlessly evil. The Powers, despite their fallenness, continue to exercise an ordering function. Even tyranny (which according to Rom. 13:1 is to be counted among the powers) is still better than chaos and we should be subject to it. The law (which according to Gal. 4:5 prevents us from attaining to filial maturity) is nevertheless righteous and good and we should obey it. Even the pagan and primitive forms of social and religious expression, although obviously unworthy of being imitated, remain a sign of the preserving patience of God toward a world that has not yet heard of its redemption

(Acts 17:22-28). Thus, before moving on to declare the impact of the work of Christ, Paul has made three fundamental declarations, in the language of his time, concerning the structures of creaturely existence:

(a) These structures were created by God. It is the divine purpose that within human existence there should be a network of norms and regularities to stretch out the canvas upon which the tableau of life can be painted.

(b) These powers have rebelled and are fallen. They did not accept the modesty that would have permitted them to remain conformed to the creative purpose, but rather they claimed for themselves an absolute value. They thereby enslaved humanity and our history. We are bound to them; "slavery" is in fact one of the fundamental terms used in the New Testament to describe the lost condition of men and women outside of Christ. To what are we subject? Precisely to those values and structures which are necessary to life and society, but which have claimed the status of idols and have succeeded in making us serve them as if they were of absolute value.

(c) Despite their fallen condition the Powers cannot fully escape the providential sovereignty of God, who is still able to use them for good.

Before continuing the analysis of "values" and of "structures," let us follow Berkhof in suggesting some concrete modern phenomena which he considers to be structurally analogous to the Powers. At one point (p. 22) he enumerates: "Human traditions, the course of earthly life conditioned by the heavenly bodies, morality, fixed religious and ethical rules, the administration of justice and the ordering of the state." In another list (p. 25) there appear: "The State, politics, class, social struggle, national interest, public opinion, accepted morality, the ideas of decency, of democracy. . . ." And in still another list (p. 27) we find: "The place of the clan or the tribe among primitive peoples, the respect for ancestors and the family . . . [in] Chinese life, the Hindu social order . . . , the astrological unity of ancient Babel . . . , the manifold moral tradition and codes of which moral life is full . . . , the powers of race, class, state and *Volk*."

If we can analyze more abstractly this wealth of allusions, we might say that we have here an inclusive vision of religious structures (especially the religious undergirdings of stable ancient and primitive societies), intellectual structures (-ologies and -isms), moral structures (codes and customs), political structures (the tyrant, the market, the school, the courts, race, and nation). The totality is overwhelmingly broad.[6] Nonetheless, even here with careful analysis we observe that it can be said of all of these "structures" what the apostle was saying concerning the powers:

(a) All these structures can be conceived of in their general essence as parts of a good creation. There could not be society or history, there could not be humanity without the existence above us of religious, intellectual, moral, and social structures. *We cannot live without them.* These structures are not and never have been a mere sum total of the individuals composing them. The whole is more than the sum of its parts. And this "more" is an invisible Power, even though we may not be used to speaking of it in personal or angelic terms.

(b) But these structures fail to serve us as they should. They do not enable humanity to live a genuinely free, loving life. They have absolutized themselves and they demand from the individual and society an unconditional loyalty. They harm and enslave us. *We cannot live with them.* Looking at the human situation from within, it is not possible to conceive how, once unconditionally subjected to these Powers, humankind can ever again become free.

(c) We are lost in the world, in its structures, and in the current of its development. But nonetheless it is in this world that we have been preserved, that we have been able to be who we are and thereby to await the redeeming work of God. Our lostness and our survival are inseparable, both dependent upon the Powers.

Thus, far from being archaic or meaningless, the "exousiology" of the apostle, that is, his doctrine of the Powers, reveals itself to be a

6. Borrowing explicitly and expressly from the thought structure of Berkhof, Albert H. van den Heuvel wrote what he called a "funny book" on mission for young adults. Under the heading *These Rebellious Powers* (New York: Friendship, 1965), van den Heuvel sketches an approach to social ethics in what he considers a modern translation of the thought structure of Paul. William Stringfellow, in his *Free in Obedience* (New York: Seabury, 1964), esp. pp. 49ff., makes more extensive use of the "principalities" language in a similar intent. Both demonstrate the fruitfulness of the Pauline imagery to render the idolatrous-demonic claims of the fallen powers; Stringfellow gives less attention to what can be said affirmatively about them from the perspective of creation and redemption, and van den Heuvel gives less note to their collective and structural nature.

very refined analysis of the problems of society and history, far more refined than the other ways in which theologians have sought to describe the same realities in terms only of "creation" or "personality." Some traditional theologies have sought to treat this theme under the heading of "orders of creation." But rarely, if ever, has it been possible under this heading to combine with such clarity and precision the simultaneous recognition of humankind's fallen condition and the continuing providential control. Nor has it generally been the case within traditional thought regarding the orders of creation that religion or ideology has been included. Nor has it generally been affirmed that it is in Christ that these values all find their meaning and coherence. As a matter of fact, the theology of the orders of creation has generally affirmed that Jesus Christ has little directly to do with them, but that rather these several orders (the state, family, economy, etc.) have an autonomous value unrelated to redemption and the church, by virtue of their being the product of a divine act of creation.[7]

The Work of Christ and the Powers

If our lostness consists in our subjection to the rebellious powers of a fallen world, what then is the meaning of the work of Christ? Subordination to these Powers is what makes us human, for if they did not exist there would be no history nor society nor humanity. If then God is going to save his creatures *in their humanity,* the Powers cannot simply be destroyed or set aside or ignored. Their sovereignty must be broken. This is what Jesus did, concretely and historically, by living a genuinely

7. Perhaps the most explicit contemporary statement of this view is the "trinitarian" ethical argument of H. Richard Niebuhr: "The Doctrine of the Trinity and the Unity of the Church," *TT,* 3/3 (Oct. 1946), 371ff. Here the distinction of persons in the Trinity is correlated with the distribution of different kinds of ethical thought, with God as Father the specific authority behind what an earlier theology would have called "the orders of creation" or "providence." This appeal to the trinitarian formulas has as its special polemical point an effort to counteract what Niebuhr called a "unitarianism of the second person," namely an ethic too directly oriented around Christ. Well before Niebuhr, much Lutheran theology made a similar point by affirming the moral autonomy *(Eigengesetzlichkeit)* of the several realms of culture. Dooyeweerd, the Reformed philosophical theologian, calls it "sphere sovereignty."

free and human existence. This life brought him, as any genuinely human existence will bring anyone, to the cross. In his death the Powers — in this case the most worthy, weighty representatives of Jewish religion and Roman politics — acted in collusion. Like everyone, he too was subject (but in his case quite willingly) to these powers. He accepted his own status of submission. But morally he broke their rules by refusing to support them in their self-glorification; and that is why they killed him. Preaching and incorporating a greater righteousness than that of the Pharisees, and a vision of an order of social human relations more universal than the Pax Romana, he permitted the Jews to profane a holy day (refuting thereby their own moral pretensions) and permitted the Romans to deny their vaunted respect for law as they proceeded illegally against him. This they did in order to avoid the threat to their dominion represented by the very fact that he existed in their midst so morally independent of their pretensions. He did not fear even death. Therefore his cross is a victory, the confirmation that he was free from the rebellious pretensions of the creaturely condition. Differing from Adam, Lucifer, and all the Powers, Jesus did "not consider being equal with God as a thing to be seized" (Phil. 2:6). His very obedience unto death is in itself not only the sign but also the firstfruits of an authentic restored humanity. Here we have for the first time to do with someone who is not the slave of any power, of any law or custom, community or institution, value or theory. Not even to save his own life will he let himself be made a slave of these Powers. This authentic humanity included his free acceptance of death at their hands. Thus it is his death that provides his victory: "Wherefore God has exalted him highly, and given him the name which is above every name . . . that every tongue might confess that Jesus Christ is Lord" (2:9-11).

> And you, who were dead in trespasses and the uncircumcision of your flesh, God made alive together with him, having forgiven us all our trespasses, having cancelled the bond which stood against us with its legal demands; this he set aside, nailing it to the cross. He disarmed the principalities and powers and made a public example of them, triumphing over them in him.[8] (Col. 2:13-15)

8. Or: "in it [the cross]."

The apostle uses three complementary verbs to describe what Christ and his death did to the Powers. The way these three terms fit together reciprocally is masterfully summarized in the words of Berkhof (pp. 30-31):

> By the cross (which must always, here as elsewhere, be seen as a unit with the resurrection) Christ abolished the slavery which, as a result of sin, lay over our existence as a menace and an accusation. On the cross He "disarmed" the Powers, "made a public example of them and thereby triumphed over them." Paul uses three different verbs to express more adequately what happened to the Powers at the cross.
>
> He "made a public example of them." It is precisely in the crucifixion that the true nature of the Powers has come to light. Previously they were accepted as the most basic and ultimate realities, as the gods of the world. Never had it been perceived, nor could it have been perceived, that this belief was founded on deception. Now that the true God appears on earth in Christ, it becomes apparent that the Powers are inimical to Him, acting not as His instruments but as His adversaries. The scribes, representatives of the Jewish law, far from receiving gratefully Him who came in the name of the God of the law, crucified Him in the name of the temple. The Pharisees, personifying piety, crucified Him in the name of piety. Pilate, representing Roman justice and law, shows what these are worth when called upon to do justice to the Truth Himself. Obviously, "none of the rulers of this age," who let themselves be worshipped as divinities, understood God's wisdom, "for had they known, they would not have crucified the Lord of glory" (I Cor. 2:8). Now they are unmasked as false gods by their encounter with Very God; they are made a public spectacle.
>
> Thus Christ has "triumphed over them." The unmasking is actually already their defeat. Yet this is only humanly visible when they know that God Himself has appeared on earth in Christ. Therefore we must think of the resurrection as well as of the cross. The resurrection manifests what was already accomplished at the cross: that in Christ God has challenged the Powers, has penetrated into their territory, and has displayed that He is stronger than they.
>
> The concrete evidence of this triumph is that at the cross Christ has "disarmed" the Powers. The weapon from which they heretofore

derived their strength is struck out of their hands. This weapon was the power of illusion, their ability to convince us that they were the divine regents of the world, ultimate certainty and ultimate direction, ultimate happiness and the ultimate duty for small, dependent humanity. Since Christ we know that this is illusion. We are called to a higher destiny: we have higher orders to follow and we stand under a greater protector. No powers can separate us from God's love in Christ. Unmasked, revealed in their true nature, they have lost their mighty grip on us. The cross has disarmed them: wherever it is preached, the unmasking and the disarming of the Powers takes place.

The Work of the Church and the Powers

If this victory over the powers constitutes the work of Christ, then it must be also a message for the church to proclaim. "To me, less than the least of all the saints," says Paul, "was given the grace to proclaim among the Gentiles the gospel of the inscrutable riches of Christ, and to declare to all what is the dispensation of the mystery hidden since the ages in God, who created all things; so that the manifold wisdom of God should henceforth be made known by means of the church to the principalities and powers in heavenly places, according to the eternal purpose which he set in Jesus Christ our Lord" (Eph. 3:8-11). Again here I cannot improve on the résumé of Berkhof (pp. 41-42):

> Paul's statement is made in connection with the truth that since Christ a new force has made its entry on the stage of salvation history: the church. The church is something quite different from Israel as God's people, namely an undreamed-of synthesis of the two sorts of persons who people the world, Jews and Gentiles. That Christ has brought together both into one body is the mystery, which for ages had remained hidden (v. 9) but has come to light, thanks to Paul's ministry. In this ministry is manifested "the unsearchable wealth of Christ" (v. 8) and the "manifold wisdom of God" (v. 10).
>
> This is what the church announces to the Powers. The very existence of the church, in which Gentiles and Jews, who heretofore

> walked according to the *stoicheia*[9] of the world, live together in Christ's fellowship, is itself a proclamation, a sign, a token to the Powers that their unbroken dominion has come to an end. Thus even this text says nothing of a positive or aggressive approach to the Powers. Such an approach is superfluous because the very presence of the church in a world ruled by the Powers is a superlatively positive and aggressive fact. We have already dealt with what this fact means to the Powers, for whom it is a sign of the end time, of their incipient encirclement and their imminent defeat.
>
> This same fact is also freighted with meaning for the Christians. All resistance and every attack against the gods of this age will be unfruitful, unless the church itself is resistance and attack, unless it demonstrates in its own life and fellowship how believers can live freed from the Powers. We can only preach the manifold wisdom of God to Mammon if our life displays that we are joyfully freed from his clutches. To reject nationalism we must begin by no longer recognizing in our own bosoms any difference between peoples. We shall only resist social injustice and the disintegration of community if justice and mercy prevail in our own common life and social differences have lost their power to divide. Clairvoyant and warning words and deeds aimed at state or nation are meaningful only insofar as they spring from a church whose inner life is itself its proclamation of God's manifold wisdom to the "Powers in the air."

It is thus a fundamental error to conceive of the position of the church in the New Testament in the face of social issues as a "withdrawal," or to see this position as motivated by the Christians' weakness, by their numerical insignificance or low social class, or by fear of persecution, or by scrupulous concern to remain uncontaminated by the world. What can be called the "otherness of the church"[10] is an attitude rooted in strength and not in weakness. It consists in being a herald of liberation and not a community of slaves. It is not a detour or a waiting period, looking forward to better days which one hopes might come a few centuries later; it was rather a victory when the

9. Or "elements"; the components of which reality is composed: Berkhof, *Christ and the Powers,* p. 58n.6.

10. Cf. my "The Otherness of the Church," *MQR,* 35 (Oct. 1961), 286, to be reprinted in *The Royal Priesthood* (Grand Rapids: Wm. B. Eerdmans, forthcoming).

church rejected the temptations of Zealot and Maccabean patriotism and Herodian collaboration. The church accepted as a gift being the "new humanity" created by the cross and not by the sword. Once more Berkhof (p. 43):

> This is not to say that Paul is ignorant of a more direct encounter between the faithful and the Powers. Ephesians 6:10-18 proves the contrary. The believer strives ultimately not against tangible persons and objects ("flesh and blood," v. 12), but against the Powers they obey. This war with the Powers must be waged seriously. One must arm oneself for it. The arms named (truth, righteousness, the readiness of the Gospel of peace, faith, salvation, and the Word of God) show that Paul is not contemplating an offensive against the Powers. Though surely the believer must be on the defense against them; but this can be done only by standing, simply, for one's faith. One is not called to do more than one can do by simply believing. Our duty is not to bring the powers to their knees. This is Jesus Christ's own task. He has taken care of this thus far and will continue to do so. We are responsible for the defense, just because He takes care of the offense. Ours it is to hold the Powers, their seduction, and their enslavement, at a distance, "to be able to stand against the wiles of the devil" (v. 11, cf. 13). The figurative allusion to weapons points to this defensive role. Girdle, breastplate, shoes, shield, helmet, and sword (*machaira,* the short sword) are all defensive arms. Lance, spear, bow and arrow are not named. They are not needed; these are the weapons Christ Himself bears. Our weapon is to stay close to Him and thus to remain out of the reach of the drawing power of the Powers.

The Priority of the Church in Christian Social Strategy

We have asked whether the New Testament provides any concept with which it would be possible to interpret the structures and the history of a secular society. In the Pauline understanding of the powers we have discovered a line of thought very apt to deal with this kind of matter.

In this view of things the condition of the creature, our fallen state, the continual providential care of God which preserves us as human, the saving work of Christ, and the specific position of the

Christian community in the midst of history are all described in terms of social structure and their inherent dynamics. Thus there can be easily established a correlation with contemporary ways of understanding society and history. This in turn drives us to suggest that we can describe more specifically the place of the church within the larger society.

For Paul, as interpreted by Berkhof, the very existence of the church is its primary task. It is in itself a proclamation of the lordship of Christ to the powers from whose dominion the church has begun to be liberated. The church does not attack the powers; this Christ has done. The church concentrates upon not being seduced by them. By existing the church demonstrates that their rebellion has been vanquished.[11]

This Pauline vision of the place of the church in the world bears decisive implications for the contemporary ecumenical discussion of the place of the church in a world in the midst of rapid social change. The phrase "responsible society" became very current since its occurrence in the preparatory documents for the Amsterdam Assembly of 1948. In these documents it was strongly affirmed that if the church is to have a ministry to society in general, the first step of this duty is toward its own identity. "Let the church be the church," was the slogan. "Let the church be a restored society," we could have said equally well. The church must be a sample of the kind of humanity within which, for example, economic and racial differences are surmounted. Only then will it have anything to say to the society that

11. Scholarly debate about the sense in which the early church's expectations of the parousia may or may not have been disappointed (cf. pp. 109ff.) has diverted attention from the unanimity of conviction about the novelty of what had already come. "Thus the confession of Jesus as Lord and Savior, and the claim of Christ over the whole civilized world as dramatized in Paul's far-reaching missionary goals, represented a continuation of the hopes of the prophet, psalmist, and the devout poor for the time when God's will would be done on earth as in heaven. . . . It is true that the early church looked for the imminent parousia of Christ. This was an inevitable aspect of their picture of history. But this cannot set aside the fact that the believers were shaping a new pattern of the human community and realizing very concrete social values in a widening movement which collided increasingly with existing institutions and vested interests economic, social and political." Amos Wilder, *Otherworldliness and the New Testament* (New York: Harper, 1954), p. 116. The entire life work of Wilder, in his rehabilitation of New Testament language and imagery, lies generally along the lines of the present study.

surrounds it about how those differences must be dealt with. Otherwise preaching to the world a standard of reconciliation which is not its own experience will be neither honest nor effective.[12]

The position paper from which the phrase "responsible society" was taken was drafted by J. H. Oldham.[13] He began his discussion of "the practice of common life" by declaring that:

> The first indispensable task is to restore substance to the human person through the revitalization of personal life in the living give-and-take, the mutual obligation and responsibility of a society of persons. If our diagnosis is true, the world cannot be set right from the top but only from the bottom upwards.
>
> There is no way of restoring substance and depth to the life of man except by living. . . . Human living is living in relations with other persons and can acquire meaning and depth only in those relations. Since the number of persons with whom an individual can have direct and close relations is limited, the art of social living has to be learned and practiced in small groups, of which the family is the chief.
>
> > . . . These little groups are the forces out of which the new Europe must be built, if democracy is to be its ruling spirit. They are the nuclei of the new social consciousness on which alone the practical architects of the social order of tomorrow can hope to build a society in which men's higher faculties of love and creative service will have soil to grow.

12. Franklin H. Littell, *From State Church to Pluralism* (New York: Doubleday Anchor, 1962), p. 120, points out how Protestant church leaders condemn themselves when they seek to use political sanctions to enforce upon all society moral obligations which they cannot with theological and ecclesiastical motivations commend to their own membership. Littell says this of the prohibition and evolution controversies; he could say it of open housing. ". . . Politicians in the churches attempted to secure by public legislation what they were unable to persuade many of their own members was either wise or desirable. . . . Lacking the authenticity of a genuinely disciplined witness, the Protestant reversion to political action was ultimately discredited, and the churches have not to this day recovered their authority in public life."

13. J. H. Oldham, "A Responsible Society," in *The Church and the Disorder of Society,* vol. III in the Amsterdam Assembly Series *Man's Disorder and God's Design* (New York: Harper, 1948). The internal quotation within the following passage is from an article by G. D. H. Cole in the *Christian News-Letter.*

> The church is concerned with the primary task of recreating a true social life in two ways. In the first place, its greatest contribution to the renewal of society is through the fulfillment of its primary functions of preaching the Word and through its life as a worshipping community. It is the worship of God that is the source of all genuine renewal. It is only in response to the demands of His perfection that it can reach out to new tasks. It is His grace and truth which in the last resort guarantee and sustain the personal and cultural values which are essential to the health of society.
>
> There is nothing greater that the Church can do for society than to be a center in which small groups of persons are together entering into this experience of renewal and giving each other mutual support in Christian living and action in secular spheres. Such groups will find their vital inspiration in Word and Sacrament and in the fellowship of such gatherings as the parish meeting.

This centrality of the church continued to be affirmed in the basic documents of ecumenical social strategy in succeeding years. But it did not remain equally clear when studies on specific social problems came into view.[14] These concrete studies were necessary to relate to problems of social organization concerning which often it appeared that there would not be such a thing as a specifically *Christian* point of view. It seemed that in such cases there would exist only the *correct* point of view of the expert — the economist, the agronomist, the sociologist, who could not necessarily be found within the church. Furthermore, it seemed that the basis of social cooperation between Christians and non-Christians would have to be something other than a specifically Christian standard. We cannot be sure that in all this process of study the central importance of the Christian community as a new humanity

14. Since 1961 (New Delhi) the phrase "responsible society" dropped out of currency in ecumenical meetings and journals. A few ethicists, notably H. D. Wendland and Walter Muelder, had adopted the term, giving it their own meaning. A few others, notably Keith Bridston, Max-Alain Chevallier, and Charles West, had raised doubts on the level of systematic-theological logic. Perhaps an equally significant, though less apparent reason for the phrase's failure to find permanent usefulness and conceptual clarity might be its rootedness in the Christendom or post-Christendom context, where it is natural for Christians to conceive of themselves as holding a determining power in society and the state.

was kept in view, not only as a verbal affirmation, but also as an instrument of social change.

In the published documents arising from the ecumenical conversation on social ethics since 1948 there has been a degree of success in avoiding the temptations of which Christians accuse the Pharisees. There is little tendency to seek to resolve these problems by trusting in some kind of immutable law or a loophole-free casuistry. But one cannot be so sure that there has been equal success in discerning and avoiding the temptation of the Sadducees, which is also a form of servitude to the Powers. By this we mean the assumption that the forces which really determine the march of history are in the hands of the leaders of the armies and the markets, in such measure that if Christians are to contribute to the renewal of society they will need to seek, like everyone else — in fact in competition with everyone else — to become in their turn the lords of the state and of the economy, so as to use that power toward the ends they consider desirable.[15]

The "Pietistic" Misunderstanding

Let us avoid with great care the two possible misunderstandings of this critical statement about social pressure to which the apostle Paul has led us. What he says is not, as some conservative religious groups would say, that the gospel deals only with personal ethics and not with social structures. Nor does he say that the only way to change structures is to change the heart of an individual, preferably the one in power, and

15. The form in which this thought pattern gathered the most attention recently was the proposal that violent revolution might be justified if directed against hopelessly unjust social situations in (for instance) Latin America. Jacques Ellul in his study *Violence* (New York: Seabury, 1969) has effectively punctured the logic of the assumption that violence, while wrong in the oppressor, becomes right when used by Christians for desirable social change. What the hasty, theologically conservative critics of this "theology of revolution" often fail to notice is that it constitutes only a modest reformulation of the concepts of the just war that are held to by most nonrevolutionary Christian groups. One of the earliest very perceptive criticisms of this kind of theological affirmation of revolution was made by the contributions of Max-Alain Chevallier and Keith Bridston to the World Student Christian Federation study, *The Christian in the World Struggle* (Geneva: WSCF, 1952), ed. M. M. Thomas and D. J. McCaughey.

then see that he or she exercises control of society with more humility or discernment or according to better standards. What needs to be seen is rather that the primary social structure through which the gospel works to change other structures is that of the Christian community. Here, within this community, people are rendered humble and changed in the way they behave not simply by a proclamation directed to their sense of guilt but also by genuine social relationships with other persons who ask them about their obedience; who (in the words of Jesus) "bind and loose."

Neither should we be understood as stating here an extreme application of some particularly radical ethical commitment, such as the argument that everything having to do with the structure of this world is impure or unworthy for the Christian because of the coercion or violence that governs society.[16] There may well be certain circumstances in which the Christian, in order to be morally faithful, would refuse certain functions within society. Every ethical system draws some kinds of lines. But if the disciple of Jesus Christ chooses not to exercise certain kinds of power, this is not simply because they are powerful; for the Powers as such, power in itself, is the good creation of God. The disciple chooses not to exercise certain types of power because, in a given context, the rebellion of the structure of a given particular power is so incorrigible that at the time the most effective way to *take* responsibility is to refuse to collaborate, and by that refusal to take sides in favor of the victims whom that power is oppressing. This refusal is not a withdrawal from society. It is rather a major negative intervention within the process of social change, a refusal to use unworthy means even for what seems to be a worthy end.

Frequently the faithfulness of the church has been put to the test the moment believers were asked to follow the path of costly conscientious objection in the face of the world's opposition. Yet we should not

16. There is widespread agreement among the historians of ethics, in the wake of Ernst Troeltsch, Max Weber, and H. Richard Niebuhr, that such a "withdrawn" or "purist" position is represented by the General Epistles of the New Testament, by Tertullian, the Anabaptists, and Tolstoy. Niebuhr's description of what he calls the "Christ against Culture" position, in his vastly influential *Christ and Culture,* is seriously distorted by his prior polemical stance. Whether or not such a characterization be fair to the persons and movements just named, it in any case does not describe the position of the present study.

overdramatize the normal expression of our mission in and through society. The church's calling is to be the conscience and the servant within human society. The church must be sufficiently experienced to be able to discern when and where and how God is using the Powers, whether this be thanks to the faithful testimony of the church or in spite of its infidelity. Either way, we are called to contribute to the creation of structures more worthy of human society. But the church will also need to be sufficiently familiar with the manifest ways in which God has acted to reconcile and call together a people for himself, so as not to fall prey to the Sadducean or "German Christian" temptation to read off the surface of history a simple declaration of God's will.[17] God is working in the world and it is the task of the church to know how he is working. The church should be the first to distinguish between this kind of divine work — which can be discerned definitively and faithfully, not only in the light of faith — and the to and fro on the surface of current events, concerning which many, even many in the church, will exclaim, "Behold, here is the Christ." "This is where God is at work!" This task of discernment is much less simple than seems to be assumed by many who in the last decade have been encouraging us to look for God at work in "the World Revolution" (whatever that is).

The Relevance of Christ to the Powers Today

It is often said that the Christian understanding of the human individual, which considers him or her at the same time fallen yet redeemable, offers a point of departure more adequate, that is, more correct and more realistic, than that which was provided by the Utopian

17. Lest it be assumed that this temptation is one that besets the church especially in unique fascist situations, we should remember that it probably happens far more often in the situation of a comfortable establishment (like the churches of the American Bible Belt) or in the crusade, the revolution which very good people proclaim to be a holy cause because of the nobility of the purposes to which it is committed. The accommodation of the Bible Belt is fittingly denounced by Samuel S. Hill, "Culture-Protestantism in the South," *CC* (Sept. 12, 1962), and by George H. Shriver, "When Conservatism Is Liberalism," *CC* (Aug. 6, 1969).

idea, where humanity is seen as almost ready to complete its own redemption, or by the mechanistic idea, where humanity is nothing but the product of its circumstances. We are now ready to affirm that the biblical understanding of the powers in history can give us a more adequate intellectual framework of the task of *social* discernment to which we are especially called in our age. This discernment is not simply a way of helping the needy with their social problems, a kind of updated philanthropy, nor does it mean simply to guide individual Christians by helping them to do good deeds or to avoid sin. It is rather a part of Christians' proclamation that the church is under orders to make known to the Powers, as no other proclaimer can do, the fulfillment of the mysterious purposes of God (Eph. 3:10) by means of Jesus in whom their rebellion has been broken and the pretensions they had raised have been demolished.[18]

This proclamation of the lordship of Christ is not a substitute for nor a prerequisite to the gospel call directed to individuals. Nor is it the mere consequence within society of the conversion of individuals one by one. Nor does it dispense with, or guarantee, or always necessarily facilitate such conversions. Such phrasings of alternatives are commended to us by traditional Protestant thought. But the New Testament does not begin at such a dilemma nor do we need to be hobbled by it.[19] That Christ is Lord, a proclamation to which only

18. The use Charles West makes of "powers language" is typical of the taken-for-granted meaning it has for a few, yet without having been exposited or tested widely. In his *Ethics, Violence, and Revolution* (New York: Council on Religion and International Affairs, 1969), pp. 45-46, West speaks of "the continual de-mythologizing and disarming of the powers by God — more specifically by Christ — in order that they may be legitimized as servants of his purpose for man." The term "legitimized" risks being understood too simply and affirmatively, forgetting the note of continuing struggle, relapse, and, worse, rebellion; but my point in citing West here is simply as a document of the agreed (yet not fully exposited or tested) fruitfulness of the *exousia* imagery.

19. Protestant theology has long been divided about the sense in which the work of Christ is "objectively" real as over against the sense in which it depends for its reality upon being "appropriated" by the believer. Is the victory over the powers something that has happened "out there" whether or not everyone knows it or believes it? Has the shape of the universe really been changed? Or is there only a change in the orientation of the individual believer or the church, so that we should say that the sovereignty of the powers is broken "only for faith" and that its continuing defeat is dependent upon the faithfulness of the church in living out its liberation? As Graydon Snyder has argued in an unpublished

individuals can respond, is nonetheless a social, political, *structural* fact which constitutes a challenge to the Powers. It thus follows that the claims such proclamation makes are not limited to those who have accepted it, nor is the significance of its judgment limited to those who have decided to listen to it. It was Johann Christoph Blumhardt who rediscovered for German Protestantism a century ago the wondrous power of the gospel in individual lives and at the same time the eschatological foundation of Christian involvement in politics. We may echo his battle cry: "Dass Jesus siegt ist ewig ausgemacht. Sein ist die ganze Welt!" "That Jesus is conqueror is eternally settled: the universe is his!" This is not a statement concerning the benevolent disposition of certain individuals to listen or of certain Powers to be submissive. It is a declaration about the nature of the cosmos and the significance of history, within which both our conscientious participation and our conscientious objection find their authority and their promise.

It cannot be the task of this chapter to spell out at length samples of the relevance of this kind of approach for concrete social and ethical thought. Berkhof himself suggests only very sketchily some directions, especially with reference to the foreign missionary enterprise of the church and to that particular Western totalitarianism which arises when the Powers are no longer cowed by the proclamation that had originally humbled them. Probably Jacques Ellul, in his writing on money, the law, violence, and technology, thinks the most consistently within the framework of this approach, though often without direct allusion to the Pauline vocabulary.[20] Scientifically oriented Westerners are poorly

---

paper, this set of alternatives is foreign to the apocalyptic and mythic literary context in which these statements are found. This kind of language is not interested in dealing with realities that are "out there" but do not transform our situation, nor can it conceive of our situations as being transformed by the mere force of our own believing. This set of alternatives, which echoes down the halls of Christian controversy in social ethics, from the classic Lutheran-Catholic debate through the Lutheran-Reformed debate to the contemporary "evangelical-liberal" debate, is the fruit of a warped initial phrasing in the question. This dilemma is a product of the modern Protestant individualistic ontology, not a conceivable distinction within the biblical text itself.

20. Cf. below, p. 159n.25. Perhaps the earliest effort to make sense of the concept of the powers in modern theology was that of Otto Piper, *Die Grundlagen der Evangelischen Ethik* (Gütersloh, 1928), pp. 122ff., "Die Mächte." The book is preoccupied, however, with theodicy and with philosophical anthropology, locating the awareness of the rebellious-

equipped to perceive other points of relevance which this approach might have to occultism, psychodynamics, or the mass media. The creative translation of the Pauline mood into the language of today, however, need not be completed for us to be able to perceive that such a translation would be not only conceivable but natural.

With this observation we have found one more point at which the ethical relevance of the stance of Jesus breaks through in a segment of the apostolic literature with which for generations most Protestants did not know how to deal. The Powers have been defeated not by some kind of cosmic hocus-pocus but by the concreteness of the cross; the impact of the cross upon them is not the working of magical words nor the fulfillment of a legal contract calling for the shedding of innocent blood, but the sovereign presence, within the structures of creaturely orderliness, of Jesus the kingly claimant and of the church which is itself a structure and a power in society. Thus the historicity of Jesus retains, in the working of the church as it encounters the other power and value structures of its history, the same kind of relevance that the man Jesus had for those whom he served until they killed him.

EPILOGUE

Few themes in recent New Testament interpretation have "taken off" in the popular theological culture as has the vision of the rebellious

---

ness of the powers in "believing contrition" rather than in history itself. It does not attempt to unfold in any detail the actual inner structure of the thinking of Paul about the powers, nor to sketch contemporary relevance. In Piper's later writing, *God in History* (New York: Macmillan, 1939), there is a continuing accent upon the reality of a satanic power, but the same is not done with the wider realm of distinct rebellious created powers. Without being so labeled, the "principalities and powers" thought pattern is present in Piper's *Christian Meaning of Money* (Englewood Cliffs, N.J.: Prentice-Hall, 1965); it is not explicit in his *Biblical View of Sex and Marriage* (New York: Scribner, 1960). Cf. the more popular treatments above, n. 5. John Swomley in his *Liberation Ethics* (New York: Macmillan, 1972), esp. chs. 3 and 10, interprets "principalities and powers" as oppressive social structures.

powers. The kind of popularization represented in my original notes by the references (n. 6) to Albert van den Heuvel and William Stringfellow continued to grow in popularity since the 1970s. The vision of a dialectical interlocking of created goodness and rebelliousness, in what makes the world the way it is, has been found illuminating by many.

A simple example: in the major addresses presented at the 1980 Assembly of the Division of World Mission and Evangelism of the World Council of Churches, gathered at Melbourne, allusions to "the principalities and powers" were in every major address.[21] Hendrikus Berkhof updated his booklet (n. 5 above).[22]

The most thorough review of the theme is the trilogy by Walter Wink.[23] Anthony Tyrell Hanson devoted to it an insightful chapter.[24] Jacques Ellul, the prolific French Reformed sociologist and lay theologian, made the dialectic of creatureliness and rebellion the key to his entire *oeuvre* of critical social thought.[25] It would not be too much to claim that the Pauline[26] cosmology of the powers represents an alternative to the dominant ("Thomist") vision of "natural law" as a more biblical way systematically to relate Christ and creation.

But for our purposes it suffices to observe that exegetical scholar-

21. Jacques Matthey (ed.), *Your Kingdom Come: Mission Perspectives* (Geneva: World Council of Churches, 1980), pp. 4, 36, 67, 177, 209ff.

22. Rev. ed. (Scottdale, Pa.: Herald, 1977).

23. *Naming the Powers: The Language of Power in the New Testament* (Philadelphia: Fortress, 1984); *Unmasking the Powers* (Philadelphia: Fortress, 1986); *Engaging the Powers* (Minneapolis: Fortress, 1992).

24. "Militia Christi"; ch. 6, pp. 99-128, in *The Paradox of the Cross . . .* (see n. 38, p. 131 above).

25. Because of his desire to keep his social critical thought from being set aside by social scientists as confessionally biased, Ellul made little of this connection in most of the writings which made him famous. Its foundational place in his thought has been laid bare with great thoroughness, exploiting some of his (as yet untranslated) earliest writings, by Marva J. Sandberg Dawn in her Ph.D. dissertation *The Concept of the "Principalities and Powers" in the Work of Jacques Ellul,* approved by the Department of Theology, University of Notre Dame, 1992.

26. There is no more reason now than there was twenty years ago, for our purposes, to make much of the difference between the original authentic apostle Paul and the further developments of his thought by his disciples in Ephesians and Colossians; the trajectory is one of organic development.

ship has continued to confirm that in the Pauline witness Jesus is confessed as foundationally relevant to the political realm — not only in the biographical sense which we saw at work above in chapters 2 and 3 of this book, but in the cosmological sense that "cross and resurrection" designates not only a few days' events in first-century Jerusalem but also the shape of the cosmos.

This is not to say that there is any *detailed* consensus among scholars on the simplest levels, as to the sense in which the powers are "real."[27] Are they a metaphor for constructs in the human mind? Are they "real super-human spiritual entities" something like angels?[28] Walter Wink tries a new answer of his own to this question;[29] Jacques Ellul seems to have shifted his answer recently from something more realistic to something more metaphorical.[30] None of these debates about nuance would seem to undermine the thesis that this set of passages from the Pauline corpus demonstrates an astoundingly sweeping and coherent "translation" of the political meaning of Jesus into the worldview of the audience of Paul's missionary witness.

I doubt that our concern to interpret the witness of the apostolic

27. Dawn (*Concept of the "Principalities and Powers,"* 36ff.) itemizes at length the several items in the exegetical debate and the variety of dominant answers currently being offered.

28. The Anglican evangelical Bible teacher John Stott best represents the thesis that what Paul is really talking about is "personal, demonic intelligences" (most fully in *God's New Society* [Downers Grove: InterVarsity Press, 1979], pp. 263-75). Yet Stott, for whose gracious readiness to converse on the theme by letter I am most grateful, does not support with any documentation his taken-for-granted claim that there has in fact been a serious deposit of scholarly evangelical exegesis spelling out how that claim is to be taken. The student of the ancient world is less clear than is the person in the pew about what would have to be meant by "intelligences" or by "personal" (or even by "real"). What underlies Stott's critique of Berkhof, Rupp, et al. would seem to me to be a set of unquestioning assumptions about the worldview behind these texts, a worldview which persists uncritically in our popular culture, so that Stott can assume a greater univocality in the evangelical tradition than any scholar has in fact spelled out.

29. Beginning pp. 104ff. in his first volume, Wink projects his own ontology of "inner" and "outer" realities, which he believes can do justice both to ancients texts and to our world.

30. Cf. again Dawn, *Concept of the "Principalities and Powers,"* pp. 337ff., 348ff. The shift is a matter of nuance, in how seriously to take metaphors like "personality" and "existence" behind the functional descriptions.

Scriptures *in their setting* is much served by our importing this kind of modern question into the interpretation of first-century literature, however much we as moderns are driven to ask them. Whether Jesus' work and witness were and are politically relevant for the witnesses of the first generations does not depend on our answering our contemporary question, "In what sense are the powers real? In what sense are they 'persons'?" The growing bulk of serious social thought using these concepts, referred to at the beginning of this epilogue, should be sufficient demonstration that the Pauline vision is realistic and illuminating.

If it could be our task here to enter modern conversations about social ethics, the point to make would be that this Pauline vision is far more nuanced and helpful than much contemporary discussion about "the problem of power" in Christian social ethics. For many who use that phrase it designates little more than a sense of guilt about "realistically" having to "take responsibility" for harming some persons in the interest of desirable social ends. The Pauline perspective is far more clear about the intrinsic complexities of institutional and psychodynamic structures, such that basically good creaturely structures can nonetheless be oppressive, and basically selfish decisions can sometimes nonetheless have less evil outcomes. Neither guilt about losing personal purity, nor pragmatism about doing lesser evils to achieve greater goods, is then at the heart of "the problem of power" for "Paul," as they are for our contemporaries.[31] The challenge to which the proclamation of Christ's rule over the rebellious world speaks a word of grace is not a problem within the self but a split within the cosmos.

31. A representative specimen of an inappropriate concentration on the problem of guilt is Leslie Griffin, "The Problem of Dirty Hands," *Journal of Religious Ethics* 17/1 (Spring 1989), 31-61. Part of the misunderstanding is its describing as "moral purity" my reading of the New Testament ethic.

CHAPTER 9

Revolutionary Subordination

I began this book by taking issue with the recent scholarly consensus about the relevance of Jesus, according to which he took such a short view of the existence of society that he taught no relevant social ethic. I sought to provide an alternative to the reading of the Gospels which that consensus both assumes and reinforces. Yet the argument is not concluded with a new reading of the Gospels. Another major segment of the case for a low view of Jesus' relevance argues from a particular view of the ethical teaching that actually arose in the early church. Since Jesus did not provide a social ethic relevant to the continuing life of human communities, it is claimed, the early church found itself obliged to borrow one from somewhere else.

A key aspect of this claim as it relates to the ethic of the early church is symbolized by that particular type of ethical instruction which scholars have come to refer to as the *Haustafeln.*[1] The New Testament has numerous traces of a particular type of ethical teaching, most purely represented by Colossians (3:18–4:1):

> Wives, be subject to your husbands,
> as is fitting in the Lord.

1. The German term *Haustafeln,* literally "house tables" or "household tablets," has usually been rendered "household precepts." The term "tables" is cognate to the English usage which refers to the "two tables" of the Decalogue, i.e., a listing of rules. "Household precepts" is not an accurate rendering since it points to a plurality of individual rules, whereas *Tafel* identifies the format of a *series* of stated rules standing in some parallel relationship to each other. The present study does not seek to establish a new standard usage, but will use sometimes the German term and sometimes the various English paraphrases.

Husbands, love your wives.
Children, obey your parents in everything, for this pleases the Lord.
Fathers, do not provoke your children, lest they become discouraged.
Slaves, obey in everything those who are your earthly masters, . . . fearing the Lord.
Masters, treat your slaves justly and fairly, knowing that you also have a master in heaven.

A similar line of instruction is found in Ephesians (5:21–6:9):

Be subject to one another out of reverence for Christ.
Wives, be subject to your husbands, as to the Lord.
Husbands, love your wives, as Christ loved the church and gave himself up for her. . . .
Children, obey your parents in the Lord, for this is right. . . .
Fathers, do not provoke your children to anger, but bring them up in the discipline and instruction of the Lord.
Slaves, be obedient to those who are your earthly masters, as to Christ. . . .
Masters, do the same to them, . . . knowing that he was both their Master and yours.

Very similar again in thought content, but differing in detail, is the admonition of 1 Peter (2:13–3:7). Here the reference to children and parents is lacking but a reference to government is found instead:

Be subject for the Lord's sake to every human institution, . . .
For it is God's will that by doing right you should silence the foolish. . . .
Servants, be submissive to your masters in all respect. . . .
Likewise you husbands, live considerately with your wives, bestowing honor on the woman as the weaker sex.

Any effort to reconstruct imaginatively the life of the churches from which these texts arose will surmise that when we find thoughts and even expressions this nearly parallel in quite distinct literary contexts, the only sensible hypothesis is that there must have been some patternedness in the moral teaching of the earliest churches.[2] At least since Martin Luther these outlines have come to be discerned by scholars as representing a particular literary form.[3] Whether the practical focus of the use of these phrases was in a catechism or a baptism liturgy,[4] the parallelism in content and in logic fully supports the surmise that there was a regular way of thinking about these questions in the early church.

If we have once established the probable existence of a recurrent pattern of thought and instruction, what does this then mean for the question with which we began? Here we well begin with the classic statement of the widely accepted thesis by Martin Dibelius, father of the form-critical analytical method.

> These collections of proverbs intend to define the duties of the several groups [i.e., categories of persons] in the household. Their existence in the early Christian writings testifies to the need of the young Christian movement to establish itself within ordinary daily life. This need is not self-evident; for that [particular kind of] Christianity which burst into the world and especially into the Hellenistic world (I Thess. 1:9f) could apparently do without any basic attitude to the cultural communities of Family and Fatherland, as toward Culture itself. (Cf. Paul's personal attitude to marriage, I Cor. 7:29ff.) Thus Christianity was unprepared for meeting these needs, or to say the

2. This essay borrows heavily, with permission, from the unpublished dissertation of David Schroeder, *Die Haustafeln des Neuen Testaments, Ihre Herkunft und ihr theologischer Sinn,* accepted by the Evangelical Theological Faculty of the University of Hamburg in 1959, and from a series of lectures *New Testament Ethics* (unfortunately also unpublished) derived from the dissertation. Schroeder makes clear on critical grounds that no literary dependence of these texts upon each other can be demonstrated or assumed; the parallelism is explainable only by assuming that there was in the pre-literary life of the earliest churches a far-reaching commonality in the use of this pattern of moral instruction. Schroeder's writings will henceforth be referred to as *Die Haustafeln and Ethics.*

3. Luther may be the creator, and at least was a major popularizer of the label *Haustafeln.*

4. After reviewing the various scholarly conjectures as to the place of the *Haustafeln* in early church life, Schroeder (*Ethics,* ch. 3) concludes that they must have arisen within the ethical preaching/teaching life of the congregations rather than from a particular liturgical setting.

least, could not adequately deal with them in terms of the gospel of Jesus. Resort to the moral instructions which Hellenistic and Jewish propaganda had developed was inevitable. . . . Thus early Christianity began, by a very gradual process, to come to grips with the World. The *Haustafeln* are especially fitting specimens of this process. They do show that Christian paraenese preserved for the common ethic of the West both the moral family principles of Greek popular philosophy and those of Jewish halakah.[5]

We have here again, in classic form, the statement that the ethic derived from the meaning of Jesus was inadequate or irrelevant to meet the practical needs of the church as it went on living in society while the kingdom did not arrive, so that the stuff of moral discrimination and discernment had to be borrowed elsewhere, wherever it could be found, namely from both Jewish and Gentile thinking. In the case of the *Haustafeln* it is from Stoicism that such borrowing must have come.[6]

The fact of this borrowing, if it be a fact, has three significant implications. One of them has to do with the relationship of revelation and nature, or of Jesus on one hand and reason on the other, as sources of ethical organization. If the early church could borrow from non-biblical sources of moral insight, then our accepting the appropriateness of such free borrowing (in any age), and the inadequacy (which this demonstrates) of the resources we have available if we do not resort to borrowing, will go a long way toward setting the ground rules for Christian ethical thought.

Second: not only does this demonstrate that borrowing ethical guidance from nonbiblical, non-Christian sources is necessary, possible,

5. *An die Kolosser, Epheser, und Philemon,* HzNT 12 (3rd ed. 1953), 48-49.

6. In the Dibelius text just quoted, the Jewish ethical tradition *(halakah)* and the Hellenistic *(stoa)* were mentioned as parallels. They were properly parallel in Dibelius's mind, in the sense that he could appeal to either to fill in the gap where the overheated eschatology of Jesus had failed to provide an ethic. They may also have been somewhat parallel in content, since any ethical teaching that reckons with social continuities must say some of the same things. They were not parallel, however, in their literary and logical form. Schroeder makes clear (*Die Haustafeln,* pp. 29ff.) that the Jewish tradition provides no immediate literary models for the *Haustafeln;* it is too clearly bound to specific commands of God, their application and interpretation, to be guided by lists of given social structures. I thus appropriately will restrict my continuing discussion for now to the Stoic side of the alleged borrowing.

and legitimate; it also suggests what kind of insight we will find there. In seeing ethical obligations as defined by the *status* of persons (wives and husbands, children and parents, slaves and masters . . .), the *Haustafeln* are saying in effect that it is possible to ascertain one's duties by finding out who one is, that is, by asking what is one's *role.* At this point, as did Dibelius, many others have pointed out that the Stoics offered a very similar kind of instruction:

> He [the philosopher] should bring his own will into harmony with what happens, so that neither anything that happens happens against our will, nor anything that fails to happen fails to happen when we wish it to happen. . . . The result of this . . . [is] that each person passes his life to himself, free from pain, fear, and perturbation, at the same time maintaining with his associates both the natural and the acquired relationships, those namely of son, father, brother, citizen, wife, neighbor, fellow traveller, ruler, and subject.[7]
>
> The second field of study deals with duty; for I ought not to be unfeeling like a statue, but should maintain my relations, both natural and acquired, as a religious man, as a son, a brother, a father, a citizen.[8]
>
> See whether they [those who get ahead of you] observe what becomes them as men, as sons, as parents, and then, in order, through all the other terms for the social relations.[9]

The third lesson that would follow is that by moving from the radicality of the ethic of Jesus to the guidance the early church found in the structures of society in their givenness, the early church took on a position that was essentially conservative. It chose not to challenge the subjugation of woman or the institution of slavery.[10] Thereby it

7. *The Discourses of Epictetus as Reported by Arrian,* trans. W. A. Oldfather, Loeb Classical Library, CIV, 308-9.

8. *Ibid.,* CV, 23.

9. *Ibid.,* CV, 355. Similar listings can be found in Marcus Antonius, Plutarch, Diogenes Laertius, Cicero, Horace, and others; Schroeder, *Die Haustafeln,* pp. 32ff.

10. A full statement of the traditional interpretation of Paul's failure to challenge the institution of slavery is: P. R. Coleman-Norton, "The Apostle Paul and the Roman Law of Slavery," in his anthology *Studies in Roman Economic and Social History* (Princeton University Press, 1951), pp. 155ff. Coleman-Norton gathers a wealth of background material for the interpretation of slavery as an institution and the treatment of runaway

prepared itself gradually to become the religion of the established classes, a development that culminated in the age of Constantine three centuries later.

This development can be evaluated either positively or negatively. Martin Dibelius considered it a kind of progress that the early church moved away from the timeless radicality of Jesus and began coming to grips with "the world" — by which he meant what Martin Luther earlier had called the "orders of creation."

One strand of social ethical thought ever since the Reformation has accordingly taken the borrowings of Paul from Stoicism as representing a precedent or a mandate for the continued legitimacy in Christian ethics of insights drawn from "the nature of things" as any philosopher can see them.[11] More recently, especially within the context of "progressive" Protestantism, the evaluation has often turned the other way; the apostles, and Paul in particular, can be rapidly and vigorously condemned for having had such a low view of women or for having failed to attack the institution of slavery head-on as we now know he should have.

The same kind of negative judgment can also be reached in another way: it can be claimed from the perspective of the radical Protestant "theology of the word of God" that in borrowings like this we see the beginning of a relapse into "natural theology." Such an evaluation would support a critical conviction that these texts are not genuinely representative of the theology of the apostle Paul, and were probably written by some of his later disciples who no longer had his

---

slaves. He wrongly suggests that the *Haustafeln* type of teaching appears only once in the New Testament (p. 164). By failing to ask in any historically relevant way what it would have meant for Paul to challenge the institution of slavery, he keeps himself from observing the extent to which both the *Haustafeln* and the Epistle to Philemon do provide an alternative to the contemporary way slavery functioned as an institution. Cf. below, n. 37.

11. Probably the most perceptive interpretation of the *Haustafeln* in the framework of these assumptions is that of Heinz-Dietrich Wendland, "Zur Sozialethischen Bedeutung der Neutestamentlichen Haustafeln," in Otto Michel and Ulrich Mann (eds.), *Die Leibhaftigkeit des Wortes: Festgabe Adolf Köberle* (Hamburg: Furche Verlag, 1958), pp. 34ff. Through careful analysis Wendland comes to many insights parallel to those argued for later in this present text; but he does not question the basic axiom of borrowing and "Christianizing" pagan principles; this thought structure of course is very much at home in his Lutheran understanding of law and gospel and the Ethic of the Orders.

deep grasp of the meaning of revelation as an alternative to human wisdom.

These lines of argument, despite their differing conclusions, begin by agreeing in their reading of what actually happened in the early church, and therefore in their understanding of the way we must approach the problems. For both views there is in the midst of the canon a chasm separating the ethic of Jesus from that of the apostolic church, of such a nature that one must choose between the two. The reason for the church's leaping over the chasm was the lack of any adequate moral equipment on Jesus' side of the gap.

Second Thoughts

The assumption of the Stoic origin of the *Haustafeln* was accepted so rapidly and sweepingly by scholars that serious doubts have only recently come to the surface. More careful reading now sees more clearly to what extent the polarity of Jesus and Paul was imposed on New Testament criticism in the last century by the Hegelian philosophical assumptions of F. C. Baur, rather than rising necessarily out of the text.[12] The material is after all not wholly in the Pauline writings, but in 1 Peter as well, an indication that no one apostle dictated this way of teaching.[13] Nowhere in the texts is there any literary basis for the claim that the moral exhortations to wives and husbands, children and parents, slaves and masters, calling them to behave fittingly toward one another, are derived as a kind of makeshift substitute from the failure

12. The landmark study which most pointedly called into question the axiom of the chasm in the canon was Edwyn Hoskyns and Noel Davey, *The Riddle of the New Testament* (London: Faber & Faber, 1947, 3rd ed. 1957).

13. For some scholars, like Hans Lietzmann in his *Beginnings of the Christian Church* (New York: Scribner, 1937), the Petrine Epistles represent "early Catholicism," i.e., a degeneration subsequent to the early, more correct insights of the Pauline gospel. For others, like Vincent Taylor in his *The Atonement in New Testament Teaching* (London: Epworth, 1940), the level of development in the thought of the church which is represented by 1 Peter is — whatever the date of actual writing — more "primitive" or less "evolved." In either case it would be hard to explain the parallel appearance of the *Haustafeln* in both Pauline and Petrine writings as proof of a radical shift in ethical thought in the midst of the New Testament canon.

of the kingdom to come. Quite other reasons are given in these texts, as we shall observe shortly, for the behavior the *Haustafeln* call for.

Thus already on the level of careful logic and skeptical reading of sources we must begin to doubt Dibelius's view. But more serious doubts — and perhaps more helpful learnings — come to the surface if we actually look more closely and respectfully at the instructions in question. We shall discover that although in the widest sense the *Haustafeln* are vaguely like Stoicism, in that they call upon a person to fulfill the meaning of his or her special role, there are other very significant differences which forbid any simple explanation such as that of direct borrowing from an extant Stoic source.

(a) The call of Stoic morality is to live up to *my own nature.* This nature or role or function, of course, has a social side; it relates me to other persons. But the fulfillment of the authenticity of my living my role is seen by Stoic thought as centered in my person. In the *Haustafeln,* on the other hand, it is the relationship itself that we are called upon to live up to. This is evident in the literary form. Whereas for the Stoic the roles of father, friend, sibling, slave are listed one by one, in the *Haustafeln* the listing occurs in *pairs:* both the wife and the husband are spoken to; both the slave and the master. Not only does this reciprocity of relationship show in the literary structure of the listing; it is also a part of the imperative. The call to be "subject" or to "love" or to "respect" always uses a verb which relates this person not to herself or himself, or to one's image of oneself, or to one's nature or role, but to the other member of that pair.

(b) Stoic thinking uses all of these nouns in the singular, and discerns in one person as many different roles as possible. Amid the multiplicity of all these roles, it is the freedom and self-determination of the individual that shows through. It is the man himself, in a given decision, who will determine which definition of his role is to apply. Only male roles occur. There are so many such roles, and they are combined in such varied ways, that the listing of roles amounts to a relativizing of all ethical bindingness.

The *Haustafeln,* on the other hand, speak in plural terms. The admonitions are addressed to all wives or all servants or all parents in the churches receiving these epistles. There are also a limited number of such relationships to which the *Haustafeln* always speak. Thus there is in the ethical admonition of the *Haustafeln* the possibility of community discipline, of common insight and standards, around which it is possible for a whole group of persons, and not simply a meditative elite, to develop a shared moral commitment.

(c) The Stoic pattern of reasoning seeks simply to unfold or to get *insight into what is.* Its tool is reason and the basis of moral obligation is "the nature of things."[14] If a person can see what the nature of things truly is, it is assumed that he or she will act accordingly. The Stoic discourse is not in the imperative mood. In the *Haustafeln,* on the other hand, the grammatical form is uniformly imperative.

In its form, the *Haustafeln* ethic is patterned most closely on the style of the so-called "apodictic law" of the Old Testament. This is not only the case where in Ephesians 6:2 there is explicit reference to Exodus 19:25; but the imperative style is generally parallel to the construction of the ethical appeals of the Old Testament.[15] The borrowing — by the testimony of syntactic style — is not from Hellenistic Judaism (although the substance would not be greatly different therefrom) but from the prophetic imperatives recorded in the Old Testament as received from the mouth of God himself. This view is further demonstrated by the grammatical peculiarity of the imperative participle.[16]

(d) Still further demonstration of the difference between Stoic and apostolic thought shows in the vocabulary itself. Even where almost

14. Eduard Schweizer, "Die Weltlichkeit des Neuen Testamentes: die Haustafeln," in Herbert Donner, Robert Hanhart, and Rudolf Smend (eds.), *Beiträge zur Alttestamentlichen Theologie: Festschrift für Walther Zimmerli* (Göttingen: Vandenhoeck, 1977), p. 402, adds that in Stoicism the cosmic order "as it is" is identical at the same time with divinity and with one's own well-being; nothing of such a cosmic unity is present in the *Haustafeln.* Schweizer's exposition of how the *Haustafeln* transformed the substance they borrowed is substantially like my own, though far more expert. Schweizer reviews that same theme in "Traditional Ethical Patterns in the Pauline and Post-Pauline Letters and Their Development," in Ernest Best (ed.), *Text and Interpretation* (Cambridge University Press, 1979), pp. 195-209.

15. Deut. 16:21-22; 17:1; 22:5; 23:7-8; Lev. 17:10; Amos 5:4; Prov. 3:1-2 (Schroeder, *Die Haustafeln,* pp. 92ff.).

16. In addition to the *Haustafeln* of 1 Peter, this same imperative use of the participle is found in Rom. 12:9ff. Its origins are not Greek but rabbinic: Schroeder, *Ethics,* II, 11; David Daube, *The New Testament and Rabbinic Judaism* (London: University of London, 1956), pp. 90ff.; and W. D. Davies, *Paul and Rabbinic Judaism* (London: S.P.C.K., 2nd ed. 1955), pp. 329-30.

the same point is being made, the most usual terms are not the same. For the concept of obedience the New Testament uses *hypakouein* where the Stoics would use *peithesthai;* for the relation of servant and master the New Testament uses *doulos* and *kyrios* whereas the Stoics used *oiketai* and *despotai.* For love the New Testament uses *agapan* and the Stoics *philein.*[17] If the apostles had been borrowing directly from Stoic usage and counting on the terms they used to be already familiar to their readers, one would have expected a greater correlation in the actual words used.

(e) Stoicism addresses *man in his dignity* and calls upon him to live up to the highest vision of himself.[18] This call is addressed to the dominant man in society, especially to the prince or freedman or father, to the person who had time and leisure and capacity to meditate on his nature and its fulfillment.[19] Self-control and a measure of dominion over others is itself a virtuous posture. The free man should avoid coming into bondage to a woman or to his subordinates.

This concentration upon the dignity of the addressee is missing in the New Testament. The admonition of the *Haustafeln* is addressed *first to the subject:* to the slave before the master, to the children before the parents, to the wives before the husbands.[20]

Here begins the revolutionary innovation in the early Christian style of ethical thinking for which there is no explanation in borrowing from other contemporary cultural sources. The *subordinate* person in the social order is *addressed as a moral agent.*[21] She is called upon to

17. Schroeder, *Die Haustafeln,* p. 124. Schroeder adduces other linguistic and literary grounds as well for denying any direct verbal borrowing from Stoic sources (pp. 86ff.).

18. This is one point where, dealing with historic Stoicism, it would be inappropriate to make the language gender-inclusive.

19. More accurately: it is only the philosopher who can be taught to understand himself in these roles. There is no concept of an ethical vision accessible to a community or to those who have no claim on the philosopher's help.

20. The priority of the address to the subordinate party of the pair is further reinforced by Schroeder's hypothesis (*Die Haustafeln,* p. 89; *Ethics,* III) concerning the pre-literary history of these admonitions. On the grounds that they are more uniform in written traditions, he argues that they must also have become routinized in the preaching of the early churches at an earlier date.

21. Schweizer, *Beiträge zur Alttestamentlichen Theologie,* p. 405, notes that in Stoicism

take responsibility for the acceptance of her position in society as meaningful before God. It is not assumed, as it was in both Jewish and Hellenistic thought, that the wife will have the faith of her husband, or that the slave will be part of the religious unity of the master's household. Here we have a faith that assigns *personal moral responsibility to those who had no legal or moral status* in their culture, and makes of them decision makers. It gives them responsibility for viewing their status in society not as a simple meaningless decree of fate but as their own meaningful witness and ministry, as an issue about which they can make a moral choice.

(f) Not only does Stoicism address itself to the dominant or noble man and the high or noble element within man; its vision of what man truly is and should become is concentrated upon his *dignity and detachment;* his being free from bondage and obligation.[22] Subordination may apply in his relationship to God or to the state but not among men.[23] In the *Haustafeln,* on the other hand, the center of the imperative is a call to willing subordination to one's partner. The term *hypotassesthai* is not best rendered by *subjection,* which carries a connotation of being thrown down and run over, nor by *submission,* with its connotation of passivity. Sub*ord*ination means the acceptance of an *order,* as it exists, but with the new meaning given to it by the fact that one's acceptance of it is willing and meaningfully motivated.

Why did this need to be said? Why was there any point, in that ancient time, in directing an imperative to children and women to subordinate themselves? Was this not taken for granted? Was there any other choice in that society? Here we find the second revolutionary

---

the slave would not be thought about as an ethically accountable person. Thus the first "liberating" dimension of this material is the fact that the addressees, underdogs in the culture, have been convinced by the gospel of their dignity, to the point that it is relevant to urge them to be patient.

22. It is noteworthy that although Epictetus was a slave, he does not list "slave" as one of the roles to live up to.

23. The root meaning of the very *hypotassein* is "to set in line under"; in the middle voice it then means "to accept one's lower place." The verb is used 31 times in the Greek version of the Old Testament, where it renders ten different Hebrew terms — enough to indicate that there was not one such clearly focused concept in Hebrew usage. In this Old Testament usage subordination is normal in relation to God or to the king, but not generally to other men.

axiom underlying our texts. It is not enough, if we want to understand a text, that we seek the meaning of an answer it gives to the question it deals with. If we are truly to understand any answer, we must also understand the meaning of the question to which it is addressed. For the apostles to encourage slaves and women to be subordinate, there must have been some specific reason for them to have been tempted to behave otherwise. What could that have been? There must have been something in the experience of their becoming Christians, or in their education as new members of the Christian community, or in their experience in the life of that group, which had given to these subjects a vision or a breath of a new kind of dignity and responsibility. This must already have occurred if they were tempted to rise above their station. Only if something in the life or the preaching of the church had given them the idea that their subordinate status had been challenged or changed would there be any temptation to the kind of unruliness to which these texts are addressed.

A widespread tradition, present ever since the age of Lincoln but propagated still more sweepingly with the currency of civil rights and women's liberation rhetoric, sees in Paul's teaching about subordination one of the causes for Christianity's failure to seek social justice more aggressively, or more successfully.

Our present study does not focus upon the history of Christianity as a force for social justice,[24] but a parenthetical detour may be justified for the light it throws on how easily Paul is misunderstood. Those whose Christian commitment does not permit them simply to mock or ignore the apostle feel they can "excuse" or "understand" his subordination teaching (which, not understanding its fundamentally revolutionary character, they do not intend to accept) on the ground that he had not yet "matured" or "advanced" to the "higher"[25] insights

24. Ever since Ernst Troeltsch, it has been commonplace to see that *indirectly* a minority Christian movement with a nonconforming ethic can have considerable social impact.

25. An example of this condescending approach is the (in other respects quite helpful) study of Krister Stendahl, *The Bible and the Role of Women* (Philadelphia: Fortress, 1966). In order to overcome the uncritical woodenness of certain traditional interpretations, Stendahl plays off the Paul he agrees with against the one he disagrees with in the way just suggested, thereby cutting off the possibility that any new light might be received by hearing

expressed in Galatians 3:28, namely the modern-sounding egalitarianism which denies all differences between "Jew and Greek, slave and free, male and female."[26]

Paul still gets the credit for finally reaching that height, which we can recognize as a height by its modern sound; and thus we can credit the New Testament with a personalistic view which by implication was to undermine slavery and subordination; but in order to be thus indulgent with the apostle we must forgive his retention of the vestiges of the subordination idea and (for our purposes) cut them out of the canon.

Careful discussion of this kind of supercilious approach to Scripture would have to deal both with the general issue of scriptural interpretation[27] and with the character of the implicitly egalitarian personal-

---

the apostolic witness at those points where it says something that does not reinforce what we already believe. Stendahl mocks the naive exegesis that would try to "play first-century Semite" or "out-do the Amish," but does not (in this text) clarify the ground rules of another approach which would better enable Scripture to play a needed role in the life of the churches. There would seem to be other ways to make room for the ministries of women in the Church of Sweden without simply excising those elements of Scripture which seem out of step with contemporary convictions. What if, e.g., the sweeping, doctrinaire egalitarianism of our culture, which makes the concept of "the place of [anyone]" seem either laughable or boorish, and makes that of "subordination" seem insulting, should turn out really (in "the intent of God," or in long-run social experience) to be demonic, uncharitable, destructive of personality, disrespectful of creation, or unworkable? Must we still assume that in order properly to "play twentieth-century occidentals" we must let this modern myth keep us from hearing what the apostle says about the christological basis of mutual subordination? (cf. below p. 191).

26. It should be noted that the point of Gal. 3:28 is not *sameness,* in the sense of overruling all variety of roles and rights, but unity. The reference to "slave and free, man and woman" simply reinforces the "Jew and Greek" concern which is the topic of the whole book. Jew remains Jew, Greek Greek in this unity. Equality of *worth* is not identity of *role.* To make of Gal. 3:28 a "modern" statement on women's liberation, from which one can then look down on the rest of Paul's thought, not only misplaces this text logically (as is said in the text above); it also misreads the text itself.

27. Such modern judges of New Testament ethics generally do not bother to suggest what Paul in his situation should have done differently. What should an Emancipation Proclamation have looked like then? Did Lincoln's way really work? Nor do they generally note that the "established" forms of "Christendom" which legitimized slavery were not obeying the ethics of either Jesus or Paul as we find them in this study. Nor do they generally bother to test whether some other available option (Islam?) would have had over the centuries a more liberating effect. How can there be any corrective or challenge to our self-sufficiency, any continuity in the Christian community — to say nothing of any

ism which it approvingly finds in Galatians 3:28.[28] Here, however, it must suffice to stay by the context of our texts. The call to willing subordination is not explainable unless there has been a temptation to insubordination. Such a temptation to insubordination is not thinkable unless some kind of message affirming the dignity of the subordinate one had already been heard. Then the call to subordination must, in any thinkable reconstruction of the social context of Paul's message, result from — not deny or fall short of — some kind of proclamation of the dignity of every man and woman.

Thus whereas Stoicism speaks to the man who is already respectable, and encourages him to live up to the dignity he already sees in his role, the *Haustafeln* admonition is addressed first to persons on the bottom side of the social order,[29] and assumes that they have heard a message which calls into question the subjection they have hitherto not been able to challenge.[30] Where had they heard such a message if not from Paul?[31]

---

judging and redeeming Word of God — if the present insight of the bearer is to be sovereign judge of any communication one will accept?

28. The egocentric modernity of the contemporary reader distorts the texts one likes as well as the ones one doesn't (cf. above, n. 26). Not only the text of Gal. 3:28 but also its nearly literal parallel Col. 3:11 affirms not the equality of isolated individuality but the complementary unity of diverse people in one body (see below, "justification" and "new creation," pp. 215, 228).

29. This observation is underlined by William Lillie, "The Pauline House-tables," in *The Expository Times,* 86 (1974-75), 179ff.: "The New Testament generally uses the humble rather than the dominating parties . . . as figurative descriptions of true Christian believers."

30. This point is accented by Schweizer, *Beiträge,* pp. 405-6. The idea that Paul had "retained a vestige" of subordinationist thought is false also at the point of its assumption that the duty of subordination ever was being taught. Slaves and women were kept subject by superior power and by the absence of alternatives, not by moral teaching. We have already observed that moral teaching was not addressed to subordinate people. Paul did not "borrow" or "fail to overcome" his subordinationist thought. He (or the church before him) created it by the application to a universal human problem of the central theme of Christology: that Jesus' suffering is the law of his disciples' life.

31. We noted that Gal. 3:28 and Col. 3:11 are almost literal parallels, even though the points being argued in the two contexts are quite different. This gives some room for the hypothesis that in each case the writer was quoting an earlier dictum or slogan already known to his readers. If so, this would indicate that the "new-humanity" or "new-creature" or "new-person" imagery, including its illustration by the denial of differences, Jew/Greek, slave/free, was pre-Pauline tradition.

How had they heard it if not in the form of the report that in Jesus' messianity a new age had begun in which men and women alike are freed for obedience by the resurrection of the Crucified?

(g) The only "sanction" or "motivation" undergirding the Stoic ethic is the self-evident appropriateness of giving in to the way things are and living up to what one is. There is no promise of reward, there is no moving in the heart, there is no pleading. Ethical meditation counts on the readiness of the upright man to do the right, once by insight and reason he knows what that is. (The maleness of the prototypical actor is the Stoic assumption.) He is presumed to be the kind of healthy person who without discussion or question does what is fitting.

In the *Haustafeln,* on the other hand, there are several reasons, not only one, which are given to interpret and to motivate. All of them are *substantial* arguments, that is, they not only say that the right is imperative but also explain why this kind of action is right. They are all related specifically to the person of Christ and the work of the church.[32] Sometimes the example of Jesus is specifically referred to. This allusion has maximum clarity in 1 Peter 2:18-23 with regard to the slave who should subordinate himself even to the unjust master, because of the example of Christ who did the same when unjustly accused, and in Ephesians 5:22-25 where the readiness of the husband to give himself for his wife is both motivated and given substance by Christ's giving himself for his church.[33]

At other points there is a wider reference to participation in the person and the character and the movement of Christ with such phrases as "as befits one in the Lord."[34]

In still other circumstances there is additional reference to the *testimony* which the Christian seeks to give to the non-Christian. The

32. Schweizer, *Beiträge,* p. 405, accents the diversity of the motivating references to the will and righteousness of "the Lord."

33. The concept of imitation of, conformity to, or participation in the servanthood of Christ is of course widespread in New Testament thought apart from the *Haustafeln.* Cf. above, pp. 112ff.

34. Eph. 5:21, "out of reverence for Christ"; Col. 3:18, "as is fitting in the Lord." Schroeder, *Die Haustafeln,* pp. 161-70, pursues extensively the meaning of the formula *in Christ* or *in the Lord* as it is used to sanction the believer's subordination. Far from being a pagan borrowing, this call is shown by this usage to be rooted in the very center of the Christian's confession and piety.

wife is motivated in her subordination partly by the concern to win to faith in Christ her unbelieving husband.[35] In addition the parallels to the *Haustafeln* in Timothy have considerable reference to the life of the church. Then there are also references to reward or to the results of one's obedience.[36]

Once more it becomes clear at this point that the ethic of the apostles cannot possibly be defined primarily by borrowings from either Jewish or Greek sources. Neither the general imperative to be subordinate nor the specific rooting of this call in the example of Christ, or in the nature of Christ as it is shared by the believer, can have any other explanations than that they arose within the original teaching of the apostles in the earliest common life of the Christian community.

(h) After having stated the call to subordination as addressed first to those who are subordinate already, the *Haustafeln* then go on to turn the relationship around and repeat the demand, calling the *dominant* partner in the relationship to a kind of subordination in turn. Parents are asked not to irritate their children, husbands are called upon to love *(agapan)* their wives. Philemon is invited to receive Onesimus "no longer as a slave, but more than a slave, as a beloved brother, both in the flesh and in the Lord," as he would receive Paul himself. Paul even offers to pay Philemon, if that is needed for him to treat Onesimus as his peer.

That the call to subordination is reciprocal is once again a revolutionary trait. If this acceptance of the existing social order and the call to those who are subordinate to remain there were all that was said, then it might be correct when Lutheran tradition sees in these texts a reaffirmation of the creation order, which has about it the authority of revelation because God has made society thus. That same tradition could then also be right in concluding that the Christian social ethic must always be basically conservative because of the rootage of the present order in the divine imperative. But the *Haustafeln* do not

35. 1 Pet. 2:12, 15; 3:1, "so that some may be won without a word by the behavior of their wives"; cf. 1 Cor. 7:16.

36. Eph. 6:3, "That it may be well with you" (from Deut. 5:16); 6:8, "whatever good we do, we will receive the same again from the Lord"; Col. 3:24, "knowing that from the Lord you will receive the inheritance"; 1 Pet 3:7, "in order that your prayers may not be hindered."

consecrate the existing order when they call for the acceptance of subordination by the subordinate person; far more they relativize and undercut this order by then immediately turning the imperative around. For a first-century husband to love *(agapan)* his wife or for a first-century father to avoid angering his child, or for a first-century master to deal with his servant in the awareness that they are both slaves to a higher master,[37] is to make a more concrete and more sweeping difference in the way that husband or father or master behaves than the other imperative of subordination would have made practically in the behavior of the wife or child or servant.

The biblical scholar would pause at this point to concentrate on the possible origins of this particular fragment of tradition. Where did Peter and Paul get this set of imperatives which they thus worked into their epistles? If the evidence seems to be against their having devised it by simple borrowing from either Hellenistic or Jewish sources,[38] and if the evidence seems to be against the likelihood that one of them borrowed it from the other, then one has hardly any other choice than to conclude that this kind of teaching was present in the very earliest years of the church. It must have grown directly out of the meaning

37. This study does not deal directly with the Epistle to Philemon, since the particular language of the *Haustafeln* does not appear there. The interpretation of that text would, however, only support the rest of the present study. Paul's convert Onesimus, as a part of the meaning of his conversion, voluntarily returns to his master. By leading Onesimus to take this step, Paul went beyond the prescriptions of Deut. 23:15-16. (Coleman-Norton, *Studies in Roman History,* pp. 172ff., after surveying considerable material, still is not able to say whether Paul was obeying any particular Roman legal obligation to return Onesimus.) Paul's instruction to Philemon is to receive Onesimus "no longer as a slave, but as a beloved brother, both in the flesh and in the Lord," as Paul himself would be received. This amounts to Paul's instructing Philemon, in the kind of noncoercive instruction which is fitting for a Christian brother (even with the offer of Paul's payment), that Onesimus is to be set free. American experience since 1865 has demonstrated that summary release from chattel slavery is not necessarily an improvement in the status of the slave if not accompanied with a new and honorable relationship to the former master and the prevalent social structure. Then this way of dealing with Onesimus, by instructing that he be treated as a brother and a guest, documents not the conservatism but the innovative character of Paul's ethic.

38. One most careful study of the relationship between New Testament thought and Stoicism is J. N. Sevenster's *Paul and Seneca* (Leiden: Brill, 1969). Without setting out to deal specifically with the *Haustafeln,* Sevenster (esp. pp. 167-218) finds differences between Paul and Seneca very similar to those we have been observing.

for the young church of confessing Christ as Lord and the impact that proclamation had upon its listeners. The only remaining source we very logically suspect is that somehow this tradition comes from Jesus.[39]

But although leaning most gratefully upon the work of the biblical critic, it is with a more systematic ethical concern that we have read these texts. We have now tested, at another quite distinct point in the New Testament literature, the systematic axiom of modern Protestant ethics, the contrast between the ethic of stable society in the late teachings of Paul and the ethic of the immediate kingdom in Jesus. Right where we had been told that the systematic split between two kinds of ethical thought is located and symbolized, in the reasoning with which the apostle Paul speaks to the relation of persons to each other within the most stable functions of society, the family and the economy, we find an ethic that is derived in its shape and in its meaning, and even in its language, from the novelty of the teaching and the work and the triumph of Jesus.

Widening the Circle

Now that we have become familiar with the central structure of ethical thought expressed in the *Haustafeln,* we are able to observe its presence elsewhere in the New Testament as well.[40] In his first letter to the

39. For interpretation of the significance of the chain of tradition reaching back to Jesus, to which the apostle Paul refers explicitly a few times, but indirectly still more often, compare Oscar Cullmann, "The Tradition," in *The Early Church* (Philadelphia: Westminster, 1956), pp. 59ff.; and Archibald M. Hunter, *Paul and His Predecessors* (Westminster, 1961).

40. A most penetrating statement of this wider logic is that of Johannes Hamel:

> The instruction, "Let everyone be subordinate . . ." has been so seriously misunderstood, and then abused, because of the failure to respect the complete context in which both the word *hypotassesthai* and the other similar invitations to obedience, honor, [or] humiliation are found. All of these words give expression to an essential mark of Christian relations to one's fellow man: in the congregation, in the family and in the city, for brethren, for non-Christians, and also (in political contexts) toward the bearers of power. The call to "be subordinate," to "obey," to "regard another as higher than oneself" is addressed to men with regard to their wives and vice versa, slaves toward their masters (and again vice versa, compare Philemon), children toward their parents (and the parents should honor their children by not

Christians at Corinth, Paul has occasion more than once to speak to specific ethical problem cases in the realm of the household, and we can observe the same thought patterns at work.

One of the ways in which the Christian women at Corinth had felt it would be appropriate to dramatize the new dignity given to them in Christ was the gesture of throwing off, in the course of the worship

---

irritating them), the young toward the old, and the elders toward the congregation which they lead.

If then one does not regard the imperative, "Be subordinate," in isolation, it immediately loses the bad taste which the word "subject" has taken on in German history and literature. *Hypotassesthai* then does not mean playing along at every price, not slavish obedience, not bowing before the throne and the altar. It is not the attitude of the loyal citizen in the time of national absolutism. It is rather founded, in accord with an ethical theme which runs clear through the New Testament, in the person and the way of the Lord, who is at the same time the norm and the realization of this self-abasement; cf. I Tim. 2:3-7; Titus 3:3-7; 2:11-14; I Pet. 2:21-25; 3:18; Eph. 5:25-27; 4:52–5:2; Phil. 2:5-11; Col. 2:18ff; 4:1; Eph. 6:1-9; I Cor. 7:20ff; 8:11f; Rom. 14:7ff; 15:3f; Gal. 5:24; 6:2, and many other texts.

The best-known example, the christological Psalm of Phil. 2:5ff, grounds the imperative to the church to "regard one another as higher than oneself" by pointing to the self-abasement of the Lord of our salvation. The concrete definition of the meaning of *hypotassesthai* comes from the crucified and risen Lord who, being free, abased himself for our sake and gave himself for us. Since we receive our life from this deed of this Lord, it is fitting that we subordinate ourselves to one another in a way that corresponds to this gift and this example. The form of love among us is defined by *that* love which was shown toward us by the Lord who served us and rescued us.

If on the other hand one understands *hypotassesthai* in isolation, then one has made of this root word for discipleship a formal and a passive obedience which takes from the "subject" his own arbitrariness. But the blame for this misunderstanding does not belong to the New Testament but to our unbelief, which has made out of the call to freedom and discipleship and the way of the cross an invitation to duck out of danger, to get out of the way, for the benefit of whatever group may be in power. . . .

If then *hypotassesthai* (and the other substantially synonymous terms) is in principle a posture "befitting" the gospel of the self-abasing Lord of the world, then it is in every situation a free, extremely aggressive way of acting, taking very clear account of the situation, including feeling and understanding and will, always including the possibility of a spirit-driven resistance, of an appropriate disavowal and a refusal, ready to accept suffering at this or that particular point.

Johannes Hamel, "Erwägungen zur urchristlichen Paraenese. . . ," in Ernst Wolf (ed.), *Christusbekenntnis im Atomzeitalter? ThEx,* 70 (1959), 159-61.

service, the veiling or the head covering which was standard accouterment for a woman appearing in public (cf. 1 Cor. 11:2ff.). This veiling was a sign of protection (Paul calls it a "power") when she went out of the home, in that it indicated that she belonged somewhere in society; that her father or her husband was her protector; but at the same time it was a symbol of subjection.

In reading this passage, as with the *Haustafeln,* some interpreters conclude that it is regrettable that Paul had not yet come to the vision of the equality of all kinds of persons in Christ. But if we are to understand the point of this passage we must assume that the women in Corinth *had* heard that message. Otherwise they would not be taking off their veils, especially not during the worship service. Thus the retention of the veil when a woman would rise to speak in the congregation (to "pray or prophesy") also became a symbol of that double movement: first of the enfranchising impact of the gospel upon women, in that she may rise to speak and can function religiously as far more than simply a member of the household of her father or husband, and second of her acceptance of the order of society within which her role is to be lived out.

Here again as in the *Haustafeln* there is a clear reminder that this relationship of subordination and superordination is not a difference in worth: "in the Lord woman is not independent of man nor man of woman; for as woman was made from man so man is now born of woman" (1 Cor. 11:11-12). To accept subordination within the framework of things as they are is not to grant the inferiority in moral or personal value of the subordinate party. In fact the opposite is true; the ability to call upon the subordinate party to *accept that subordination freely* is, as it was in the *Haustafeln,* a sign that this party has already been ascribed a worth that is fundamentally different from what any other society would have accorded.

In chapter 7 of the same letter, Paul speaks to the specific decisions faced by two categories of subordinate persons: the woman and the slave. His counsel is illustrative both of the *freedom* with which the gospel speaks to specific ethical cases and of the *consistency* within its freedom of application. His first element of counsel is to remain in the social status within which one is; "in whatever state each was called, there let him remain with God" (v. 24). This applied to the slave's remaining a slave, to the single person's remaining single, to the married woman's remaining with her unbelieving husband, to the forsaken married woman's remaining unmarried without her husband as long as he lives; to accepting one's status as circumcised or as not circumcised. The reasoning supporting this general admonition is not that to change in any of these ways would be sinful or wrong, in the sense of an infraction of the law of God. The concern of the apostle is rather to assist everyone to remain "free from anxieties" (v. 32), in a world whose structures are impermanent, and not so important that we should concentrate our efforts upon changing our status with regard to them. ("The appointed time has grown very short; from now on let those who have wives live as though they have none, those who mourn as though they were not mourning . . . for the form of this world is passing away" [vv. 29-31].)

Yet right alongside this concern for that freedom which is maintained by not being rebellious about one's status in the present, there runs a second strand of instruction which seems at first to be opposed to it. If a slave can become free, he should avail himself of this opportunity (v. 21).[41] If the husband of the forsaken woman dies she is free to remarry (v. 39); if anyone is strongly inclined toward marriage, that is quite proper (v. 36), but a freed man must not become a slave since that would be to move away from rather than toward freedom (vv. 22-23). Thus the Christian is called to view social status from the perspective of maximizing freedom. One who is given an opportunity to exercise more freedom should do so, because we are called to freedom in Christ. Yet that freedom can already become real within one's present status by voluntarily accepting subordination, in view of the relative unimportance of such social distinctions when seen in the light of the coming fulfillment of God's purposes.

The same attitude toward society occurs again when we move to

41. In order not to open too many arguments at once, we have here accepted the predominant understanding of v. 21: "Get free if you can." This meaning is, however, by no means clear. There are good grammatical arguments supporting the opposite reading: "Even if a choice of liberation should come, it is still better to make use of your servitude" (cf. Sevenster, *Paul and Seneca,* p. 189; Stendahl, *The Bible and the Role of Women,* p. 33). This reading would reinforce the main thrust of this chapter, yet without fully removing the permissiveness toward a change in status where it is imperative.

one still wider circle, the teaching of the New Testament with regard to the state. In 1 Peter 2, the *Haustafeln* text began: "subordinate yourself for the sake of the Lord to every human institution," and then spoke first to citizens, then to servants, then to wives. Again in 1 Timothy 2, which some scholars would consider as also belonging to the list of *Haustafeln,* there is a call first to subjection to government, then subordination of women, and then acceptance by Christians of the orderly office of the bishop and the deacon in the church. Without linkage to the *Haustafeln* texts, the call to subordination to government is clear again in Romans 13. Thus government is, like the order of the family, one of the given structures of human relations within which the Christian has a role to live out. This subordination is again motivated and sanctioned by its relationship to the mission of Christ.[42]

There is one striking difference, however, at this point. After the invitation to wives we saw that the *Haustafeln* addressed a similar and immensely more novel call to husbands to love their wives; after calling slaves to be subject, the early Christian moralists called upon the masters to be equally respectful; after calling children to remain subordinate to parents, the admonition was turned about and addressed to parents as well. When, however, the call to subordination is addressed to the Christian in his status as a political subject, in these texts the exhortation is not reversed. There is no invitation to the king to conceive of himself as a public servant. Was this only because, as a matter of course, the apostolic preachers and authors recognized that there were no kings in their audiences? Or was it that, in line with the teaching of Christ, which had been preserved in several forms, Jesus had instructed his disciples specifically to reject governmental domination over others as unworthy of the disciple's calling of servanthood?[43]

42. Rom. 12:1-2 sets the entire ethical passage in the context of "the mercies of God"; 12:4-8 explains its imperatives as living up to one's assigned role; 12:17-21 commands the renunciation of vengeance, which coordinates with the acceptance of the powers that be as avengers (15:4). Markus Barth, *Acquittal by Resurrection,* pp. 45ff., exposits fully how the submission of Rom. 15 is rooted in the work of Christ. "He [Paul] reasons not from an order of creation or toward an easy life, but from the humiliation and exaltation of Christ" (p. 46).

43. Mark 10:42-43; Matt. 20:25ff.; Luke 22:25ff.

In his landmark study of NT tradition criticism, *The Primitive Christian Catechism,*[44] Archbishop Philip Carrington places the *Haustafeln* in a wider context of tradition. He lifts out didactic texts[45] in which the same sequence of imperatives recurs:

(a) put off . . .
(b) be subject . . .
(c) watch . . .
(d) resist . . .

It would seem reasonable to conjecture that this parallelism in sequence (which is much fuller than just these four verbs) might point back to a commonality in the oral catechetical tradition of the earliest churches. It would then follow that such teaching was received by every new Christian and accepted as part of his baptismal commitment, a part of "having learned Christ" (Eph. 4:20; Col. 2:6). Carrington further surmises that the early churches, as they were dealing with the Gentile problem or with Gentiles' problems,[46] were concerned to find common instructional forms (verbal and social) reaching back to pre-Christian (i.e., Jewish) models. He does not point up the novelty whereby these common patterns were Christianized. Regarding the imperative of subordination, which for the NT writers is explicitly measured and motivated by the example of Christ, Carrington[47] retains its (Jewish?) foundation in the acceptance of "the godlike status of the elders and fathers." We can agree with Carrington in finding Jewish precedent for this instructional pattern, without following him in reducing the instructional content to the foundations present in the Jewish parallel.

44. Cambridge University Press, 1940.
45. Col. 3–4; Eph. 3–6; 1 Pet. 2:1–4:11; 1 Pet. 4:12ff.; James; Heb. 12–13.
46. *Ibid.,* pp. 68, 88ff.
47. Pp. 64, 68.

A Whole New Order[48]

As scattered as are the ethical instructions of the New Testament writers, as freely as they flex to fit the varied positions of the addressees, nonetheless one finds tying them together the link of a common clear logic. The liberation of the Christian from "the way things are," which has been brought about by the gospel of Christ, who freely took upon himself the bondages of history in our place, is so thorough and novel as to make evident to the believer that the givenness of our subjection to the enslaving or alienating powers of this world is broken. It is natural to feel Christ's liberation reaching into every kind of bondage, and to want to act in accordance with that radical shift.

But precisely because of Christ we shall not impose that shift violently upon the social order beyond the confines of the church. Following his example of accepting subordination (1 Pet. 2:18; Eph. 5:22) we shall not do this because the new world or the new regime under which we live is not a simple alternative to present experience but rather a renewed way of living within the present (1 Cor. 7:20; John 17:15-16). We may have reason to hope that the loving willingness of our subordination will itself have a missionary impact; "the unbelieving husband is consecrated through his wife, and the unbelieving wife is consecrated through her husband. . . . Wife, how do you know whether you will save your husband?"[49] The voluntary subjection of the church is understood as a witness to the world.

The pattern is thus uniformly one of creative transformation. The early Christians accepted the commonsense analysis of Stoicism that the ethical duties of the Christian could best be stated with reference to living up to the meaning of one's role in society. Yet the meaning of that role was changed in its form by the encounter with the apodictic

48. This subtitle is borrowed from another Pauline context: "If one is in Christ, behold a whole new world!" (2 Cor. 5:17). There is no linguistic justification for the "new creation" in this text to be taken as referring to the regenerate individual personality, as Protestant preaching has so often done; cf. below, pp. 214ff. To confess Jesus Christ as Lord is to make a statement not only about the confessor but about the world. The Christian can transform human relationship through voluntary subordination not because (à la Troeltsch or Dibelius) Jesus did not change the world, but because he did.

49. Cf. above, n. 35.

imperative style of Old Testament law, and changed in substance by the stance of servanthood derived from the example and the teaching of Jesus himself. His motto of revolutionary subordination, of willing servanthood in the place of domination, enables the person in a subordinate position in society to accept and live within that status without resentment, at the same time that it calls upon the person in the superordinate position to forsake or renounce all domineering use of that status. This call is then precisely not a simple ratification of the stratified society into which the gospel has come.[50] The subordinate person becomes a free ethical agent in the act of voluntarily acceding to subordination in the power of Christ instead of bowing to it either fatalistically or resentfully. The claim is not that there is immediately a new world regime which violently replaces the old; rather, the old and the new order exist concurrently on different levels. It is because she knows that in Christ there is no male or female that the Christian wife can freely accept that subordination to her unbelieving husband which is her present lot. It is because Christ has freed us all, and slave and free are equal before God, that their relationship may continue as a humane and honest one within the framework of the present economy, the structure of which is passing away (1 Cor. 7:31).

Troeltsch and his disciples were right; the early church had to develop an ethic for living within the structures of society which was not immediately apparent within the discourses of Jesus himself, pervaded as they are by the expectation of the imminent reign of God. But they were wrong in assuming that it must follow from that observation that the ethic the early church then developed was contradictory to or unrelated to the ethic of Jesus.[51] It is far more accurate to say that

50. The understanding that Paul's teaching did in fact ratify uncritically the social structures of his time, and that Christians following his guidance today would do the same, is prevalent both among social conservatives and among would-be "revolutionaries" who turn away from the New Testament for just this reason. This misapprehension is due partly to the readers' failure to read in the text the elements of *moral* conscientization and of reciprocity (e and h above) but also to the modern mythical belief that righteous violence on the part of the oppressed is normally a means of liberation.

51. We referred above (p. 45) to the demonstration by Hans Werner Bartsch that, *if* any changes can be discerned in the Gospel *texts* (e.g., between Mark and Luke), those

it is the ethic of Jesus himself that was transmitted and transmuted into the stance of the servant church within society, as indicated precisely in the *Haustafeln.* Since in the resurrection and in Pentecost the reign which was imminent has now in part come into our history, the church can now live out, within the structures of society, the newness of the life of that reign. The early church did not need to borrow from Stoicism the concept of living one's own role. The apostles rather transformed the concept of living within a role by finding how in each role the servanthood of Christ, the voluntary subordination of one who knows that another regime is normative, could be made concrete. The wife or child or slave who can accept subordination because "it is fitting in the Lord" has not forsaken the radicality of the call of Jesus; it is precisely this attitude toward the structures of this world, this freedom from needing to smash them since they are about to crumble anyway, which Jesus had been the first to teach and in his suffering to concretize.

This chapter might be understood as assuming that for any question of social ethics a direct solution can be sought in the casuistic teachings of the New Testament. That would be wrong. I have picked up one segment of these teachings and found it both relevant to issues of social order and coherent with the ethic of Jesus. I was especially concerned to test — and as it turns out, to negate — the widespread view that the ethic of the apostles betrays that of Jesus. But this should not be taken as suggesting that for other questions — the welfare state, or the meaning of property in an industrialized society, or ethical dilemmas in modern medicine — we could do without broader generalizations, a longer hermeneutic path, and insights from other sources. I am not affirming a specific biblical ethical content for modern questions; I am rather observing that where the New Testament did offer specific guidance for its own time, that guidance confirmed and applied the messianic ethic of Jesus.

---

changes represent not the abandon, but rather reaffirmation of the eschatological expectancy of Jesus' preaching. Luke's editing rephrased some details *in order to keep* testifying to his lively hope, not because he had lost it.

EPILOGUE

No other single chapter provoked as much angry objection as this one when *The Politics of Jesus* first appeared. The omnipresence of liberation as the preferred agenda of our age, colliding with the traditionally conservative use so often made of the *Haustafeln* in defense of patriarchal structures from the second century to the present, made it hard for readers to entertain the case made in this chapter for the initially critical and empowering impact of the apostolic witness. On grounds of their own modern ideology some readers had decided that the apostolic generation had to be wrong about "subordination," since the autonomy of the independent individual is the center of the modern liberal vision. That easy dismissal dispensed some readers from attending to the detail of the above chapter's argument.

That kind of a priori dismissal was of course facilitated by the already widespread tendency of many in our times to use the apostles' witness more as a foil than as gospel. This fits the notion of one school of readers that the witness of Jesus was lost sight of very soon in the development of the apostolic church. This view is commonsensical on the surface, since the notion of a founder's unique vision being betrayed or diluted by his less powerful or less creative successors is a sociological commonplace. Yet for a realistic understanding of the first century it is odd, since the epistles may well be just as old as the Gospels.[52]

Since the studies cited above in my original chapter, New Testament scholars have continued to attend to the *Haustafeln*.[53] Debate

52. The epistles clearly written by Paul are obviously the oldest writings we have. When Colossians, Ephesians, and 1 Peter were written is, just as with the Gospels, a matter of scholarly surmise, and the dating process is partly circular, in that the scholar's primary criterion for dating an anonymous or eponymous text has to be the way its vocabulary and its ideas fit on the trajectory of how the scholar thinks those ideas must have evolved.

53. A few citations from the summary by E. Schweizer have been added to the annotation of the chapter proper. Cf. James E. Crouch, *The Origin and Intention of the Colossian Haustafel* (Göttingen: Vandenhoeck, 1972). An overview in the light of contemporary agenda is presented by Elisabeth Schüssler Fiorenza, *In Memory of Her* (New York: Crossroad, 1984). Cf. also David Lee Balch, *Let Wives Be Submissive: The Domestic Code in I Peter* (Chico, Calif.: Scholars Press, 1981); Robert Scott Nash, "Heuristic Haustafeln," in Jacob Neusner et al. (eds.), *Religious Writings and Religious Systems* (Atlanta: Scholars

still continues about the sources of the notions of orderly society from which the apostolic witness borrowed; specialists seek to disentangle those derivations (from classical Greek thought, Stoicism,[54] Hellenistic Judaism . . .) with more confidence than their expositions evoke in the amateur reader.[55] It is possible, if one contrasts the several passages,[56] rather than seeing them as relatively parallel witnesses to a standard approach to a general problem, to argue that the transformation which the theme of subordination undergoes in the light of the cross is not equally evident in all of the texts. The subordination is explicitly reciprocal in Ephesians 5:21; less so in the other texts.[57]

There is in the expansion of the amount of scholarly attention given this topic since 1970 no substantial refutation of the starting point of my exposition above, namely that these passages testify to a collision between the liberating core of the Jesus message and the patriarchal assumptions of the cultures into which that message came. In a setting like that of 1 Peter the concern is more to avoid giving occasion for persecution by hostile authorities;[58] in Colossians and Ephesians a "thicker" description

---

Press, 1989), pp. 25-50; Karlheinz Müller, "Die Haustafel des Kolosserbriefes und das antike Frauenthema," in Gerhard Dutzenberg et al. (eds.), *Die Frau im Urchristentum* (Freiburg: Herder, 1983), pp. 263-319; Klaus Thraede, "Zum historischen Hintergrund der 'Haustafeln' des NT," in Ernst Dassmann and Suso Frank (eds.), *Pietas: Festschrift für Bernard Kotting* (Münster: Aschendorff, 1980), pp. 359-68.

54. There are expert debates about such questions as whether "Stoicism" was a definable entity with clear outlines, or a mood, or a cultural stream.

55. Schweizer, *Beiträge,* 400-401, reviews the scholarly opinions on the derivation of the *Haustafeln* substance from the several environing cultures. For our purposes this does not matter much; why should there not have been borrowings from all kinds of sources? Can we really disentangle three quite separate streams? What matters is how those borrowed materials were transformed as they were taken into the witness of the apostles.

56. Scholars differ about the dating of the several "Pauline" sources (and the Petrine one) and about whether the Saul/Paul of history himself held to these ideas. For our purposes that is not decisive.

57. According to Schüssler Fiorenza's reading ("Christian Mission and the Patriarchal Order of the Household," in *In Memory of Her* [New York: Crossroad, 1983], pp. 251ff.) the body of the text in Ephesians is less marked by the call to reciprocity than is the superscription (5:21), and Ephesians is in general less egalitarian than the witness underlying the use of the *Haustafeln* in Colossians. She assigns Ephesians a later date.

58. Some scholars accentuate the "apologetic" dimension of not wanting to scandalize the surrounding society by flaunting too visibly their freedom. For others the fear of disruption was also internal to the churches.

of the setting can illuminate more concretely just how the message adjusted to the setting. This fuller, more complex analysis reinforces our awareness that without the initial messianic thrust the entire subject would not have arisen. In none of the three settings[59] would there have had to be a warning against overdoing enfranchisement, if there had not in the first place been good news pointing in that direction.[60] The appeal "don't overdo celebrating your liberation" is only pertinent if somehow the vision of empowerment had authentically arisen. The one thing the *Haustafeln* cannot have meant originally is what they have mostly been used for since the second century, namely to reinforce extant authority structures as divinely willed for their own sake,[61] by borrowing propatriarchal arguments either from a Stoic or a Jewish world vision, from an appeal either to creation or to nature.

59. The studies we are here reviewing deal only with the *Haustafeln* proper. Yet it should be remembered (above, p. 179) that the same themes apply no less in other apostolic writings (subordination to the authorities in Romans, the return of Onesimus to Philemon, the place of women and slaves in households and in worship according to 1 Corinthians, and the place of the "weak" and "foolish" in 1 Cor. 1).

60. The basic stance of the study of Schüssler Fiorenza, *In Memory of Her,* is that the reading of the New Testament should generally be guided by the awareness that Jesus' original emancipatory message can only be discerned by watching its trajectory through the oppressive culture with which it interacted. The most original texts are therefore those in which the emancipatory impact has been the least diluted. Retrieving for more attention the fact that women did experience more liberation in the first century than was remembered later will liberate the gospel. That approach is parallel to mine. The difference is that my objective in 1972 was to gather inductively what scholars were already saying, claiming no authority of my own to debate with them. Schüssler Fiorenza goes back independently and critically to the sources. She and I (and E. Schweizer) agree that within a short time the emancipatory vision was lost, so that the moral meaning of "subordination" was reversed. Her reconstruction shows the loss beginning sooner, as she can work with a much more detailed and confident reconstruction of the trajectory.

61. Schweizer, *Beiträge,* p. 407, describes as "paganization" the several changes which are discernible in the next two generations, in such a way that the emancipatory thrust was diverted or spiritualized, so that the initial acceptance, on missionary-tactical grounds, of "subordination" yielded later to the reinforcement of the present order. "Don't overdo your liberation" soon slid back into "stay in your place." Schüssler Fiorenza describes the same slippage as "The Gnostic-Patristic Trajectory." My interpretation differs from theirs only in that I would describe the motivation for the initial adoption of these concepts as not only "missionary-tactical" but also christological (analogue to the cross as model: e.g., 1 Pet. 2:20-21). I must therefore also see the ensuing loss of the empowering impact as linked to a waning of the vision of the cross as ethical, and of Jesus as Servant.

A quite different and perhaps more difficult dimension of responding to the *Haustafeln* is not about ancient origins or original meanings but about how or whether to let these texts speak through the grid of twentieth-century assumptions. After all the care he has taken with early texts Crouch concludes[62] as a modern: ". . . the gospel is not a reform movement and . . . Christian faith does not imply social change." He calls this "an affirmation of finitude within the social order,"[63] as if the only way to be finite were to be conservative. This simple statement is not the product of any of his study of either the society or the literature of the first century. Crouch avows that his own moral vision is simply the product of his own conditioning. If he had been born in Switzerland he might oppose women's franchise and if in Arabia he might favor slavery.[64] Then he takes back the claim that the early church did not care about social reform by conceding that any alternative strategy, which would have sought to change the imperial social order from the top, would not have worked.

The reader remembers that the intention of this book is not to innovate in New Testament scholarship, but rather to free the results of scholarship from the grids imposed on it by customary unthinking assumptions about ethics. When Crouch moves beyond his first-century expertise he becomes a good example of traditionalism about ethical axioms.

Footnote 25 above was too brief to be appropriate in this setting, since it moves from interpreting the text to challenging the contemporary fashion of doctrinaire egalitarianism which some bring to the text as a grid from the present. That oblique reference to cultural fads was out of place.

I am no more convinced of the adequacy of oversimple egalitarianism than I was in 1970, but of course the setting in which its adequacy needs to be challenged keeps changing. The notion that those components of the scriptural heritage which modernity finds incongruous should simply be screened out rather than wrestled with is no more convincing now than when I first wrote.[65]

62. *The Colossian Haustafeln,* p. 160n.31.

63. P. 158.

64. P. 159n.27.

65. Krister Stendahl's mocking the Amish, as if they represented the "comprehensive and pervasive view of the Bible" whose inadequacy in the European theology of the time he was arguing, is still a distraction.

Elisabeth Schüssler Fiorenza cited this sentence[66] but reversed its meaning into "it motivates Christian slaves and women to accept 'things as they are.'"[67] In that passage the formulation of "things as they are" was that in Christ (and in baptism) the differences between "Jew and Greek, slave and free, male and female" have been transcended. That is in some important sense "real." Yet Jews are still jewish and Greeks greek; that also is "real." Both reality claims and social strategies need to be more nuanced. What the Haustafeln texts project is a tactic for change in the light of the new christological reality.

As I have already shown, I agree with Schüssler Fiorenza (and with Eduard Schweizer before her) that in the first century an original vision of equality[68] soon came to be modified by less revolutionary interpretations of the Gospel setting in which subordination made sense. Our difference is in the details; for Schüssler Fiorenza and Schweizer the explanation for the dilution was primarily an "apologetic" concern for the perception of the Christian movement by outsiders as being disorderly, whereas while not disagreeing with that I also note that for the New Testament writers there was a christological component to the appeal as well.

66. *Bread Not Stone: The Challenge of Feminist Biblical Interpretation* (Boston: Beacon, 1984), p. 83.

67. Her reference to Reaganism as where America is going demonstrates that my shorthand reference to cultural fashionableness would have needed fuller elaboration to be clear. She italicizes "things as they are" and telescopes quotations from different contexts so as to give these utterly nontechnical words a meaning opposite to what I am arguing.

68. That original vision was both "in Jesus" in the simple sense of reaching back to the founding experience, and "in Christ" in the Pauline sense of being supported by the eschatological promise of baptism.

CHAPTER 10

Let Every Soul Be Subject: Romans 13 and the Authority of the State

Until the crisis of Nazism struck into the heartland of Protestant theological scholarship, there was little question about the centrality and adequacy of Romans 13:1-7 as the foundation of a Christian doctrine of the state. It seems to be said here quite unambiguously that civil government is established by God and that Christians are therefore to obey their respective rulers, not only because they fear the state's sanctions but because they conscientiously support its function of repressing evil and encouraging good. Especially within the Post-Constantinian context which Catholic and Protestant theology had long been taking for granted, this text served as a sort of capsule constitution to guide the Christian statesman (who should punish evil and reward good) and the Christian citizen (who should conscientiously obey). When a government thus divinely instituted wields the sword, this action is therefore exempted from the general prohibition of killing. There might remain some imaginable borderline problems, such as a government waging an unjust war, or a government asking its citizens to commit sin; but within Christendom such eventualities were not definite enough to demand that the borders be traced concretely. This definition presumably would apply to all states, but preeminently of course to the governments of Christian Europe and America.

New Testament exegesis has long since abandoned such a simple concept of divine institution in the order of creation; but it persists in the systematic-theological and ethical thought of Protestants, especially of theologically conservative Protestants. It is therefore important that the traditional commonplaces be challenged here in a systematic, even argumentative way, in addition to the verse-by-verse rereading done by the textual scholars.[1] This outline must run the risks of simplification in order to point up the polemic issues. Let me then put most precisely the challengeable claim of the tradition I intend to challenge; it is that by virtue of the divine institution of government as a part of God's good creation, its mandate to wield the sword and the Christian's duty to obey the state combine to place upon the Christian a moral obligation to support and participate in the state's legal killing (death penalty, war), despite contrary duties which otherwise would seem to follow from Jesus' teaching or example. Every general affirmation I can make about this text must therefore be pointed up by its impact upon that standard tradition.

(1) The New Testament speaks in many ways about the problem of the state; Romans 13 is not the center of this teaching.

There is a very strong strand of Gospel teaching which sees secular government as the province of the sovereignty of Satan. This position is perhaps most typically expressed by the temptation story, in which Jesus did not challenge the claim of Satan to be able to dispose of the rule of all the nations. If one makes this perspective central, all the New Testament texts appear in another light.[2]

1. Reviews of exegetical discussion are offered for the classic theological traditions by Fritzhermann Keienburg, *Die Geschichte der Auslegung von Römer 13:1-7* (Basel theological dissertation, Gelsenkirchen, 1956), and for recent studies by Ernst Käsemann, "Römer 13:1-7 in unserer Generation," *ZTK,* 56 (1959), 316-76. A thorough verse-by-verse restatement, without reaching out into wider theological interpretation, is that of Rolf Walker, "Studie zu Römer 13:1-7," *ThEx,* 132 (1968). Even more for this present chapter than for those which preceded, it must be said that no attempt is made, or need be made for our purposes, to survey thoroughly the scholarly consensus. The general outlines of our interpretation are not original; to argue them in depth would interest a different readership than that for which this text is prepared. The present view is much like those of Markus Barth, *Acquittal by Resurrection,* pp. 34 and 159; of Herbert M. Gale, "Paul's View of the State," *Interpretation,* 6 (1952), 409ff.; and of Hans Werner Bartsch, "Die Neutestamentliche Aussagen über den Staat," *EvT,* 19 (1959), 375ff. The first draft of this presentation arose from a "Peace Witness Seminar" on "Evangelicals in Social Action" convened Nov. 30–Dec. 2, 1967, by Eastern Mennonite College, Harrisonburg, Virginia.

2. One serious expression of this perspective is Archie Penner's *The New Testament, the Christian, and the State* (Scottdale, Pa.: Herald, 1959).

This position is offensive to the modern mind because it stands in judgment on modern democratic humanism and because it is held to in an extreme way by Jehovah's Witnesses; but certainly no one can deny that it is part of the biblical material, or that it remained a significant thrust of the teaching of the early postapostolic church. When it is seen from this perspective, we are reminded that Romans 13 was written about pagan government.[3] It constitutes at best acquiescence in that government's dominion, not the accrediting of a given state by God or the installation of a particular sovereign by providential disposition.

There is a strong strand of apostolic thought that sees the state within the framework of the victory of Christ over the principalities and powers. This position is stated by Hendrikus Berkhof and G. B. Caird.[4] Instead of a stable institution, dating from creation, the "state as such," this text tells us to think of a dynamic process related to and reflecting the saving work of Christ, as this work reaches even beyond the realm of the church. This wider perspective is especially significant because of the language of "powers" present in the Romans text[5] — an observation that should keep us from taking for granted that the text can be interpreted standing alone, as is habitually done. It is in this christological-cosmological context that Oscar Cullmann finds the New Testament understanding of the state to be expressed most clearly.

3. If, as a strong variant textual tradition suggests, we should read "*all* authorities," the reference would probably be not to other governments (than Rome) but rather to other kinds of authority.

4. Fuller interpretation and bibliography relating to the theme "victory over the powers" is provided above, pp. 140ff., and by Markus Barth, *loc. cit.*

5. The term "powers" in Rom. 13:1 *(exousiae)* may have the specific cosmological sense dealt with by Berkhof and Caird; this is the opinion of O. Cullmann, following K. L. Schmidt. It is like the other passages of this kind in that the word appears in the plural and (perhaps) with the adjective "all." It differs from those other contexts in the absence of a string of synonyms (rulers, thrones, angels, principalities . . .) and in the absence of express reference to Christ. Thus it is also possible that it may have the simpler functional sense of "authorities." Elsewhere in the New Testament the cosmological sense predominates when the term appears in the plural; in the singular both meanings are possible. Robert Morgenthaler, "Rome — Sedes Satanse," reinforces by detailed comparison with Luke's usage the claim of Oscar Cullmann that *exousia* has a political sense. The scholarly debate on this issue is very significant as it relates to the "Powers" problem (cf. ch. 8) and the "Subjection" theme (ch. 9), but it is immaterial to the thesis of the present chapter.

In the book of Revelation, most pointedly in chapter 13, we find an image of government largely comparable to the one we referred to in the earliest portions of the Gospels. The "Powers" are seen as persecuting the true believers; the same is true in the assumed background of Peter and James. We shall return later to the issue of the relation between Revelation 13 and Romans 13; for now it suffices to indicate that here again there is a statement of the church's view of government which is strikingly less simple and affirmative than the *traditional* interpretation of Romans 13. It is therefore in principle already challengeable when Protestant political ethical thought is dominated as much as it has been by this one text, as if it were a kind of charter or constitution for the political realm.

(2) In the structure of the Epistle, chapters 12 and 13 in their entirety form one literary unit. Therefore, the text 13:1-7 cannot be understood alone.

Chapter 12 begins with a call to nonconformity, motivated by the memory of the mercies of God, and finds the expression of this transformed life first in a new quality of relationships within the Christian community and, with regard to enemies, in suffering. The concept of love then recurs in 13:8-10. Therefore any interpretation of 13:1-7 which is not also an expression of suffering and serving love must be a misunderstanding of the text in its context. There are no grounds of literary analysis, textual variation, or style to support the claim that we have here to do with a separate chunk of teaching which constitutes foreign matter in the flow of the text.[6]

6. The foreignness of the passage to its context has been most sweepingly argued by James Kallas, "Romans 13:1-7: An Interpolation," in *NTS,* 11, 365-74. The argument is all based on Kallas's views as to the compatibility of the passage's teaching with other ideas he thinks were held by Paul. Some scholars argue insertion by a later writer; others see Paul himself as quoting a tradition foreign to the rest of his thought. In order to be so convinced that the text does not fit the rest of Paul, most of these scholars must first assume for it a meaning that has been imposed on it by later readers, rather than the emphasis the present study finds in it. Those who challenge the authenticity of the passage first interpret it to mean something Paul probably would not have said. If the text were read with more openness to its wording and less acceptance of later tradition about its meaning, the argument would fall away.

The beginning of the unit of text (12:1) ties its thought firmly back to the "mercies of God" as the theme of the previous portion of the Epistle. These "mercies" included the unmerited calling of the Gentiles to the new life in God (chs. 1–5), the unmerited renewal of even the "body" through the Spirit (chs. 6–8), and the continuing unmerited redemptive concern of God for ethnic Israel (chs. 9–11).[7] The continuation of our passage (13:11-14) looks forward in hope to a salvation so concretely imminent and historical as to be "nearer than when we first believed." It issues in a new quality of concern for the "weak" (14:1–15:21) and in the gathering of financial and spiritual resources to support one another (15:26-29) and Paul (15:22-25, 30-33). The entire text thus sees Christian nonconformity and suffering love as driven and drawn by a sense of God's triumphant movement from the merciful past into a triumphant future. Any interpretation of 13:1-7 that would make it the expression of a static or conservative undergirding of the present social system would therefore represent a refusal to take seriously the context.[8] Any interpretation in which God's mercies are not seen as overcoming hostilities through the creation of community, reaching even to the nuts and bolts of financial sharing and missionary support, has covered over the meaning of each part of the text by not seeing it whole.

In addition to this kind of implication which follows from the broader frame of the passage, there are specific verbal cross-references which link the text with what preceded and what follows. As we shall see later at length, 13:8 begins with a verbal echo of verse 7. As Oscar Cullmann and others have indicated, the submission to the powers in 13:1 is motivated and exposited by the hope in 13:11-14. Verse 10, by expositing verse 8, also gives a definition of the "good" in verse 3, whereby the behavior of Christians under government is guided.

7. Cf. below, pp. 219ff. nn. 6, 7, and 12, the word of Bartsch and Minear concerning the "political" aspect of all of Romans.

8. A broader way to put the same question would be to apply the traditional distinction between creation and redemption. The opening chapters of Romans may be seen as positing a duality between creation and redemption. Then 13:1-7, describing the "Powers" as the order of creation (cf. the phrase "creatures" in the parallel text of 1 Pet. 2:13), would be out of place in a context of redemption. I do not pursue this question further here because the prior assumptions it makes about the distinct orders of creation and redemption themselves need to be examined before they can be assumed to throw light on the question.

There is a most specific dialectical interplay around the concepts of vengeance and wrath. Christians are told (12:19) never to exercise vengeance but to leave it to God and to wrath.[9] Then the authorities are recognized (13:4) as executing the particular function which the Christian was to leave to God. It is inconceivable that these two verses, using such similar language, should be meant to be read independently of one another. This makes it clear that the function exercised by government is not the function to be exercised by Christians. However able an infinite God may be to work at the same time through the sufferings of his believing disciples who return good for evil and through the wrathful violence of the authorities who punish evil with evil, such behavior is for humans not complementary but in disjunction. Divine providence can in its own sovereign permissive way "use" an idolatrous Assyria (Isa. 10) or Rome. This takes place, however, without declaring that the destructive action by pagan powers which God thus "uses" is morally good or that participation in it is incumbent upon the covenant people. That God turns human wrath to praise (Ps. 76:10) is an affirmation of providence overriding human rebellion, not ratifying it. If the statements of 12:19 and 13:4 were not in the same passage, we might not necessarily cross-refer from one to the other. Then we might not have to conclude that the prohibition of vengeance in the one verse excludes the sharing of Christians in the outworking of vengeance as described in the other. One could then say that the contexts are sufficiently different that the terms need not have exactly the same meaning. But within the sustained reasoning of one passage, with the same words being used in the midst of the same text, certainly it is a most likely interpretation that the "vengeance" or "wrath" that is recognized as being within providential control is the same as that which Christians are told not to exercise.

(3) The subordination that is called for recognizes whatever power exists, accepts whatever structure of sovereignty happens to prevail. The text

9. In general NT usage human wrath is a passion to be avoided (Eph. 4:31; Col. 3:8; Matt. 5:22; 1 Tim. 2:8; Titus 1:7) or to be held in check (Eph. 4:26; James 1:19). Divine wrath is not to be understood in anthropomorphic analogy to human passion (cf. Anthony T. Hanson, *The Wrath of the Lamb* [London: S.P.C.K., 1957], esp. pp. 178ff.) and is not served by human wrath (James 1:20).

> *does not affirm, as the tradition has it, a divine act of institution or ordination of a particular government.*

One of the ways of understanding the "institution" of government by God is to claim that whatever government exists, it is by virtue of an act of institution, that is, a specific providential action of God, that it came into being. Therefore this government exists by revelation. The events whereby it came to rule are themselves providential. If Germany finds itself under the control of Adolf Hitler, this very fact demonstrates that his government is "of God." The events whereby this came to be thereby constitute a revelation given to the German people in the course of their history, by virtue of which they can know that they are to be subject to Hitler's authority and consider his cause to be divinely mandated. This concept of the givenness of a particular government as itself constituting its legitimacy we might call the "positivistic" view. It has tended in the past to be held in certain Lutheran circles. It certainly need not lead so far as to accredit Hitler; but it is significant and expressive of its theological structure that it could go that far, without anything within the theological system necessarily needing to object. Whatever is, is the will of God. When we see what exists, we know thereby what God desires us to do. This position has evidently been discredited by the lengths to which it was taken by some in Hitler's Germany; but it remains very much alive in popular piety and patriotism.

The weakness of the "positivistic" view is that the text of Romans makes no affirmative moral judgment on the existence of a particular government and says nothing particular about who happens to be Caesar or what his policies happen to be.

The other option, the alternative both logically and historically, is more at home in the Calvinistic tradition. We might call this the "normative" view. It runs from Huldrych Zwingli through Cromwell to Karl Barth and Emil Brunner. What is ordained is not a particular government but the concept of proper government, the principle of government as such. As long as a given government lives up to a certain minimum set of requirements, then that government may properly claim the sanction of divine institution. If, however, a government fails adequately to fulfill the functions divinely assigned to it, it loses its authority. It then becomes the duty of the preacher to teach that this has become an unjust government, worthy of rebellion. It can become the duty of Christian citizens to rise up against it, not because they are against government as such but because they are in favor of *proper* government. The concept of just rebellion, in which the preacher as such does not become a revolutionary but does preach the moral obligation to rise up against unjust government in the name of proper government, finds its rootage in Huldrych Zwingli. In the second generation of the Reformed tradition, the generation of Calvin, it was already being worked out in some detail in its application to the position of the Huguenots in France. It continues through John Knox and Cromwell and through the American Revolution, and is currently being applied in a very consistent way by a particular current of ecumenical thought which would justify the rebellion of subject peoples in Latin America or Africa against white American and Western European cultural and economic imperialism.

The shortcoming of this view is partly internal. Who is to judge how bad a government can be and still be good? How much deviation from the norm is justifiable on the grounds of human frailty? At what point is a government disqualified? But a greater weakness is the simple fact that nothing in the text of Romans 13 justifies the concept of just rebellion. The conception of a "state properly so called," in the name of which one would reject and seek to overthrow the state which exists empirically, is totally absent in the passage. In the social context of the Jewish Christians in Rome, the whole point of the passage was to take out of their minds any concept of rebellion against or even emotional rejection of this corrupt pagan government. There is no definition of the theoretical "proper state," by contrast with which some other, "real" state would stand condemned to be overthrown.[10]

10. In this section I have taken "rebellion" in the current sense of violent overthrow. It is of course possible to redefine rebellion to cover any disavowal of a government's legitimacy, even without violence and without the creation of a counter-government. In this sense nonviolent noncooperation might be spoken of as a form of rebellion. If this usage were accepted we would still need to challenge the integral distinction between good governments, which Christians should bless, and bad ones against which they should rebel. They should rather rebel against all and be subordinate to all; for "subordination" is itself the Christian form of rebellion. It is the way we share in God's patience with a system we basically reject. Cf. ch. 9 above.

One very frequent expression of the "legitimist" or "normative" view is the balancing against one another of Romans 13 (the good state) and Revelation 13 (the evil state which glorifies itself religiously and must be resisted). Christians are first to measure which kind of state they have, and then to support it if it is the orderly state of Romans and oppose it if it is the evil state of Revelation.[11] For this there is no ground in either text. Neither text calls for active moral support or religious approval of the state; both texts call for subordination to whatever powers there be.

If both the "positivistic" and "normative" interpretations do violence to the text, what does the passage say? The apostle is making a moral statement, not a metaphysical one. He is speaking to the present situation of the Roman Christians as representative of Christians throughout the empire, and not to the nature of all political reality, nor does he prescribe an ideal social order.

God is not said to *create* or *institute* or *ordain* the powers that be, but only to *order* them, to put them in order, sovereignly to tell them where they belong, what is their place. It is not as if there was a time when there was no government and then God made government through a new creative intervention; there has been hierarchy and authority and power since human society existed. Its exercise has involved domination, disrespect for human dignity, and real or potential violence ever since sin has existed. Nor is it that by ordering this realm God specifically, morally approves of what a government does. The sergeant does not produce the soldiers he drills; the librarian does not create nor approve of the book she or he catalogs and shelves. Likewise God does not take the responsibility for the existence of the rebellious "powers that be" or for their shape or identity; they already are. What

11. This posing of the alternatives is clearest in O. Cullmann, *The State in the New Testament,* pp. 73ff., but is found very widely, from Karl Barth to Eberhard Arnold. Cf. my *Christian Witness to the State,* p. 76.

The criticism of this "normative" approach has been made especially strongly by a circle of German Protestant theologians around Ernst Wolf. Their way of putting their point is their denial that the New Testament, or Rom. 13 in particular, contains a "doctrine of the state." By this is not meant that nothing is said about the state in the New Testament, nor that what is said on the subject is not clear, or not coherent. What they mean is that there is not one dogmatically authorized and unchanging statement of what the state must always be, which could then be used to accredit, but also to disqualify, particular states.

the text says is that God orders them, brings them into line, providentially and permissively lines them up with divine purposes.

This is true of all governments. It is a statement both *de facto* and *de jure.* It applies to the government of dictators and tyrants as well as to constitutional democracies. It would in fact apply just as well to the government of a bandit or a warlord, to the extent to which such would exercise real sovereign control.[12]

That God orders and uses the powers does not reveal anything new about what government should be or how we should respond to government. A given government is not mandated or saved or made a channel of the will of God; it is simply lined up, used by God in the ordering of the cosmos. It does not mean that what individuals in government do is good human behavior. As we noted, the librarian does not approve of the content of a book he or she shelves; God did not approve morally of the brutality whereby Assyria chastised Israel (Isa. 10).[13]

The immediate concrete meaning of this text for the Christian Jews in Rome, in the face of official anti-Semitism and the rising arbitrariness of the Imperial regime, is to call them away from any notion of revolution or insubordination. The call is to a nonresistant attitude toward a tyrannical government.[14] This is the immediate and

12. The medieval and the classic Protestant idea of government as being specifically instituted by an act of the divine will always assumes that if it were not for this creative act "anarchy" would reign. But in real history there is no such thing as anarchy. Where one power does not rule, another does.

Having discerned the difference between "ordain" and "order" in this way, we may now be able to state more clearly what would be needed if the traditional view were to be right after all. To support the standard Protestant concept of orders revealed in creation it would have to be affirmed by Paul not only that the powers *exist,* but that there exists a standard, known to everyone by nature, to govern the functions of governments. Yet in the rare places (e.g., Rom. 2) where Paul seems (according to some interpreters) to be affirming that pagans possess some kind of moral insight, he never says that the standards for the civil order are included in this natural knowledge.

13. Herbert M. Gale ("Paul's View of the State") uses the comparison between the state and the law to show that divine ordering or origin does not bestow unconditional authority.

14. By "nonresistant" here, as in this entire study, is not meant compliance or acquiescence in evil, but what Paul means in 12:7 and Jesus in Matt. 5:39, the suffering renunciation of retaliation in kind. It does not exclude other kinds of opposition to evil. Cf. above, n. 10.

concrete meaning of the text; how strange then to make it the classic proof for the duty of Christians to kill.

(4) The instructions to the Romans are to be subject to a government in whose administration they had no voice. The text cannot mean that Christians are called to do military or police service.

The functions Rome asked of its subject peoples did not include military or police service, which were considered either as hereditary professions or as citizens' privileges. There was no general military obligation. As slaves and as Jews, most early Christians would have been liable to no such obligation even if it had applied to Roman citizens. The functions the government did actually ask of its citizens did not include participation in bearing the sword of government. The functions described in verses 3-4 did not include any service that the Christian is asked to render. The "things due to the authority" listed in verses 6-7 do not include any kind of participation or service.

This observation is not simply about the substance of the text but also about the political situation at that time. It is therefore illegitimate to extend the meaning of the text as if it self-evidently applied as well to other kinds of services which other kinds of governments in other ages might ask of their citizens. Especially is it out of place for those who feel that simple literalism suffices to include unquestioning acceptance of the modern institution of conscription, as belonging under the heading of "being subject."

(5) The function of bearing the sword to which Christians are called to be subject is the judicial and police function; it does not refer to the death penalty or to war.

The sword *(machaira)* is the symbol of judicial authority. It was not the instrument of capital punishment, since the Romans crucified their criminals. It was not the instrument of war since it was but a long dagger. Like the pistol worn by a traffic policeman or the sword worn by a Swiss citizen-officer, it was more a symbol of authority than a weapon. This is not to say that the Roman government was mild or that this weapon was only symbolically present. But what it symbolizes is the way a given government exercises dominion over its subjects by appeal to violence, not the execution of capital offenders or the waging of hostilities against other nations.[15] At this time Rome was not carrying on major military hostilities against other nations. There were in fact no neighbor "nations" with whom Rome could very meaningfully wage war. The brushfire hostilities along the frontiers were more like police action than like war.

The distinction made here between police and war is not simply a matter of the degree to which the appeal to force goes, the number of persons killed or killing. It is a structural and a profound difference in the sociological meaning of the appeal to force. In the police function, the violence or threat thereof is applied only to the offending party. The use of violence by the agent of the police is subject to review by higher authorities. The police officer applies power within the limits of a state whose legislation even the criminal knows to be applicable to him. In any orderly police system there are serious safeguards to keep the violence of the police from being applied in a wholesale way against the innocent. The police power generally is great enough to overwhelm that of the individual offender so that any resistance on the offender's part is pointless. In all of these respects, war is structurally different. The doctrine of the "just war" is an effort to extend into the realm of war the logic of the limited violence of police authority — but not a very successful one. There is some logic to the "just war" pattern of thought[16] but very little realism. At the very most the only relevance of Romans 13 to war would be to a very precise operation carried on within the very clear limitations of all the classic criteria that define the "justifiable war." The more we would attempt honestly to define and to respect such criteria, the more clearly we would see that as far as any real or conceivable war is concerned, in the name of any real or thinkable

15. On the other hand, it is the normal weapon in hand-to-hand combat (Matt. 26:51-52) and in insurrection (Luke 22:36ff.). In non-Roman contexts it was used to put people to death (Heb. 11:37; Acts 12:2).

16. The use of the *term* "just war" has become unpopular in many circles since Hiroshima; but the logic it refers to is still the only serious way of dealing with the moral problem of war apart from pacifism. Even many who call themselves pacifist are in fact still using "just war" reasoning. Cf. Ralph Potter, *War and Moral Discourse* (Richmond: John Knox, 1969), and my own *When War Is Unjust* (Minneapolis: Augsburg, 1985).

government, it is not honestly possible to include that function under the authorization given government by Romans 13.

(6) The Christian who accepts subjection to government retains moral independence and judgment. The authority of government is not self-justifying. Whatever government exists is ordered by God; but the text does not say that whatever the government does or asks of its citizens is good.

(A) "The authorities are ministers of God, attending to this very thing." What is the grammatical construction of the participle "attending" *(proskarterountes)?* Most translations consider it a simple further predication: "the authorities are ministers of God *and* they busy themselves with this very function (of meting out good to the good and evil to the evil)." But this is from a grammatical viewpoint not the most likely meaning of such a participial construction. It is more likely that the participle represents an adverbial modifier of the previous predication. We should then read "they are ministers of God *to the extent* to which they busy themselves" or "*when* they devote themselves" or "*in that* they devote themselves" to the assigned function. In the strictest sense we might take this adverbial modifier restrictively: "they are ministers of God *only to the extent to which* they carry out their function"; or we could take it more affirmatively: "they are ministers of God *by virtue of* their devoting themselves" to it. In any case, whichever of these meanings be Paul's intent, all of them assume that there are criteria whereby the functioning of government can be measured. According to the totality of the passage, we cannot measure whether we should revolt against the government, as if certain governments could fall short of the status of legitimacy, and therefore need to be revolted against. Nor can we measure by this yardstick whether a government has been permitted by God, because all government has been permitted by God. All the powers that be are subject to the ordering of God, and Christians are to be subject to them all. But we can judge and measure the extent to which a government is accomplishing its ministry by asking namely whether it persistently (*present* participle) attends to the rewarding of good and evil according to their merits. To be "minister to you for good" is a criterion, not a description.

Thus far we have been reading verse 6 as if the rest of the traditional interpretation were correct. There are, however, two further difficulties of interpretation, each of which, if inspected carefully, would move us further away from the traditional affirmation.

The verb *proskartereo* normally does not take an accusative object. The verb may appear with no object or its object may be in the dative case. Its most current New Testament usage is in the phrase which the Authorized Version translates "continuing instant [in prayer]" (Acts 1:14; 6:4; Col. 4:2; Rom. 12:12). But that then means that the sentence cannot simply affirm concerning the authorities that "they do devote themselves to this very thing," since the accusative "to this very thing" cannot be the object of this verb. It has to modify "they are servants." Therefore the translation would have to read "they are servants of God to this very end, devoting themselves persistently." In this construction it is even more likely that the participle has the adverbial sense and even less that it is a predication. This consideration then further supports the interpretive hypothesis already made above.

But a greater difficulty is that it is not immediately clear what is the antecedent of "they are." Interpreters in general assume that the *rulers* of verse 3 and the *powers* of verses 1 and 3 are somehow all merged together in one grammatical subject, which may be either feminine singular or masculine plural and always has the same meaning. This is, however, a most unusual way to disregard the keys to interpretation that gender and number provide. It is more appropriate to ask concretely what plural noun can be the subject of "they are" in verse 6. The most recent such plural noun referring to the realm of government was the "rulers" in verse 3, but that is rather far back to reach for an antecedent. Thus some serious scholars, including M. Dibelius, have argued that it is more likely that "ministers of God" should be itself the subject.[17] Then we would read: "the ministers of God are there for this very purpose (as they persist)." Then we must further choose between two meanings of the noun "ministers." In secular Greek usage of the time the term translated "ministers" *(leitourgoi)* referred to government functionaries, most currently to those who gathered tax

17. Martin Dibelius, "Rom und die ersten Christen im Ersten Jahrhundert," in *Botschaft und Geschichte,* II (Tübingen: Mohr, 1956), 181n. 9.

money. Since the preceding sentence referred to the voluntary payment of taxes, it would be quite appropriate (with Dibelius) to move on to speak of government officials as ministering to God in this way; thus "tax collection agencies exist for this very purpose when they are zealous." But the most current biblical usage of the word, like its near synonym *diakonos,* refers to the priest or the Christian who "serves" God in the sense of worship and sacrifice. There is thus nothing in the text to make sure that Paul does not intend "ministers of God" to refer to Christians. This would also fit quite smoothly in the context: The Christian is subject for the sake of conscience; Christians pay taxes because Christians also, as ministers of God, devote themselves to the end that the good be approved and evil reprimanded.

All grammatical interpretations of the verse must be subject to the risks of probability; the main thrust of our present paragraph is not dependent upon any one of these hypotheses. This grammatical detour should, however, have permitted us at least to overcome the naive sense of self-evidence with which the reader of the English text has often heard it being said as a simple affirmation that, whatever government does, it is serving God and therefore what it is doing is a ministry which the Christian should always share.

Let it be noted that "good" and "evil" here cannot be understood in some wide historical sense such as to cover the preservation of democracy or the interests of the nation. The ministry for good is "to thee," that is, it is to be measured by the welfare of each individual subject (not only of the full citizens).[18]

(B) Whatever be the kind of criteria and discrimination to which *proskarterountes* points in verse 6, it is all the more clear in verse 7 that we are being instructed to discriminate. "Render to each his due" cannot normally be assumed to mean "render everything to government."

18. Jean Lasserre points out ("Note complementaire sur Rom. 13,4," *CR* [Oct. 1968], pp. 39-40) that thus to link the legitimacy of the exercise of governmental power to the welfare of the subject (not only to the formally defined rights of the full citizen) is a very substantial judgment upon the autonomy of the authorities (and, we might add, historically a very progressive one).

It might be recalled that according to the account of Acts, Paul's experiences with the authorities were that they had protected his missionary freedom against hostile Gentiles (19:35-41), and his life in the face of hostile Jews (23:12-24) and soldiers (27:42-43).

Often this text is read as a sort of list of the four kinds of things that are due to government: taxes, revenue, respect, and honor. Such an interpretation is quite common. It makes nonsense, however, of the prior invitation to be discriminating and to render to each just what is his due. It is therefore a much more serious reading of the entire passage to hear in this text, as do Cullmann and Cranfield, an implicit allusion to the words of Jesus. "Render to each what is due to him" means to render to Caesar what belongs to him and to God what belongs to him. Taxes and revenue, perhaps honor, are due to Caesar, but fear is due to God.[19]

Thus once again there are criteria that come into play in our attitude toward government. We are instructed to refuse to give government certain types of "honor" or "fear." The place of government in the providential designs of God is not such that our duty would be simply to do whatever it says. This discrimination commanded in verse 7 is further reinforced in verse 8. In English usage we do not note that the words "that which is due" in verse 7 and "owing" of verse 8 have the same root. (This similarity is incidentally a significant argument against those who claim that verses 1-7 constitute a foreign body within chapters 12–13.) Verse 7 says "render to each his *due*"; verse 8 says "nothing is *due* to anyone except love." Thus the claims of Caesar are to be measured by whether what he claims is due to him is part of the obligation of love. Love in turn is defined (v. 10) by the fact that it does no harm. In this context it therefore becomes impossible to maintain that the subjection referred to in verses 1-7 can include a moral obligation under certain circumstances to do harm to others at the behest of government.

It is not by accident that the imperative of 13:1 is not literally one of *obedience.* The Greek language has good words to denote obe-

19. C. E. B. Cranfield, "Some Observations on Romans XIII:1-7," *NTS,* 6 (1959-60), 241ff., argues convincingly (p. 248) that for Paul "fear" *(phobos)* is due only to God. Ethelbert Stauffer reports (*Christ and the Caesars,* p. 137) that the Carthaginian Christian martyr Donata, asked to swear "by the divine spirit of the Lord our Caesar," responded that she would "honor Caesar as Caesar but fear only God." This kind of discrimination was probably a settled usage. Cranfield, p. 247, agrees that Paul is here explicitly referring to Jesus' call to discrimination (Mark 12:7; Matt. 22:21; Luke 22:35); the verb "render" *(apodote)* is the same in both contexts.

dience, in the sense of completely bending one's will and one's actions to the desires of another. What Paul calls for, however, is sub*ordi*nation. This verb is based upon the same root as the *ordering* of the powers of God. Subordination is significantly different from obedience.[20] The conscientious objector who refuses to do what government demands, but still remains under the sovereignty of that government and accepts the penalties which it imposes, or the Christian who refuses to worship Caesar but still permits Caesar to put him or her to death, is being subordinate even though not obeying.

The imperative and the enablement of this subordination are found not in fear or in calculations of how best to survive, but, as we saw, "in the mercies of God" (12:1) or in "conscience" (13:5). But how does conscience motivate subordination? If the ground of our subordination is not God's having created the government, what is it? Further attention to the motif of subordination as it is urged upon the slave (1 Pet. 2:13ff., 19ff.), or upon wives and children (Eph. 5:21ff.; Col. 3:18ff.), shows the reason to be that Jesus Christ himself accepted subordination and humiliation (Phil. 2:5ff.).[21] The willingness to suffer is then not merely a test of our patience or a dead space of waiting; it is itself a participation in the character of God's victorious patience with the rebellious powers of creation. We subject ourselves to government because it was in so doing that Jesus revealed and achieved God's victory.

A Conclusion

The purpose of this outline has not been to furnish a full or balanced exposition of the text in question,[22] but only to respond to the points

20. Cranfield, "Some Observations on Romans XIII:1-7," p. 242, underlines the difference between obedience and subordination.

21. Cf. ch. 9 above on the wider meaning of "subordination" in New Testament ethics. It bears repeating that the appeal at the outset of the passage Rom. 12–13 was not to God's working as creator or as providential governor over the state, but to the "mercies of God" and to the reconciling of Jew and Greek in one people.

22. I have not intended to speak of every verse and every grammatical problem. I have, however, identified the central purpose of the apostle's writing to the Romans (at the end of section 3 above, p. 202).

at which the predominant traditions of interpretation seek to find support in this text for a view of government and of the Christian's obligation to it which can include the obligation to participate in war. In this mainstream tradition, which has prevailed in the churches since Constantine, Romans 13 and the other texts like it stand in tension with Matthew 5. This is said alike by Protestants and Catholics, by conservative and liberal theologies. They then conclude that in the tension between these two kinds of obligations or two kinds of statements, the duties of Romans 13 take precedence in the social realm and the duties of Matthew 5 in the personal one. Then it is easy to turn the interpretation back on one's interlocutor and to say that the pacifist is one who gives precedence to the personal realm over social obligation, preferring Jesus to Paul or eschatology to responsibility.

Some pacifists have accepted this analysis and gone on to argue that personal faithfulness is more important than social responsibility. This lets it be forgotten that the logic of the post-Constantinian position holds only under the assumption that the imperatives of Matthew 5 and Romans 13 are actually contradictory. If that were the case, there might well be some good reasons to stand with Jesus against Paul or with eschatology against responsibility; but the above exposition should have shown that the assumption itself does not hold. It is not the case that two imperatives are affirmed in the New Testament, obedience to government on one hand and loving the enemy on the other, between which we must choose when they contradict. Romans 12–13 and Matthew 5–7 are not in contradiction or in tension. They *both* instruct Christians to be nonresistant in all their relationships, including the social. They *both* call on the disciples of Jesus to renounce participation in the interplay of egoisms which this world calls "vengeance" or "justice." They *both* call Christians to respect and be subject to the historical process in which the sword continues to be wielded and to bring about a kind of order under fire, but not to perceive in the wielding of the sword their own reconciling ministry.

EPILOGUE

This chapter calls for less revision than some of the others, not because Romans 13 has not continued to be studied since 1972, but because the text has become less central in the thought of some. The notion that out of this one apostolic passage there could be derived a normative and timeless divine pattern for what "The State" both is and should be, which dominated Protestant thought since the Reformation, was not a promising base for further development. Those who hold to that hope, on the grounds of their theory of Scripture, need say no more, and have said no more recently, than they said generations ago. On the other hand, those who read the letter to the Romans with critical concern for what mattered to the author and his addressees no longer tend to put these seven verses at the center of their concern.

Many scholars who have been reading Romans most carefully over the last generation find the author to be most concerned for the reconciliation of Jews and Gentiles in the new community. This theme brings Romans closer to Galatians and Ephesians, and thus to the topic of my chapter 11.

Another set of critical readers see in this passage its cross-references to the themes both of the principalities and powers (my chapter 8) and of subordination (chapter 9). They then study (a) whether Paul, when he thought about the Roman government, was essentially politically conservative and, if so, (b) whether he thereby betrayed the radicality of Jesus or applied it to a new agenda. Thus the deeper reading of the Romans passage overlaps at each point with concerns this book works with more thoroughly under other headings.

CHAPTER 11

Justification by Grace through Faith

I have followed up my reading of the story of Jesus with several sample soundings in the thought of the apostolic church. I have observed the prevalence of the language of discipleship, imitation, and participation, and seen how this characterized not only the motivation but also the shape of early Christian behavior. I have observed a parallel expression in the cosmology of the apostle where the "principalities and powers" language, which might be called "mythological," nonetheless has a very precise and fruitful burden of meaning with regard to understanding the church's faithfulness within the structured power relationships of society. I have observed that the willingness of the apostles (sometimes embarrassing for moderns) to live within the limits of a society marked by slavery and radical social stratification also has a meaningful foundation in their understanding of the work of Christ and the place of the church in the continuation of that work.

If the reader has followed thus far, it may not be too much to claim that what we have been observing are several significant strands of corroborative evidence for the survival of the social stance of Jesus into the church of the Apostolic Age. But, the critic may well say, this still leaves aside one fundamental observation. The apostle may well have retained within his thought the vestiges of the Jesus kind of ethos; after all, he did not claim to be uniquely pioneering on every subject. But was not his major *original* contribution to the life of the early church the position he took with regard to justification and the law? Is not the center of Pauline theology the argument, called forth by "Judaizers" and stated in different ways, especially in Romans and

Galatians, that a person may be made righteous before God only on the grounds of faith, with no correlation to his keeping of the law?

Just as a guilty thief or murderer is still a thief or a murderer after a declaration of amnesty has freed him from his punishment, the argument runs, so a guilty sinner is still a sinner when God declares, on the ground of the work of Christ which no person could have accomplished for himself or herself, that he or she shall henceforth be considered a new person, forgiven and restored to fellowship. But this "being considered" is, spiritually speaking, a legal fiction. It is valid only on the grounds of the sovereign authority of the judge who declared it to be so. The act of justification or the status of being just or righteous before God is therefore radically disconnected from any objective or empirical achievement of goodness by the believer.

This "disconnection" is only a part of the wider phenomenon of separation between body and soul, objective and subjective realities, outward and inward history, which are the key, are they not, to all the specific emphases of the apostle Paul?

Was not the central message of the apostle Paul his rejection of any objective dimension to the work of God which could be focused in piety, religious practices, or ethical behavior in such a way as to turn the believer's attention toward the human works instead of toward the gift of God? Does not the insistence that justification is by faith alone and through grace alone, apart from any correlation with works of any kind, undercut any radical ethical and social concern by implication, even if Paul himself might not have been rigorous enough to push that implication all the way? If we truly join with classic Protestantism in considering the proclamation of justification by grace through faith to be the point at which the gospel stands or falls, must we not then interpret the ethical tradition which Paul took over from Jewish Christianity and shared with his Gentile churches as a vestige of another system, destined to fade away? Was it not, after all, at the cost of forgetting Paul's emphasis upon grace that a later generation again made good works and a certain social stance very important in the preaching of the church?

Paul and the Question of the Modern Reader

This sweeping set of assumptions about what the apostle Paul must certainly have meant when he spoke about the righteousness of God becoming effective in making people righteous was so self-evident for centuries of Protestant thought, and seemed so necessary as a corrective over against certain tendencies attributed to Catholic piety, that it scarcely could occur to anyone to think that it might be otherwise. It rhymed so well with the heritage of Augustine, and fit so neatly into Protestant preaching patterns, that there was no chink in the armor of self-evidence through which a doubt could insinuate itself.

Or so it seemed, at least, until the advent of the biblical scholarship of this century, which found more freedom to distinguish between the initial cultural context of a biblical passage on one hand and the contribution it makes to contemporary thought on the other.[1] If we may be freed by self-critical scholarly objectivity no longer to have to assume that the authority of the Bible resides in its saying things that we agree with, we may be free as well to hear more clearly what it really says instead of giving it credit for saying what we already think.

Once the entering wedge of this capacity for critical self-awareness had made possible a freer and less apologetic reading of the ancient documents, it became possible to call into question the far-reaching assumption that the apostle Paul was preoccupied with personal self-acceptance. It is understandable that Martin Luther could have found this preoccupation in the apostolic message since it was his own question. Luther had been taught by his monastic training to be personally in need of knowing that he had found a God who would be gracious personally to him. Thus it was perfectly natural for Luther to assume that this was also the preoccupation of the apostle. It was also perfectly natural for a John Wesley, a Kierkegaard, or today for an existentialist or a conservative evangelical reader to make the same assumption and find the same message — for all of these are in their variegated ways children of Luther, still asking the same question of personal guilt and righteousness.

1. Krister Stendahl, article "Biblical Theology," *Interpreter's Dictionary of the Bible* (Nashville: Abingdon, 1962), I, 418ff.

But let us set aside for purposes of discussion the assumption that the righteousness of God and the righteousness of humanity are most fundamentally located on the individual level. Let us make this, instead of an axiom, a hypothesis to be tested. Let us posit as at least thinkable the alternate hypothesis that for Paul righteousness, either in God or in human beings, might more appropriately be conceived of as having cosmic or social dimensions. Such larger dimensions would not negate the personal character of the righteousness God imputes to those who believe;[2] but by englobing the personal salvation in a fuller reality they would negate the individualism with which we understand such reconciliation.

Krister Stendahl set about to call this axiom into question in his article "The Apostle Paul and the Introspective Conscience of the West."[3] Stendahl demonstrates one by one that all the constitutive elements of the classic "Luther-type experience" are missing in both the experience and the thought of the apostle. Paul was not preoccupied with his guilt and seeking the assurance of a gracious God; he was rather robust of conscience and untroubled about whether God was gracious or not. He never pleads either with Jews or Gentiles to feel an anguished conscience and then receive release from that anguish in a message of forgiveness.

Second, Paul's understanding of the meaning of Hebrew law as taught is not that its function was to make people know their guilt, to prepare listeners for the message of forgiveness by deepening their awareness of their sinfulness. The law was rather a gracious arrangement made by God for ordering the life of his people while they were awaiting the arrival of the Messiah. It is true that, once present, law makes its opposite, sin, more visible; but that is not its first purpose nor its primary effect for the believer.

Third, faith was for Paul not a particular spiritual exercise of

2. In view of the corrective intent of the present argument it should be reiterated that my purpose is not to reverse a prior error by claiming that justification is *only* social. I am objecting to a particular polemical application of the traditional doctrine, which used it to *exclude* the ethical and social dimensions. By echoing scholars who have rediscovered the missing dimensions I am not denying the personal. I am doubting that the personal can most adequately be spoken about in abstraction from the rest, as certain recent Western traditions have assumed. This chapter is not expositing all of Paul's thought on justification; it is asking only whether that thought supports the arguments against a "messianic ethic" as it has been held to do.

3. *HTR,* 56 (July 1963), 199ff.

moving from self-trust through despair to confidence in the paradoxical goodness of the judgment of God; faith is at its core the affirmation which separated Jewish Christians from other Jews, that in Jesus of Nazareth the Messiah had come. A Jew did not become a Christian by coming to see God as a righteous judge and a gracious, forgiving protector. The Jew believed that already, being a Jew. What it took for him or her, to become a Christian was not some new idea about his or her sinfulness or God's righteousness, but one about Jesus. The subjective meanings of faith for the self-aware person, and its doctrinal meanings for the believing intellect, build upon this prior messianist affirmation. They cannot precede or replace it.

The heresy Paul was struggling against was not that the Jewish Christians continued to be committed to keeping the law; Paul was quite tolerant of those who held to such a conviction. He taught respect for their dietary scruples. He went out of his way to share their ritual faithfulness when in Jerusalem. Nor was it their thinking that by keeping the law they would be saved, for Jewish Christians did not believe that. The basic heresy he exposed was the failure of those Jewish Christians to recognize that since the Messiah had come the covenant of God had been broken open to include the Gentiles. In sum: the fundamental issue was that of the social form of the church. Was it to be a new and inexplicable kind of community of both Jews and Gentiles, or was it going to be a confederation of a Jewish Christian sect and a Gentile one? Or would all the Gentiles have first to become Jews according to the conditions of premessianic proselytism?

Stendahl exemplifies this difference with one of the classic texts, Galatians 3:24, which states that the law was a "custodian" to order the life of the Jewish community until the Messiah should come. The point of Paul's explanation is that now that the Messiah has come, the Gentiles do not need to pass by way of the law, but can be incorporated directly into the new community. For Luther, on the other hand, "custodian" was interpreted as "schoolmaster," as representing a necessary step which even now the Gentiles must go through. They do not need to be educated by way of the details of the Jewish legislation, but in order to be able to receive grace one must first be broken under the yoke of some kind of law. All must pass by the *usus elenchticus,* by the way of the judging impact of the righteousness of God.

What then was Paul's understanding of sin? When he does speak of himself as a serious sinner at all, this is not because of his existential anguish under the righteousness of God in general, but very specifically because, not having recognized that Messiah had come in Jesus, he had persecuted the church and fought the opening of God's covenant to the Gentiles. What is now set right in his life is not that he has overcome his inner resistances and has become able to trust in God for his right status before God; it is rather that through the inexplicable intervention of God on the Damascus Road and in later experiences, Paul has become the agent of the action of God for the right cause. He has become the privileged bearer of the cause of the ingathering of the Gentiles.

This was perfectly clear not only to Paul but also to his readers. What was at stake in the "proclamation of the righteousness of God to both Jew and Gentile" was precisely that it was to be proclaimed to both and that both were to become parts of the new believing community, some having come by way of the law and some not. It was only when in later generations the Jew-Gentile relationship was partly forgotten and partly distorted into a polemic one that the Pauline language of justification could be reinterpreted, especially in the heritage of Augustine, and translated into the terms of Western self-examination and concern for authenticity. Since this transformation stated the justifying purpose of God in terms translatable for and accessible to every individual, it could be considered somehow eternally or universally relevant, whereas the reconciling of Jew and Gentile can be understood and celebrated only particularly in the uniqueness of salvation history in given times and places.

Stendahl is quite tolerant. He does not reject outright the possible claim that the new "Western" meaning might be, by certain criteria which we might consider useful, more "valid" or more "relevant" than the original one. The further "development of doctrine" may in some way be a good thing. But he nevertheless closes with the suggestion that *perhaps* the meaning enshrined in the salvation-history concern of the early church as a social reality might also be relevant for modern Christians, in addition to doing more justice to the biblical documents and the thought which they report.

The New Person

The most presumptuous and the clearest statement of the particular apostolic ministry of Paul is stated in the letter to the Ephesians.[4]

Here the apostle makes claims to a knowledge and to a ministry that is not merely on the level of the other apostles but unique among the apostles. It is a particular grace which was given just to him to steward for the churches (Eph. 3:2), a "mystery" which was made known to him (3:3). "Mystery" is to be understood not as a spooky secret forever hidden from view, but rather as the strategic purpose of God, which was not widely known until the point of its execution.[5]

The "plan of the mystery" was hidden for ages in God, but now it is known and in fact it is being made known beyond the church by the church, proclaimed even to the "principalities and powers in the heavenly places" (3:9-10).

Just what is this divine purpose, hidden for a time and made known by revelation to Paul? It is precisely that Jew and Gentile are now reconciled in one community.

> At one time you Gentiles in the flesh . . . were separated from Christ, alienated from the commonwealth of Israel and strangers to the covenant of promise . . . but now in Christ Jesus you who once were far off have been brought near in the blood of Christ. For he is our peace, who has made us both one, and has broken down the dividing wall of hostility, by abolishing in his flesh the law . . . that he might create in himself the one humanity instead of two, so making peace, and might reconcile us both to God in one body through the cross, thereby bringing the hostility to an end. (Eph. 2:11-26)

The hostility brought to an end in Christ is first and foremost in this passage not the hostility between a righteous God and the creature

4. I need not discuss here whether the present text of Ephesians is from the pen of Paul, or his amanuensis, or a later writer claiming to write in the same spirit. For a later writer to make these statements about Paul's ministry would be no less germane to our discussion.

5. The usual context for this usage of "mystery" would seem to have been military. A battle plan is kept secret until the battle; but once the battle has begun it is public knowledge.

who has trespassed against his rules, but the hostility between Jew and Greek. The overcoming of this hostility, the making of peace by eliminating the wall that had separated them, namely the Jewish law to which Jews were committed and which Gentiles ignored, is itself the creation of a new humanity. This is why the unique ministry of Paul as "prisoner for Jesus Christ on behalf of you Gentiles" (3:1) is inseparable from his own unique revealed insight into the "mystery" of God's purpose. The work of Christ is not only that he saves the soul of individuals and henceforth they can love each other better; the work of Christ, the making of peace, the breaking down of the wall, is itself the constituting of a new community made up of two kinds of people, those who had lived under the law and those who had not. The events the book of Acts narrates as the recent initiative of the Holy Spirit in opening up the churches, first at Jerusalem and then in Samaria, then in Damascus and Antioch, to the fellowship of believing Jews and believing Gentiles, are here interpreted by Paul, a major actor in that drama and its accredited interpreter, as being the extended meaning of the cross and resurrection of Jesus.[6]

We have identified this message in the book of Ephesians, a relatively late document, where the word "justification" actually is not central, only in order to be able to perceive more readily its presence in the earlier writings where it is not equally developed. As elsewhere, we lean heavily upon a few contemporary scholars, testifying again to

6. The recorded workings of the Holy Spirit in the book of Acts are always related to the opening up of the church to a wider view of her mission. The Holy Spirit is made known in those divine initiatives which drive the church to proclaim to a wider world. Cf. Harry Boer, *Pentecost and Missions* (Grand Rapids: Eerdmans, 1961). A current interpretation of Paul's understanding of the place in history of his own mission posits a temporal-causative relation between the evangelizing of the nations and the return of Christ; *when* the gospel has been proclaimed to all the nations, *then* the end will come (Matt. 24:14). This is the understanding especially of Oscar Cullmann and Johannes Munck (summarized in John Knox, "Romans 15:14-53 and Paul's Conception of His Apostolic Mission," *JBL*, 83 [Mar. 1964], 1ff.). Krister Stendahl's understanding and that of Eph. 2–3 advocated here would turn it the other way around; because the end time is here, the Gentiles are now in the covenant. The ingathering of the Gentiles is not a means to an end or a precondition of the fullness of time; it is the beginning of the end. The fullness of time is the precondition of the Gentile mission. Cf. as well Paul Minear, "Paul's Missionary Dynamic," in his *The Obedience of Faith: The Purposes of Paul in the Epistle to the Romans*, SBT, 2nd ser., 19 (1971), 91ff.

the fact that the thrust of the present book is not original except perhaps in the consistency with which it attempts to draw ethical conclusions from what more specialized scholars have already found.

The New Righteousness That Is Valid Before God

Markus Barth[7] plunges right to the heart of the classic discussion in Galatians (2:14ff.).

> We have believed in Christ Jesus in order to be justified by faith in Christ and not by works of the law, because by works of the law no one shall be justified.

What does "justified" mean here? Can it really mean, as Protestant tradition assumes (Lutheranism most sweepingly, but the Anglican and Reformed liturgies give the same testimony), that it refers only to the quasi-judicial status of the sinner's guilt before God, which is annulled or amnestied by a declaration of the judge in response to the act of faith?

Through very careful analysis of this classic passage, Markus Barth clarifies that the particular issue at stake, carried on unbroken from the earlier part of chapter 2, was whether Jewish and Gentile Christians were to live together acceptingly in one fellowship. To be "justified" is to be set right in and for that relationship. "Justification" is, in other words, in the language of Galatians the same as "making peace" or "breaking down the wall" in the language of Ephesians.

> Sharing in the death and resurrection of Jesus Christ is the means of justification: only in Christ's death and resurrection is the new man created from at least two, a Jew and a Greek, a man and a woman, a slave and a free man, etc. . . . The new man is present in actuality where two previously alien and hostile men come together before God. Justification in Christ is thus not an individual miracle

7. Markus Barth, "Jews and Gentiles: The Social Character of Justification in Paul," *JES,* 5/2 (Spring 1968), 241ff. Cf. as well Barth's *Justification* (Grand Rapids: Eerdmans, 1971).

> happening to this person or that person, which each may seek or possess for himself. Rather justification by grace is a joining together of this person and that person, of the near and far; . . . it is a social event.[8]

Barth has thus confirmed, beginning his analysis from another direction and dealing with another text, what we have already seen to have been demonstrated by Stendahl and in Ephesians: that the relationship between divine justification and the reconciliation of persons and groups to one another is not a sequential relationship. It is not that "faith" occurs first as an inner existential leap of the individual past concern for his or her finitude, and then God operates a change in the person who becomes able to love others. Barth characterizes Albrecht Ritschl as having "considered forgiveness and justification as sort of psychic release which enabled the individual member of the church to participate in an ethical process," whereas for Paul this relationship of prelude and sequence cannot thus be distinguished.[9]

The "New Creature"

If there is any one biblical text that focuses for lay understanding the individualism of the Pietist heritage it is the statement of 2 Corinthians 5:17: "If anyone be in Christ *he is* a new creature" (AV). It has seemed self-evident that we were being promised here, overlapping with the language of a new birth (John 3:5-6), a metaphysical or ontological transformation of the individual person. The miracle of being made a new person has been promised in evangelistic proclamation and has served in turn to illuminate traditional understandings of the rootage of Christian social concern. It is because only a transformed individual will behave differently that some kinds of social activism are fruitless; it is because a transformed individual will definitely behave differently

8. *Ibid.*, p. 259.

9. In general the New Testament word *pistis* would better not be translated "faith," with the concentration that word has for modern readers upon either a belief *content* or the *act* of believing; "faithfulness" would generally be a more accurate rendering of its meaning.

that the preaching of the gospel to individuals is the surest way to change society.

It is not the concern of the present study to deny that such a thrust has had a wholesome corrective impact in certain contexts in the history of Protestant thought and Protestant church life. Like Stendahl, we may concede a certain usefulness to nonbiblical thought patterns. Nor are we setting aside the "new birth" imagery of John 3 or parallel themes elsewhere. Our question is only whether this is what *Paul* is saying in *this* text. This becomes extremely doubtful when we look more carefully at the text itself.

As the italics in the AV indicate, the words "he is" are not in the original text. Now it can regularly be necessary to add the English "is" in order to make clear a predication which in the Greek requires no copulative verb. But to add "he" (or "she"), thereby identifying an antecedent in the previous clause, is quite another matter. It is grammatically not impossible to reach back to the "anyone" earlier in the verse as the understood subject of this predication; but that is not the only interpretation, and others should be tried first.

A second shortcoming of this traditional interpretation of "the new creature" as the transformed individual personality is that the word *ktisis,* here translated "creature" or "creation," is not used elsewhere in the New Testament to designate the individual person. It in fact most often is used to designate not the object of creation but rather the act of creating (e.g., Rom. 1:20), "from the creation of the world." Secondarily it may mean the entire universe (Mark 16:15; Col. 1:15, 24; Rom. 8:19-22; Heb. 9:11). The single reference to "human creation" refers to social institutions (1 Pet. 2:13). In the one other place where the phrase "new creation" is used, it is quite parallel to the "new humanity" of Ephesians 2:15, not a renewed individual but a new social reality, marked by the overcoming of the Jew/Greek barrier; "neither circumcision nor uncircumcision but a new creation" (Gal. 6:15).[10]

Putting together these strictly linguistic observations, it becomes enormously more probable that we should lean to the kind of translation favored by the more recent translators; literally, "if anyone is in

10. Even the verb *ktizo* tends to be used in the sense of the "new humanity": "created in Christ for good works" (Eph. 2:10; cf. 2:15; 4:24; Col. 3:10).

Christ, new is creation," or more smoothly, "there is a whole new world" (NEB). The accent lies not on transforming the ontology of the person (to say nothing of transforming his or her psychological or neurological equipment) but on transforming the perspective of one who has accepted Christ as life context.

This is certainly the point of the rest of the passage in question. Paul is explaining why he no longer regards anyone from the human point of view;[11] why he does not regard Jew as Jew or Greek as Greek, but rather looks at every person in the light of the new world which begins in Christ. "The old has passed away, behold the new has come," is a social or historical statement, not an introspective or emotional one.

To the Jew First but Also to the Greek

A quite different segment of Paul's writings is the framework of introduction and conclusion around his letter to the Christians at Rome. Hans Werner Bartsch points out[12] that Paul never calls the total Roman community a "church"[13] and that the issue of the polarity of Jew and Gentile is present at major turning points throughout the argument of the book, as well as in the introduction and conclusion. The foreground meaning of the issue of the place of the law was not systematic theological speculation about how human beings are to be made acceptable to God,

11. One standard interpretation of this passage has Paul defending his apostolate against those who argue that he had not known the earthly Jesus as the other apostles had. This meaning is excluded by Paul's going on to deny that he "knows" anyone else in this way. Cf. J. B. Souček, "Wir kennen Christus nicht mehr nach dem Fleisch," *EvT,* 19/7 (July 1959), 300ff. 1 Cor. 3:3-4 also uses "after the flesh" to describe the practice of placing people in categories, with the effect of dividing the church. "After the flesh" can simply mean "by biological descent" (Rom. 1:3; 4:3; 9:3-5; 1 Cor. 10:18; 11:18; Gal. 4:23).

12. Hans Werner Bartsch, "Die Historische Situation des Römerbriefes," *Communio Viatorum,* 8/4 (Winter 1965), 199ff. Cf. also Étienne Trocmé, "L'Église Romaine et la méthode missionnaire de l'Apotre Paul," *NTS,* 7/1 (Oct. 1960), 148ff. Paul Minear *(The Obedience of Faith),* working quite independently of Bartsch, Barth, and Trocmé, comes to the same conclusion.

13. In ch. 16 Paul greets twenty-four individuals by name, plus two families (or house fellowships? vv. 10, 11) and another group of saints (v. 15); but only for the group gathered in the house of Aquila does he use the name "church."

but rather the very concrete Roman situation in which Jew and Greek, legalistic Christian and pagan Christian needed to accept one another. "Law" is written about neither as a means of soul salvation, nor as a hindrance thereto, but as the historically concrete identity of the Jewish separateness which made the problem that justification resolves.

We could in fact most properly say that the word "justification" (like the word "creation" examined above) should be thought of in its root meaning, as a verbal noun, an action, "setting things right," rather than as an abstract noun defining a person's quasi-legal status as a result of a judge's decree. To proclaim divine righteousness means to proclaim that God sets things right; it is characteristic of the God who makes a covenant with us to be a right-setting kind of God.

Bartsch supports this interpretation of the concern of Romans with a wealth of detailed textual observations. That the Christians in Rome are not referred to as a "church," in view of Paul's usage elsewhere, is presumed to indicate that the insufficient unity of that group constitutes a problem to them and to him. Bartsch emphasizes the recurrence of reference to Jew and Greek at all the turning points of the document, to say nothing of the special significance of chapters 9–11, whose entire concern is the place of Jewish identity in view of God's having created the church. From the obedience of faith (1:5) through the "accepting one another" (14:1; 15:7) to Paul's concern for collecting funds for Jerusalem (15:28), his desire is that there should come into being in Rome this kind of new community where the brokenness of humankind is set right and where persons who were not born under the law obey it from the heart.[14]

If the reader can grant that in the company of Stendahl, Barth, Bartsch, and Minear we may properly understand Paul's concept of justification as a social phenomenon centering in the reconciliation of different kinds of people, what has that to do with the problem with which our study began, namely the ethic of revolutionary nonviolence which Jesus offers to his disciples?

14. The difference between the function of the law in Paul and that in Luther is not merely that the Gentiles do not pass by way of the law to come to the gospel; it is also that the law continues to have a validity for all believers. Thus the law is not done away with but rather restored in its life-giving, nondivisive intent.

Perhaps most evident is a kind of double negative impact upon the state of the debate in theological ethics. This debate has been dominated by a negation, which appealed in its support to what was supposed to be unique about the message of Paul. Because Paul is different from Jesus or because justification is different from social ethics, therefore the way of Jesus, it was classically held, has lost its bindingness for our age. It is this negation which a more open reading of the apostles in turn negates. The negation of this negation is all the more significant because the scholars I have been quoting were simply going about their erudite business, with no predisposition to support my reading of Jesus' or of Paul's ethics.[15]

But the proclamation that God reconciles classes of people is in itself far more than a double negative. To proclaim it as Paul did in his writings years and even decades after Pentecost is to confirm that such reconciliation is a real experience and therefore a real invitation. Paul is saying, somewhere toward the *end* of the evolution of apostolic Christianity, what Jesus had said somewhere near the beginning. That he can still say it now is proof that, at least to some modest degree, experience had confirmed it. Paul says that it characterizes the victory of God's creation-sustaining love that insider and outsider, friend and enemy are equally blessed, in such manner that the genuineness (Jesus said, "perfection")[16] of our love is also made real at the point of its application to the enemy, the Gentile, the sinner. There is a sense

15. This outline has thus leaned on the lessons offered by contemporary New Testament scholars, who themselves did not intend to support my thesis. This should defend against any suspicion of special pleading. But it should not be thought that this view of Romans first arose in the 1960s.

The argument that the message of Paul is more social, less "existential" than it has been made by Protestant tradition, has been present in the academic underground for a century, especially in Johann Christoph Blumhardt and in the "religious socialism" of European Protestantism *ca.* 1910-25. The movement broke up on the rocks of personal and theological conflict between its two strongest spokesmen, Leonhard Ragaz and Karl Barth, both of whom had made this point about Paul.

16. The "perfection" to which Jesus calls his hearers in the Sermon on the Mount (Matt. 5:48; cf. Luke 6:35-36) is not flawlessness nor impeccability, but precisely the refusal to discriminate between friend and enemy, the in and the out, the good and the evil. It is revealed in the indiscriminateness in which God loves the good and the evil alike (cf. above, p. 116).

in which the ethics of marriage and the prohibition of adultery, or the ethics of work and the regulation of attitudes toward slavery, or the opening up of communication and the prohibition of falsehood are all part of the promise of a new humanity enabled and created by God, and already being received by men and women of faith. But it is *par excellence* with reference to enmity between peoples, the extension of neighbor love to the enemy, and the renunciation of violence even in the most righteous cause, that this promise takes on flesh in the most original, the most authentic, the most frightening and scandalous, and therefore in the most evangelical way. It is the Good News that my enemy and I are united, through no merit or work of our own, in a new humanity that forbids henceforth my ever taking his or her life in my hands.

Perhaps a retrospective word should extend to all of this section on the thought of Paul what was said with regard to "justification." My presentation, in order to correct for the one-sided social ethic which has been dominant in the past, emphasizes what was denied before: Jesus as teacher and example,[17] not only as sacrifice; God as the shaker of the foundations, not only as guarantor of the orders of creation; faith as discipleship, not only as subjectivity. The element of debate in the presentation may make it seem that the "other" or "traditional" element in each case — Jesus as sacrifice, God as creator, faith as subjectivity — is being rejected. It should therefore be restated that — as perusal of the structure of our presentation will confirm — no such disjunction is intended. I am rather defending the New Testament against the exclusion of the "messianic" element. The disjunction must be laid to the account of the traditional view, not of mine. It is those other views that say that because Jesus is seen as sacrifice he may not be seen as sovereign, or that because he is seen as Word made flesh he cannot be seen as normative person.

17. The theme of obedience and imitation in response to Jesus as teacher and example has not been absent from scholarship or piety (cf. above, p. 112); but it has seldom entered into formal ethical discourse, and its relevance has been more to motivation than to substance. "Be like Jesus, this my song . . ." usually refers to unselfish purpose, not to distinctive behavior. Cf. my fuller attention to this theme in the epilogue to chapter 7.

EPILOGUE

I had occasion to review and extend the theme of the present chapter, with more attention to the key text of 1 Corinthians 5, in my "The Apostle's Apology Revisited."[18] Its point has been largely taken for granted (not because of my text, but thanks to the growing prevalence of the insights I was reporting) in much continuing Pauline scholarship. Much of this study is located within the renewal of Jewish-Christian dialogue about first-century origins. The way in which the anti-Roman and anti-Jewish biases of the North European scholarship of earlier generations kept Paul's own message from getting through the screen of individualistic and neo-Platonistic notions of salvation is now widely recognized.

The last paragraph of the above text should perhaps have been placed at a more prominent place in the book. Some readers, who missed that paragraph or did not believe it, have described *The Politics of Jesus* as reductionistic or materialistic, some intending that description as praise, but more of them as blame.

In an apologetic or missionary perspective, I am not sure that I should be sorry, if it were to turn out to be the case that my retrieval of the straightforward gospel message should be found understandable or interesting to contemporaries not at home in classical Christian understandings of transcendence or inwardness. Yet such a potential apologetic value was, as the reader of my first chapters knows, not the point of my exercise.

18. In Wm. Klassen (ed.), *The New Way of Jesus* (Newton, Kans.: Faith and Life Press, 1980), pp. 115-34.

CHAPTER 12

The War of the Lamb

Jesus and Paul have been the foci of our exposition. They must represent the centers of any New Testament theological synthesis, due both to their originality and to the amount of the material that makes them knowable to us. But there are other figures, other minds at work. A thorough treatment would demand that we test there as well the reading we have taken already. There would be the thought of the author of Matthew or of the writer to the Hebrews; there would be the mind of Peter, of John, of Jude, or of the seer of the Apocalypse. There is reason to trust that the reading there would confirm the orientation already sketched. Here, however, I must renounce the further cross-referencing and leap ahead to a summary, rooted nonetheless especially in the last-named Apocalypse. I shall seek briefly to characterize the stance of that book, as it might by contrast throw some light on our contemporary agenda and at the same time draw together the argument of the entire book.

One way to characterize thinking about social ethics in our time is to say that Christians in our age are obsessed with the meaning and direction of history. Social ethical concern is moved by a deep desire to make things move in the right direction. Whether a given action is right or not seems to be inseparable from the question of what effects it will cause. Thus part if not all of social concern has to do with looking for the right "handle" by which one can "get a hold on" the course of history and move it in the right direction. For the movement called Moral Rearmament, ideology was this handle; "ideas have legs," so that if we can get a contagious new thought moving, it will make its own way. For others, it is the process of education that ultimately determines the character and course of the civilization; whoever rules the teachers' colleges rules the world.

Rambunctious students believe that the office of the dean or the president is the center of the university and therefore they occupy that office. Che Guevara believed the peasant to be the backbone of the coming Latin American revolution, so he went to the hills of Bolivia. The Black Economic Development Conference directed its Manifesto to the administrators of denominations because it believed that the point of decision making for white racist American society was there. Conservative evangelicalism focuses its call for change upon the will of the individual because it believes that when the individual heart is turned in another direction the rest is sure to follow. For still others it is the proletariat or geopolitics that explains everything.

Whichever the favored "handle" may be, the structure of this approach is logically the same. One seeks to lift up one focal point in the midst of the course of human relations, one thread of meaning and causality which is more important than individual persons, their lives and well-being, because it in itself determines wherein their well-being consists. Therefore it is justified to sacrifice to this one "cause" other subordinate values, including the life and welfare of one's self, one's neighbor, and (of course!) of the enemy. We pull this one strategic thread in order to save the whole fabric. We can see this kind of reasoning with Constantine saving the Roman Empire, with Luther saving the Reformation by making an alliance with the princes, or with Khrushchev and his successors saving Marxism by making it somewhat more capitalistic, or with the United States saving democracy by alliances with military dictatorships and by the threatened use of the bomb.

If we look more analytically at this way of deriving social and political ethics from an overview of the course of history and the choice of the thread within history that is thought to be the most powerful, we find that it involves at least three distinguishable assumptions.

1. It is assumed that the relationship of cause and effect is visible, understandable, and manageable, so that if we make our choices on the basis of how we hope society will be moved, it will be moved in that direction.

2. It is assumed that we are adequately informed to be able to set

for ourselves and for all society the goal toward which we seek to move it.

3. Interlocked with these two assumptions and dependent upon them for its applicability is the further postulate that effectiveness in moving toward these goals which have been set is itself a moral yardstick.

If we look critically at these assumptions we discover that they are by no means as self-evident as they seem to be at first. There is for one thing the phenomenon Reinhold Niebuhr has called "irony": that when people try to manage history, it almost always turns out to have taken another direction than that in which they thought they were guiding it. This may mean that we are not morally qualified to set the goals toward which we would move history. At least it must mean that we are not capable of discerning and managing its course when there are in the same theater of operation a host of other free agents, each of them in their own way also acting under the same assumptions as to their capacity to move history in their direction. Thus even apart from other more spiritual considerations, the strategic calculus is subject to a very serious internal question. It has yet to be demonstrated that history can be moved in the direction in which one claims the duty to cause it to go.

The other question we must raise at the outset about the logic of the "strategic" attitude toward ethical decisions is its acceptance of effectiveness itself as a goal. Even if we know how effectiveness is to be measured — that is, even if we could get a clear definition of the goal we are trying to reach and how to ascertain whether we had reached it — is there not in Christ's teaching on meekness, or in the attitude of Jesus toward power and servanthood, a deeper question being raised about whether it is our business at all to guide our action by the course we wish history to take?

It is, however, not the concern of our present study to deal logically or systematically with this kind of question within the traditional or contemporary idioms of theological debate. In recent centuries debate around the question of the meaning of history, and the place of Christian decision within that meaningfulness, has generally been a conversation of the deaf, with some so committed to pre-Enlightenment understandings of the stability of the proper social order that any sense of movement is only a threat, and others committed with an equally unquestioning irrationality to the progressivist assumptions of post-Enlightenment Western thought, according to which the discernible movement of history is self-explicating and generally works for good, and therefore is the only terrain of significance from which ethics should self-evidently be derived. From neither direction has there been any expectation that light might be thrown upon the question from the New Testament. What medieval Christendom, with its vision of the divine stability of all the members of the *corpus christianum,* has in common with post-Enlightenment progressivism is precisely the assumption that history has moved us past the time of primitive Christianity and therefore out from under the relevance of the apostolic witness on this question.

The earlier portions of this book have sought to spell out in considerable detail the elements of a vision of the Christian's place in the world that can claim rootage in the thought of Jesus and Paul. It remains, we have seen, to test the concordance of this approach in the remaining sections of the canonical literature. This literature (the General Epistles and the Apocalypse) is less unified, less easy to understand, and there is also less of it; so we cannot ask for the fullness of delineation toward which we have pointed in the earlier sections of the study. We can, however, ask whether that which it is possible to discern in these writings is concordant with the other strands of apostolic witness we have been pursuing; and it is fitting to center this question upon the concern for history's meaning.

For a sense of the apostolic perception of the meaning and course of history and especially of the interplay of trust and coerciveness within history, we shall find that the most immediate resource comes from that segment of the biblical literature from which we are least accustomed to learn, namely from the liturgical literature which is embedded in the New Testament at certain scattered points, but which especially dominates in the book of the Revelation of John.

In his first vision (Rev. 4–5) the seer of Patmos is presented with the image of a sealed scroll in the hand of the "one that was seated upon the throne" (a circumlocution for God himself, who cannot be looked at directly, but whose presence is known as Light).

The question laid before John by his vision of the scroll sealed with seven seals is precisely the question of the meaningfulness of history. This is a question that, the vision says dramatically, cannot be answered by the normal resources of human insight. Yet it is by no means a meaningless question or one unworthy of concern. It is worth weeping, as the seer does, if we do not know the meaning of human life and suffering.

Speaking more generally we can affirm, as numerous historians of philosophy are arguing, that to be concerned about history, to assume that history is meaningful, is itself a Judeo-Christian idea. The concern to know where history is going is not an idle philosophical curiosity. It is a necessary expression of the conviction that God has worked in past history and has promised to continue thus to be active among us. If God is the kind of God-active-in-history of whom the Bible speaks, then concern for the course of history is itself not an illegitimate or an irrelevant concern. No mystical or existentialistic or spiritualistic depreciation of preoccupation with the course of events is justified for the Christian.

But the answer given to the question by the series of visions and their hymns is not the standard answer. "The lamb that was slain is worthy to receive power!" John is here saying, not as an inscrutable paradox but as a meaningful affirmation, that the cross and not the sword, suffering and not brute power determines the meaning of history. The key to the obedience of God's people is not their effectiveness but their patience (13:10). The triumph of the right is assured not by the might that comes to the aid of the right, which is of course the justification of the use of violence and other kinds of power in every human conflict. The triumph of the right, although it is assured, is sure because of the power of the resurrection and not because of any calculation of causes and effects, nor because of the inherently greater strength of the good guys. The relationship between the obedience of God's people and the triumph of God's cause is not a relationship of cause and effect but one of cross and resurrection.

We have observed this biblical "philosophy of history" first of all in the worship life of the late New Testament church, since it is here that we find the most desperate encounter of the church's weakness (John was probably in exile, Paul in prison) with the power of the evil rulers of the present age. But this position is nothing more than a logical unfolding of the meaning of the work of Jesus Christ himself, whose choice of suffering servanthood rather than violent lordship, of love to the point of death rather than righteousness backed by power, was itself the fundamental direction of his life. Jesus was so faithful to the enemy-love of God that it cost him all his effectiveness; he gave up every handle on history.

Not only does the New Testament church claim knowledge about the meaning of history or the meaning of meekness in history; it relates this very specifically to the coming and the ministry of the man Jesus. If we had only the book of Revelation we would not necessarily know what is meant by this Lamb in whom all sovereignty is said to reside. What therefore matters ultimately is how this Lamb relates to the rest of the human history of the people who praise him. The answer lies of course in the person of Jesus himself, of whom this same early church said in another context that "the Word became flesh and dwelt among us."

Thus early Christian confession means two things for our present concern. Speaking negatively, it means that the business of ethical thinking has been taken away from the speculation of independent minds each meditating on the meaning of things and has been pegged to a particular set of answers given in a particular time and place. Ethics as well as "theology" (in the sense in which in the past they have been distinguished) must, if it is to be our business as Christians to think about them, be rooted in revelation, not alone in speculation, nor in a self-interpreting "situation."

But still more important is the other side, the positive side of this confession. This will of God is affirmatively, concretely knowable in the person and ministry of Jesus. Jesus is not to be looked at merely as the last and greatest in the long line of rabbis teaching pious people how to behave; he is to be looked at as a mover of history and as the standard by which Christians must learn how they are to look at the moving of history.

The War of the Lamb

Thus the most appropriate example of the difficult choice between effectiveness and obedience, and the most illuminating example, is that of Jesus himself. What it means for the Lamb to be slain, of whom then we sing that he is "worthy to receive power," is inseparable from what it meant for Jesus to be executed under the superscription "King of the Jews."

The name "Christ," that is, the one anointed to rule, will have to suffice for present purposes to express symbolically that his ministry among his contemporaries was inseparable from the political concerns then related most intimately to fulfilling the hopes of his people in their oppression. The possibility that he might have guaranteed political efficacy and what some call "relevance" by undertaking a political alliance with the forces of the Zealots or with some other power group in Palestinian society was according to the most careful Bible study a genuine option. The choice that he made in rejecting the crown and accepting the cross was the commitment to such a degree of faithfulness to the character of divine love that he was willing for its sake to sacrifice "effectiveness." Usually it can be argued that from some other perspective or in some long view this renunciation of effectiveness was in fact a very effective thing to do. "If a man will lose his . . . life he shall find it." But this paradoxical possibility does not change the initially solid fact that Jesus thereby excluded any normative concern for any capacity to make sure that things would turn out right.

This renunciation is most profoundly stated in the hymn of the early church, which we already noted: "He counted equality with God not a thing to be seized hold of" (Phil. 2:6)

In other ages, we observed, theology understood these words as having to do with the divine nature of the eternal Son of God and his condescending to take on human nature. This was the best way to say it when people could think most meaningfully in terms of "essences" and "substances." But it is equally relevant — and much closer to the substance of the text of this hymn, as we shall see in a moment — to see in "equality with God" also the element of providential control of events, the alternative being the acceptance of impotence. Christ renounced the claim to govern history.

The universal testimony of Scripture is that Christians are those who follow Christ at just this point. The text we were just reading, Philippians 2, was cited by the apostle as part of his plea to the Christians at Philippi to live together more unselfishly. The visions of the book of Revelation go on from the heavenly throne room, where the Lamb is praised, to a vision of triumph (ch. 12) where the multitude of "our brethren" has defeated the dragon "by the blood of the lamb and by the word of their testimony, for they loved not their lives even unto death." Elsewhere, Paul can describe the entire apostolic ministry with its inner and outer sufferings as a matter of "carrying about in our bodies the putting to death of Jesus, so that in our bodies the life of Jesus also may be made manifest" (2 Cor. 4:10). This is what Jesus himself meant by recognizing as disciple only the one who is ready to take up a cross and follow him.

The reason Paul drew upon the hymn to the servant Lord was that he sought to move the Christians in Philippi to a more unselfish attitude to one another, in the interests of more brotherly relationships within the congregation. It was in this connection that we referred to the hymn, since it is one more example of the call to the Christian to imitate his or her Master.

But the original meaning of the hymn was far more than we perceive if we note only the point at which a Christian can be invited to respect the example of Christ. The initial confession of the hymn to the servant Lord was the dramatic juxtaposition of his condescension to the point of death with his victory. The renunciation of equality with God (v. 6) has been understood in later Christian doctrinal development as referring to the metaphysical meaning of deity and incarnation, but probably the first meaning in the hymn was the more concrete Godlikeness promised by the serpent to Adam in the garden, which would have consisted in unchecked dominion over creation. Or perhaps it refers as well to the kind of Godlikeness claimed by Caesar. What Jesus renounced was thus not simply the metaphysical status of sonship but rather the untrammeled sovereign exercise of power in the affairs of that humanity amid which he came to dwell. His emptying of himself, his accepting the form of servanthood and obedience unto death, is precisely his renunciation of lordship, his apparent abandonment of any obligation to be effective in making history move down the right track.

But the judgment of God upon this renunciation and acceptance of defeat is the declaration that this is victory. "Therefore God has greatly exalted him and given him the title, which every creature will have to confess, *the Lord.*" "Lord" in the earliest Christian confessions was not (as it is in so much modern piety) a label to state a believer's humility or affection or devotion; it is an affirmation of his victorious relation to the powers of the cosmos. That ancient hymn, which since it could be incorporated as a block in the apostolic writings is one of the earliest extended snatches of Christian worship on record, is thus affirming that the dominion of God over history has made use of the apparent historical failure of Jesus as a mover of human events.

We said before that this text affirms a philosophy of history in which renunciation and suffering are meaningful. After the further ground our thoughts have covered we can affirm still more roundly that for the apostle this renunciation must have been seen as profoundly linked to the human career of Jesus, who did concretely renounce the power offered to him by the tempter and by the Zealots. This hymn is then not, as some would make it, simply a Hellenistic mystery-religion text about a mythical Christ figure, coming down from heaven and returning thither; it is at the same time the account of the human Jesus whose death was the very political death of the cross. The renunciation of the claim to govern history was not made only by the second person of the Trinity taking upon himself the demand of an eternal divine decree; it was also made by a poor, tired rabbi when he came from Galilee to Jerusalem to be rejected.

This Gospel concept of the cross of the Christian does not mean that suffering is thought of as in itself redemptive or that martyrdom is a value to be sought after. Nor does it refer uniquely to being persecuted for "religious" reasons by an outspokenly pagan government. What Jesus refers to in his call to cross-bearing is rather the seeming defeat of that strategy of obedience which is no strategy, the inevitable suffering of those whose only goal is to be faithful to that love which puts one at the mercy of one's neighbor, which abandons claims to justice for oneself and for one's own in an overriding concern for the reconciling of the adversary and the estranged. 1 Peter 2 thus draws direct social consequences from the fact that Christ "when he suffered did not threaten but trusted him who judges justly."

This is significantly different from that kind of "pacifism" which would say that it is wrong to kill but that with proper nonviolent techniques you can obtain without killing everything you really want or have a right to ask for. In this context it seems that sometimes the rejection of violence is offered only because it is a cheaper or less dangerous or more shrewd way to impose one's will upon someone else, a kind of coercion which is harder to resist. Certainly any renunciation of violence is preferable to its acceptance; but what Jesus renounced is not first of all violence, but rather the compulsiveness of purpose that leads the strong to violate the dignity of others. The point is not that one can attain all of one's legitimate ends without using violent means. It is rather that our readiness to renounce our legitimate ends whenever they cannot be attained by legitimate means itself constitutes our participation in the triumphant suffering of the Lamb.

This conception of participation in the character of God's struggle with a rebellious world, which early Quakerism referred to as "the war of the lamb," has the peculiar disadvantage — or advantage, depending upon one's point of view — of being meaningful only if Christ be he who Christians claim him to be, the Master. Almost every other kind of ethical approach espoused by Christians, pacifist or otherwise, will continue to make sense to the non-Christian as well. Whether Jesus be the Christ or not, whether Jesus the Christ be Lord or not, whether this kind of religious language be meaningful or not, most types of ethical approach will keep on functioning just the same. For their true foundation is in some reading of the human situation or some ethical insight which is claimed to be generally accessible to all people of goodwill. The same is not true for this vision of "completing in our bodies that which was lacking in the suffering of Christ" (Col. 1:24). If Jesus Christ was not who historic Christianity confesses he was, the revelation in the life of a real man of the very character of God, then this one argument for pacifism collapses.

Accepting Powerlessness

We thus do not adequately understand what the church was praising in the work of Christ, and what Paul was asking his readers to be guided by, if we think of the cross as a peculiarly efficacious technique (probably effective only in certain circumstances) for getting one's way. The key to the ultimate relevance and to the triumph of the good is not any calculation at all, paradoxical or otherwise, of efficacy, but rather simple obedience. Obedience means not keeping verbally enshrined rules but reflecting the character of the love of God. The cross is not a recipe for resurrection. Suffering is not a tool to make people come around, nor a good in itself. But the kind of faithfulness that is willing to accept evident defeat rather than complicity with evil is, by virtue of its conformity with what happens to God when he works among us, aligned with the ultimate triumph of the Lamb.

This vision of ultimate good being determined by faithfulness and not by results is the point where we moderns get off. We confuse the kind of "triumph of the good," whose sole guarantee is the resurrection and the promise of the eternal glory of the Lamb, with an immediately accessible triumph which can be manipulated, just past the next social action campaign, by getting hold of society as a whole at the top. What in the Middle Ages was done by Roman Christianity or Islam is now being attempted by Marxism and by democratic nationalism. In spite of all the difference in language, and in the detailed vision of just what a good society would look like (and as a matter of fact even the visions are not that different), the real uniqueness of each of these positions is only that it identifies differently the particular moral elite which it holds to be worthy of guiding its society from the top. We may well prefer a democratically controlled oligarchy to some other kind. We may well have a choice between Marxist and Islamic and other statements of the vision of the good society. But what our contemporaries find themselves practically incapable of challenging is that the social problem can be solved by determining which aristocrats are morally justified, by virtue of their better ideology, to use the power of society from the top so as to lead the whole system in their direction.

Once a desirable course of history has been labeled, once we know what the right cause is, then it is further assumed that we should be willing to sacrifice for it; sacrifice not only our own values but also those of the neighbor and especially the enemy. In other words, the achievement of the good cause, the implementation in history of the changes we have determined to be desirable, creates a new autonomous ethical value, "relevance," itself a good in the name of which evil may be done.

In the past, Christians and especially pacifists have debated the theoretical issue of whether evil may ever be done for the sake of good. But really the deeper question is the axiom that underlies the question, namely that it is a high good to make history move in the right direction. For only if that assumption is made does the further "opportunistic" justification of evil follow.

If what we have said about the honor due the Lamb makes any sense, then what is usually called "Christian pacifism" is most adequately understood not on the level of means alone, as if the pacifist were making the claim that he can achieve what war promises to achieve, but do it just as well or even better without violence. This is one kind of pacifism, which in some contexts may be clearly able to prove its point, but not necessarily always. That Christian pacifism which has a theological basis in the character of God and the work of Jesus Christ is one in which the calculating link between our obedience and ultimate efficacy has been broken, since the triumph of God comes through resurrection and not through effective sovereignty or assured survival.

This clarification, however, places before us a new question, one that would not have to be looked at if we were content to consider pacifism simply as rejection of violent means. Does it make sense to ask the public authorities in civil society to enforce standards of fraternity and equity which Christians can seek after in the church on the basis of the free assent of those who claim to be committed to Christian obedience? Does it make sense, first of all as an expression of moral consistency, since any appeal to public enforcement involves a clear calculation of efficacy and use of pressure toward that end? Does it make sense, secondly, as radical appropriateness? Assuming that we have some factual and perhaps prophetic insight into the nature of the abuses under which our society suffers and some vision of possible solutions, is it more appropriate to appeal, in order that these solutions might have some chance of being accepted and implemented, to the convincing power of truth? Or may we honestly and more fervently appeal to lesser motives, to public opinion, resentment, isolationism, fear of the bomb, or to the unrealistic hope that the enemy may be a good guy after all?

What does it mean to raise this question? Does it mean that pessimism about the appropriateness or the possibility of a Christian witness to the social order should lead us to return to the self-centeredness and lack of social concern that have characterized so many churches so much of the time? I suggest that it would rather lead us to see judgment beginning at the house of God. We should then recognize that the distortions and the misunderstandings of truth and goodness which lead to war have their origins within the Christian camp. The roots of the crusading mentality are not "secular" in the modern sense, nor are they rooted in the mores of pagan religions. They constitute a deformation of biblical faith. Because the church bears this responsibility for having contributed to the mentality in which nations make war, the polemic of a valid Christian pacifist witness must be theological and first of all be directed to the church.

Even if the roots of this witness against the crusade and in favor of the cross were not characteristically christological as I have been claiming, this would still be the context to which we should first speak. Whatever help we may receive from a growing modern understanding of social techniques, what really needs to be debated is a Christian view of human nature and the direction of history. The audience to whom it needs to be directed is the circle of those who have affirmed knowledge of and commitment to an overarching divine purposefulness active in history.

Perhaps Christians in our age are being made ready for a new awareness of the continuing relevance of the message of the Apocalypse. There is a widespread recognition that Western society is moving toward the collapse of the mentality that has been identified with Christendom. Christians must recognize that they are not only a minority on the globe but also at home in the midst of the followers of non-Christian and post-Christian faiths. Perhaps this will prepare us to see how inappropriate and preposterous was the prevailing assumption, from the time of Constantine until yesterday, that the fundamental responsibility of the church for society is to manage it.

And might it be, if we could be freed from the compulsiveness of the vision of ourselves as the guardians of history, that we could receive again the gift of being able to see ourselves as participants in the loving nature of God as revealed in Christ? Perhaps the songs of the earliest church might restore this to us if the apostolic argument cannot. A church once freed from compulsiveness and from the urge to manage the world might then find ways and words to suggest as well to those outside its bounds the invitation to a servant stance in society.

In Sum

The secularistic and the Marxist criticism of the vision of marching to Zion claims that the promise of "pie in the sky bye and bye" cuts the nerve of action today. The expectation of "fairer worlds on high" is supposed to detach the present from that which is promised.

This may well have been the case when in recent centuries the beneficiaries of the social system appealed to a future world to encourage their subjects to remain docile. But our interest is not in asking whether eighteenth-century religion could be the opiate of the people, but rather understanding the function of the apocalyptic vision in the first-century church, whose seers were not on any drug.

In the worldview of that time the gap between the present and the promise was not fundamental. What we are now doing is what leads to where we are going. Since the "this-worldly" and the "other-worldly" were not perceived in radical dichotomy, to be "marching through Emmanuel's ground" today is to be on the way to Zion. Terms like "hereafter" are in that kind of context affirmations, not negations. They do not say that that to which we look forward is in a radically different kind of world from the world in which we now live, but rather that it lies farther in the same direction in which we are being led. The unforeseeable future is farther along in the same direction as the foreseeable future for which we are responsible.

The modern critic who has no lively sense either of heaven or of Zion begins listening to a hymn like the classic gospel processional "Marching to Zion" under the shadow of the negative assumption that there is no connection between the here and the hereafter. Therefore the critic must attribute to those who speak of "a world beyond" spiritualizing intentions dominated by the chasm between this world and the other world. This interpretation can go so far (as, e.g., in Rudolf Bultmann) as to claim that mythical language (i.e., language according to which *here* and *hereafter* are in the same universe) is intentionally used with the purpose of affirming the division between the two; so that if the meaning of the myth is demythologized, what it really wants to affirm is only that religion is not of this world.

But if, on the other hand, one does not begin by assuming the unbridgeable gap between here and there, then this proclamation of a meaningful future cannot possibly have the sense of turning away from the present. They are statements of the same promising future, throwing light back upon the present imperative, for which precisely recent "secular theology" has been looking.

The future that the seer of Patmos sees ahead is a universe — that is, a single system — in which God acts and we act, with our respective actions relating to each other. The spiritual and providential laws which we expect to see at work in this system are as solid for the believer as are the laws of dialectical materialism for the Marxist.

The beginning assumption of the irrelevance of apocalyptic, which has so often made it hard to see social meaning in the book of the Apocalypse, even though its entire message has to do with kingdoms and empires, is in its ultimate impact another aspect of the relativizing of present obedience with which we have been debating through the entire book. "Whatever the early Christians meant by a fulfillment of history, it must not have been within history that they thought of it," runs the argument. Yet the closer we look at this "demythologizing" line of thought the clearer it is that the conclusion was dictated by the beginning definitions.

We are left with no choice but to affirm that the General Epistles in which the popular thought pattern of the earliest church has undergone least reflective analysis, and the liturgical elements embedded in apostolic writings which testify to the coming age, are restatements in another key of the same kind of attitude toward history that we found first in the more organized writings of the Gospels and of Paul. A social style characterized by the creation of a new community and the rejection of violence of any kind is the theme of New Testament proclamation from beginning to end, from right to left. The cross of Christ is the model of Christian social efficacy, the power of God for those who believe.

Vicit agnus noster, eum sequamur.
Our Lamb has conquered; him let us follow.

EPILOGUE

Already in its original form, this last chapter of *The Politics of Jesus* was different from the others. It offered no footnoted support from scholarship in the field. It paid more attention to the challenges of reading a different kind of literature and to the clash of worldviews represented by apocalyptic literature in general, and particularly by the apocalypse of John within the Christian canon. That was partly the case because the original lecture from which the chapter grew had been directed to an audience whose interest was in a spirituality and worldview more than in exegesis.

The peculiarity of this chapter in this respect will not be left behind after a quarter-century. Apocalyptic literature in general still poses a special challenge to the reader in at least two ways: as to how it should be read as a particular kind of literature, and as to how the worldview it expresses should be received as theology.

As a particular kind of literature, apocalyptic has come into its own in the world of scholarship in recent decades. The awareness that each kind of literature should be read in its own terms, and that apocalyptic is a *genre* which scholars of ancient literature should respect accordingly, has produced its own subdiscipline within historical and literary studies.[1]

That formal progress still leaves undecided the substantial question: namely by what rules, through what grid, shall we read this bizarre

1. As landmarks for the widespread acknowledgment of this awareness one may cite from a much wider literature Adela Yarbro Collins (ed.), *Semeia,* 36 (1986), and J. Lambrecht (ed.), *L'Apocalypse johannique et l'Apocalyptique dans le Nouveau Testament* (Gembloux: Duculot, 1980). By the nature of things, a burgeoning subdiscipline is also a subculture with its ingroup language, its "correctness" of manners, its elite. Making no claim to crash those parties, all I can do, and all I need to do for now, is to note their existence. The effort of previous scholarly generations to ignore this entire swath of the tradition, out of distaste for what fundamentalists and crazies were doing with it, has been abandoned in favor of a readiness to own this part of the canon as well, and to begin to work out modes of interpretation which befit the intent of the texts. Cf. the symposium volume "Prophetic and/or Apocalyptic Eschatology," in *Ex Auditu,* 6 (1990).

literature? To this question some interpreters offer answers with a high level of methodological self-consciousness, using this literature to demonstrate the superiority of this or that hermeneutical stance. Other answers are rather taken-for-grantedly unreflective, assuming that whatever psychodynamic or sociodynamic anthropology we are accustomed to using on other themes and other literatures must also suffice to enable us as modern historians to make sense of how those ancient texts made sense to their ancient addressees.[2]

As a university person formed during the third quarter of this century, I respect and to some extent understand most of these grids, and if I were assigned to survey or referee the literature I could list the questions raised by their use. In this brief update I cannot and should not take on that task,[3] but must rather leapfrog past it repectfully, to a review of what does belong in this study, namely its illuminating from another angle how the figure of Jesus illuminates our ethics.[4]

As we saw at the outset, one component of the modern grid which declares Jesus nonnormative for our social ethical life is the turn of mind we call "pragmatic" or "realistic." This view makes other unspoken and challengeable philosophical assumptions as well,[5] but the

2. Two oversimple responses occur often in the literature. One is to "explain" or excuse the bizarre cosmology of apocalyptic literature on the grounds, borrowed from pop psychology, that it "met the needs" of oppressed people in the first century and may become "relevant" again today because we too live in a time of crisis. Another is to be primarily concerned to evaluate the literature morally in modern terms, by finding fault with its "exclusiveness" or "vindictiveness." Both of these reflexes inappropriately modernize. They use a grid from our world instead of letting the text interpret itself.

3. For reviews of the problems of interpretation cf. G. Krodel, *Revelation* (Minneapolis: Augsburg, 1989); Elisabeth Schüssler Fiorenza, *The Book of Revelation* (Philadelphia: Fortress, 1984); Paul S. Minear, *I Saw a New Earth* (Washington: Corpus, 1968); Jacques Ellul, *The Apocalypse* (New York: Seabury, 1977).

4. My comments here were largely prefigured in my papers "Armaments and Eschatology," *Studies in Christian Ethics*, 1, 1 (1988), 43-61, and "Ethics and Eschatology," in *Ex Auditu,* 6 (1990), 119-28. A similar concern for retrieving the proper use of the genre is worked out in Christopher Rowland, *The Open Heaven* (New York: Crossroad, 1982).

5. It is usually marked by a naive or "common sense" trust that the social "reality" out there is easily readable, that the evidence is clear, and that our mind is competent to read it. The same is assumed not only for the facts of the case, but also for the way things work, for how causes produce effects (usually spoken of in mechanistic metaphors), and for one's own good intentions.

one which matters foundationally for present purposes is that the world is assumed to be a a single causal nexus, which (one assumes) deterministic assumptions about causation and control will help us most adequately to understand, and to influence effectively. When influencing the course of events is thought about in moral terms it is usually called "social responsibility." We evaluate how to discharge that responsibility by calculating and comparing costly inputs and desirable outputs.

The apocalyptic vision of things would "talk past" or "see past" this mind-set at least at two points. One formal assumption of the genre of "apocalypse"[6] is that there are things the addressee does not know by empirical or commonsense means. One cannot "do ethics" by calculating costs and benefits if one is not omniscient about the system. The substantial assumption which moves the seer is that God is an actor. *How* God acts can be expressed only in metaphors which our mechanically formed world vision can only consider fantastic or poetic. Nonetheless, the addressees of "revelation" are expected or commanded to behave differently, *within* the system of the real world, because of that "information" which has been "disclosed" to them about God as purposeful actor.

Asked abstractly: how does confidence in God's acting (or the very notion of God as actor) correlate with the way we normally think of our own behavior as causative, goal-oriented, "pragmatic"? The condescending way in which we are at first inclined to answer that is to retain our confidence that "the real world" is the social nexus we can understand and are "responsible" to manipulate for good, and that the "inward" or "poetic" perspective of the seer is helpful for secondary pastoral or therapeutic reasons, to keep people from giving up or from losing their self-respect. People who have not given up will of course be more persistent, and therefore perhaps more effective, in exercising social responsibility, but only in marginal ways which do not challenge the dominion of our deterministic vision of the world as a whole.

Although condescending, this view of the place of apocalypse is

6. The term "assumption" is our modern jargon; we use it to explain to ourselves phenomena we are watching in a world other than our own. The seers did not think about their assumptions before receiving and passing on their visions.

also more respectful, and in a scholarly sense more honest with the texts, than the view which preceded it, namely that the apocalyptic visions were in fact harmful. Previously they could be set aside unheard, as opiate. The promise of "pie in the sky," it was argued, kept people from staying in the struggle for justice, and when mistaken as a timetable for imminent this-worldly events (as was done, e.g., by the Armageddon visions of the television dispensationalists and Ronald Reagan) it abandons all common rationality.

When read carefully, none of the biblical apocalypses, from Ezekiel through Daniel to Mark 13 and John of Patmos, is about either pie in the sky or the Russians in Mesopotamia. They are about how the crucified Jesus is a more adequate key to understanding what God is about in the real world of empires and armies and markets than is the ruler in Rome, with all his supporting military, commercial, and sacerdotal networks.

Then to follow Jesus does not mean renouncing effectiveness. It does not mean sacrificing concern for liberation within the social process in favor of delayed gratification in heaven, or abandoning efficacy in favor of purity. It means that in Jesus we have a clue to which kinds of causation, which kinds of community-building, which kinds of conflict management, go with the grain of the cosmos, of which we know, as Caesar does not, that Jesus is both the Word (the inner logic of things)[7] and the Lord ("sitting at the right hand").[8] It is not that we begin with a mechanistic universe and then look for cracks and chinks where a little creative freedom might sneak in (for which we would then give God credit): it is that we confess the deterministic world to be enclosed within, smaller than, the sovereignty of the God of the Resurrection and Ascension.[9] "He's got the

7. The Gospel of John is underrepresented in this book. I gave more attention to the importance of the confession of Jesus as incarnate Logos in my "Glory in a Tent," in *He Came Preaching Peace* (Scottdale, Pa.: Herald, 1985), pp. 69ff., and in a glancing way in *The Priestly Kingdom* (Notre Dame, 1985), 50-51.

8. The phrase "sitting at the right hand" and the title "Lord" are functionally equivalent of the classical scholastic doctrine of providence. They encode the conviction that the course of human events is being "provided" for by a wisdom and power beyond our ken.

9. Cf. my "But We See Jesus," in *The Priestly Kingdom* (Notre Dame, 1984), pp.

whole world in his hands" is a post-ascension testimony. The difference it makes for political behavior is more than merely poetic or motivational.[10]

46ff., for a review of how it worked out in the first century. In the collision between the gospel and the cosmology of the wider society, which claimed to be larger than the Jewish-Christian message, the apostolic proclamation put Jesus not within but above the respective "worlds" the apostles addressed.

10. It also makes a difference for how we read intelligently the "facts" or the "lessons" of history. Cf my "The Burden and the Discipline of Evangelical Revisionism," in Louise Hawkley and James C. Juhnke (eds.), *Nonviolent America* (North Newton, Kans.: Bethel College, 1993), pp. 21-37. Cf. also Herbert Butterfield's classic *Christianity and History.* Which facts we perceive and how we weight them are matters of theological insight; history does not read itself.

Index of Names

Index of Scripture References